"Ken Puddicombe's brilliant novel Racing with the Rain evokes not only personal consequences of an historic political conflict in Guyana, during the Cold War, but also the cold cynicism and tragic irony of a small, defenceless Caribbean state being sacrificed to super-power hegemony." -Frank Birbalsingh, author of *Novels and The Nation: Essays in Canadian Literature.*

"Ken Puddicombe's RACING WITH THE RAIN is a gritty look at the politics of a nation and within a family that drive a young man from his home and from his country. Gripping and hard-hitting, this is a novel you won't want to miss." -Karen Fenech, author of *GONE*

"...From the first page...the characters come alive in ... creating enough tension to want the reader to thirst for more. As a fellow author I am impressed with this author's writing style which left me chomping at the bit to read beyond the first chapter." –Enrico Downer, author of *There Once Was a Little England,* a story about man's obsession with colour and class.

Copyright © 2012 by Kenneth Puddicombe
All rights reserved. The use of any part of this publication, reproduced, transmitted in any form or by any means, electronic, mechanical, photocopying, recording, or otherwise, or stored in a retrieval system, without the prior consent of the author is an infringement of the copyright law.

This book is a work of fiction. While certain incidents are taken randomly from historical records, the names, characters, places and for the greater part, situations, are either the product of the author's imagination or are used fictitiously, and any resemblance to actual persons living or dead, events or locales, is entirely coincidental.

Library and Archives Canada Cataloguing in Publication
Puddicombe, Ken
Racing With The Rain: a novel/ Ken Puddicombe.
ISBN 978-1-4751-4485-7
I. Title.
PS8631.U44R33 2012   C813'.6   C2012-903789-3

Cover photograph courtesy of Ram Angod
www.riskveda.com

ACKNOWLEDGEMENTS
My appreciation to fellow writers, without whose patience in suffering through several edits, this book would not have been possible: Bernard Lelliott, Debra Porter, Gary Reist, Judith Gelberger, Karen Fenech, Ros Feldman and Sue Hopcroft.
However, the author takes responsibility for all errors of omission or commission.

Dedicated

With love to my wife Rohini, daughters Karen and Kathryn, who inspire me with their faith and confidence, and to Emma who came late into my life.

To my siblings, William, Elaine, Cecil, Rudolph, Basil, Jean, Grenville, who were once there and can remember.

And, to the succeeding generations who can now read about it.

RACING WITH THE RAIN

And finds, with keen discriminating sight, Black's not so black -nor white so very white.

George Canning 1770-1827; 'New Morality' 1821

Those wretched colonies will all be independent, too, in a few years, and are a millstone round our necks.

Benjamin Disraeli; 1804-1881, letter to Lord Malmesbury, 13th August 1852

To Joyce

RACING WITH THE RAIN ©
a novel

By
Ken Puddicombe

Best Wishes. A taste of Guyana

Ken 13 Mar 2014

MiddleRoad Publishers

CONTENTS

CHAPTER 1 –News From Back Home 1

CHAPTER 2 –On The Way 17

CHAPTER 3 –In The Deep End 42

CHAPTER 4 –Arrival 63

CHAPTER 5 –A New Era 96

CHAPTER 6 –Repentigny 111

CHAPTER 7 –Black Friday 128

CHAPTER 8 –The Canal 147

CHAPTER 9 -People Past And Present 163

CHAPTER 10 -Family Values 185

CHAPTER 11 –Last Rites 196

CHAPTER 12 –The Wake 210

CHAPTER 13 –The Strike 231

CHAPTER 14 -A Life In Pictures and Words 252

CHAPTER 15 -Day Queen Victoria Lost Her Head 275

CHAPTER 16 -A Different Place And time 290

CHAPTER 17 -Refugees 307

CHAPTER 18 -Revelations 326

CHAPTER 19 -Visitors 340

CHAPTER 20 -A Party 362

CHAPTER 21 -Paradise Hotel 375

CHAPTER 22 -Thank You, Father 386

CHAPTER 1 –News From Back Home

TORONTO. MONDAY 24 NOVEMBER 1980: AM.

The clock radio sitting on the night table, just about a foot away from him was one of the items Carl had acquired after his move to the apartment on Tyndall Avenue in Toronto.

He stared at the numbers emblazoned in red against a black background: 4:45, and he continued to look while the last digit slowly moved downwards. The movement was hypnotic: one digit sliding into a cavity somewhere in the bottom of the clock, another replacing it from a reservoir at the top, a seemingly endless cycle of time. Was this what his life had come down to?

In the worst of times insomnia had never been one of his problems. His way around the long days at the bank, the ongoing cycle of deadlines and ever moving targets, was to stop off at the gym on the way home, and by the time he went to bed he was mentally and physically drained. Recently, he was finding it increasingly difficult to sleep through the early hours of the morning. Somehow, after the first few hours, his brain came alive again and refused to let his body succumb to its physical limitations. He could remember times though, when he managed to sleep late, with Natasha.

They had been lying in bed, in what seemed such a long time ago, and she had her back to him. Light streamed through the slats of the window shade. It was a Sunday, midmorning and he was close enough to feel the rhythm of her breathing as her chest expanded with the inflow of air and her shoulders drooped with the exhalation. He had lain there on his elbow, observing every rise and undulation of her form and feature. The sunlight was focused on her, creating a halo effect. He'd never really taken the time to see her this close before and felt guilty as he observed her, like seeing someone through a one-way mirror, when the person was most exposed and vulnerable, and unable to put up a defence against all the weaknesses and foibles. On her face, he could see, in the silhouette cast by the sunlight, fine strands of blond hair, so short that they almost blended with her skin.

Moving closer to her, he'd kissed her gently on her shoulder, his pulse racing at the thought of early morning intimacy. He'd traced the pattern of hair around her long neck – he'd always found this stimulating, and he remembered how it was when they started living together; her neck was smooth, no grooves marring the surface, just an enticing part of her body from which he could taste the salt if he crept up behind her in the kitchen. Looking at it, then, it was all filled with ridges and folds, which twisted and twirled due to the angle in which she was lying. He could smell her, the odour of stale cologne, hair that hadn't been washed for days, leftover makeup from the prior night still caking her face.

The phone on the night table rang, a harsh sound splintering the stillness of the early morning and he was startled, even though he had not been fully asleep. Perhaps if he ignored it, the sound would go away.

The clock changed to 4:47. Passages in time. He had always wondered if it was possible to measure an interval, and here it was, two minutes had elapsed before his very eyes. One hundred and twenty seconds during which nothing had happened. He had not stirred, had not planned or moved his life forward in any way. As far as he knew there had been no earth-shattering event unfolding in the world, and if there were, what did it matter to him anyway? He could easily remain in bed all day and not know about it, and as far as he was concerned, if it was something he knew nothing about, it hadn't happened and had no bearing on his life. Lying there in bed, dangling in a zone somewhere between sleep and consciousness, he was overcome by a strange feeling: that he was losing control of his life, and for the first time in recent years was unsure of the direction it was taking him.

He looked around at his sparsely furnished bedroom: the bed he was lying in, a chest of drawers, vanity and wardrobe. These were all identical items he'd started out with back in 1972 when he was a bachelor and had just graduated and started working at the Canadian Business Bank.

He continued to stare at the clock: 4:48. The phone hadn't stopped ringing –an ungodly hour for anyone to be trying to get hold of him. Who could it be? Panic suddenly seized him – was it Natasha? Had something happened to one of the children? He reached over quickly to pick it up.

The voice at the other end of the line said: "Collect call from Georgetown, Guyana from Mister Jules Dias for Mister Carl Dias. Will you accept the charge?"

Just over a week ago Carl had written Uncle Jules and given him his new phone number. His uncle hadn't wasted much time in contacting him. What could he want this early in the morning?

"Yes," he said.

He heard the sound of the connection being made. "Go ahead," the operator said.

"Cal, you there?" His uncle had a habit of truncating his name, as if Carl was not short enough.

"Yes, I am, Uncle Jules."

"Cal," his uncle said, "I'm sorry to call you this early in the morning."

Sometime back the *eight* had changed to *nine* and Carl had missed the movement. The *four* was now *five* and the *nine* had changed to *zero*. A late Indian summer had given false hope of a delayed winter and he had turned off the heat in the apartment. Now, a sudden chill had somehow penetrated below the comforter, had got hold of his toes and was slowly working its way up his ankles to his calves. The phone was still lying next to him in his right hand but he couldn't feel it; his fingers were numb.

"Cal, you there?"

Carl cleared his throat. "Yes, I'm here Uncle Jules," and his first thought was of the number of times he had tried to contact anyone in Guyana and had been unable due to the erratic state of the telephone system in the country. "Where are you calling from?"

"Georgetown –Telecom Building. Is the only way to make overseas phone calls these days and you have to join a long line-up. One big waste of time but is how things run nowadays in this kiss-me-ass country."

Carl could well imagine what an imposition it must have been for Uncle Jules: journey by hire-car from the East Coast all the way to Georgetown just to make a phone call. How much more of a revolting waste of time could there be, when he could be back home in his shop making money.

"What's the news, Uncle Jules?"

Even before he asked, Carl had come to the conclusion it had to be connected to his father, that something dreadful had happened to the Old Man. He tried to brace himself for the worse.

"I'm coming from Georgetown hospital," his uncle said. "We rushed your father there last night."

There was a pause. Carl detected a sniffle and a sigh. Who was it that felt the impact more; was it the bearer of the bad news or the one about to receive it?

"Your father...died, two hours ago."

Uncle Jules was like that, from as far back as he knew him: the embodiment of paucity in language and efficiency in time management, someone who rarely said two words if one sufficed, a man who had made a fortune and lost it. *Time is money and Idle hands make mischief* were catch phrases that always directed his approach to everything.

The last digit on the clock face was now showing a *One*. Carl hugged the phone closer to his ear. The numbness was slowly overtaking his entire body.

"What happened?" Carl sputtered. "I didn't know he was in hospital. I received a letter from him just last week."

"He take in with pains last night. He didn't want to go the hospital –he was saying that he would never come out alive. The people staying at the house finally call an ambulance but none arrive. They had to take him themselves. They send word to me from the hospital." A bitter note crept into his Uncle's voice. "They didn't admit him until I arrive and by then, he was in bad shape."

The bottomless reservoir had supplied more numbers. *One, two, three, four* and *five* had fallen into the chasm and been replaced by *six* –it was now 4:56.

"My God," Carl said. "How could this happen? He didn't mention any health problems in his letter."

"That's your father –stubborn as a jackass and headstrong like a mule. He always had to do things his own way. Anyway, they going do an autopsy this morning and release the body later. We have to make plans for the funeral. I can make all the arrangements with the funeral parlour this morning before I go back home. Will you and your brothers be coming?"

He always had to do things his own way. The Old Man had only been gone a few hours and already he was being referred to in the past tense.

The clock had made its way relentlessly through the last digit and had started over, the *four* having changed to *five*. One of the slats in the middle of the window shade was bent out of shape and through it he could see a new day breaking outside. A soft glow was working its way into the bedroom. How easily time had slipped through his fingers!

"Yes, I will definitely come back for the funeral. I'm going to phone Joseph and see if he wants to make the trip. I don't think that Thomas is in any shape to take that long flight, so you can count him out. As for John, well, no one knows which part of the world he is right now…"

"Okay, I will hold the funeral until I hear from you. Will you be able to make arrangements for payment when you come? Things not too good with me right now."

"Don't worry about it, Uncle Jules. I will take care of everything. Can you phone in another three hours or so? If I'm not here I will leave a message with Natasha –you have her number. She will give you flight information and arrival time. I'm going to have to do a bit of running around to prepare for the trip."

After he hung up the phone, Carl continued to lie in bed, staring at the clock, but totally oblivious to time. He felt completely drained, as if he could sleep forever, only it was now from a numbness that left him confused, caught in the interval between sleeping and waking, when there seems to be no distinction between dreaming and reality, when very little makes sense. He got up and sat at the edge of the bed, thinking of what had just happened, wondering if it were a dream from which he'd just awakened. When the reality finally sunk in, the news struck him suddenly, swiftly, like a slap in the face, and he realized, with regret, that he had only thought of himself, and nothing about what Uncle Jules was going through. He was the only surviving relative in Guyana, bearing the full brunt of his older brother's death.

My God, Carl thought, has it really been that long since I last saw the Old Man? He tried to summon an image, what his father's features were like, how he usually dressed, what characteristics stood out, but the images had been buried so long that they had grown blurred. He remembered a photo album back in British Guiana, the pictures old and faded. He concentrated hard and sure enough he was able to recall certain details: a long aquiline nose with a solid bridge, a pencil shaped moustache, thin lips, large ears sticking out from the side of his head. He could still invoke the outline of the profile and the shape of the face; they were the easiest aspects to summon from his subconscious. And, he discovered that if he thought of the features one by one and positioned them on the face, slowly, out of the mist, a complete picture appeared and filled his vision.

He remembered his son asking him: Dad, what is our Grandfather like? Will we ever get to meet him one day? He'd been unable to respond to either question.

He thought of Natasha. Instead of being shacked up in his apartment in Toronto, he wished he were with her and the kids back in Etobicoke.

His father had always been a strong man, someone who took care of his body, preached the evils of over indulgence and boasted that he would live to be a hundred and twenty years. Now, he was dead at the age of seventy, when he should still have been enjoying the fruits of his retirement.

Since leaving Guyana back in nineteen sixty-four, despite all his attempts to make contact and bridge the gap, there had been very little communication between Carl and the Old Man, something to which he had eventually grown accustomed. The letter had arrived, written on an airmail form, the way his father always corresponded, his small, precise handwriting now degenerated into nothing more than a scribble, the letters difficult to decipher, as if he were writing in shorthand. A rambling letter –it touched on many subjects: the background of the family coming from Madeira in eighteen forty-three to British Guiana, family values he tried to instil in his children, his own political ambitions –successes and failures, life as it now existed in the country that was steadily and remorselessly sliding into an abyss of poverty and dictatorship.

Carl felt a sudden void opening up in his life, as the thought filtered slowly into his subconscious that he would never again see his father alive; that it didn't matter what had transpired over the years. It wasn't really relevant, the positions they had taken, the lack of empathy they had for each other, he would never have the opportunity to look into his father's face and try to find some common ground. With his father's departure, he had lost yet another link to his past. He opened his mouth wide, sucking in large gulps of air deep within his lungs, in a desperate attempt to control his emotions, but try as hard as he could, he was unable to avoid the convulsions racking his body and he broke down in tears. He thought of Natasha and the kids again, and he couldn't help wondering what he was doing there, all alone in his apartment.

Natasha was the first person he contacted after he'd composed himself enough to pick up the phone. She must have detected a tremor in his voice immediately when he greeted her.

"Carlos, Qué pasa? Es algo malo? What is the matter? Is something wrong?" she said.

She always called him Carlos. From the very first day they met, she had labeled him *her Carlos*, and refused to change after that.

"I just received a call from Guyana. My father died early this morning," he said.

A short pause and he could hear her heavy breathing. In the first few months after they started living together, he had come to appreciate that she was a silent crier, one of those who mourned inwardly, never really letting her emotion get hold and take control. At first, he'd often made fun of this difference between them: about her being cold like the frozen Siberian tundra, while he was hot like the tropical days and nights in the West Indies. So many years later, it seemed as if they had both switched dispositions and assumed each other's personality. She had become someone who found death and its untimely appearance a lamentable event regardless of who died and how loosely connected the person was, and even though she'd never met his father, Carl had told her enough of the Old Man that she was familiar with his life and Carl's relationship with him. This is what was affecting her: he could hear her sobbing.

"я так сожалею. Lamento mucho," she said. "I am so sorry."

"El tío Jules me llamó'" he said.

His response had been automatic. After sixteen years of living with her on and off, and hearing her constantly switch back and forth between Russian and English, Spanish and English, or even sometimes between Russian and Spanish, he'd grown accustomed to her almost seamless transitions, especially when she was speaking to him or doing the translations her job required.

"Uncle Jules called me," he said. "He died early this morning."

"What are you going to do? Are you planning on going back for the funeral?" She always seemed to be one step ahead of him, thinking into the future, making plans and concocting schemes.

"Yes, I'm going to see if I can get a flight out, this afternoon if possible."

She said, after a pause: "My poor Carlos. Puedo imaginarme cómo usted se siente. I can imagine how you feel. To have to go back when you were so far away from it all. How did he die?"

"I don't have details. But, he was rushed to hospital late last night and died early this morning."

"No hay nada peor que muriéndose solo. There is nothing worse than dying alone. Is a pity no one...none of his sons was down there with him when it happened."

"Yes, it's the life we choose, isn't it? I will leave you details of the flight when I get the information. Uncle Jules will phone you if he can't get hold of me, since I have some running around to do."

"Carlos, ¿Está usted seguro que usted es bien?"

"Yes, I'm going to be okay."

"Carlos, I'm so sorry. ¿Me querría usted al com sobre? Would you like me to come over?"

"No." It came out abrupt, harsher than he meant it to sound and it made him feel guilty, that he might have appeared to have scolded her, when all she was trying to do was provide comfort for his loss.

"Arrangements have to be made. I have to phone in to work and let them know. Must get an early flight." He was thinking in flashes now, trying to concentrate on what needed to be done. "Have to pack some things. Have to phone Thomas before he goes off to work. Must phone Joseph –not sure I can get hold of him now." He looked at the clock –it was 4:59. "Close to ten o'clock in the U.K; I'm not sure I can get him. He's probably already at work."

"What about the niños? Should I tell them?"

"No. When I come over to say goodbye I will explain everything to them. I'd like to be there when they're told, If you don't mind."

"Of course I don't mind. I'll keep the kids home today. ¿Debo preparar yo el desayuno para usted?"

"No, I don't think I'll be able to get there that early in time for breakfast."

The clock was showing 5:45 by the time Carl was through with the British West Indian Airways agent on the phone.

The problem, the travel agent had told him, would not be so much one of getting into Guyana –the real hurdle would be in getting out since there was always a long list of people who were waiting to join the exodus from the country. Even though they would issue a ticket, he would have to confirm his return flight in person at the airline office in Georgetown and there was always the possibility that someone who had good connections with some official in the office might be given Carl's seat. That was the way things worked there now: having a contact ensured priority in everything, whether it was booking a flight or buying groceries, obtaining a passport or getting a driver's license.

Carl didn't have much of a choice. He booked the flight.

He looked up his address book, found Joseph's work number in England and dialled.

When the switchboard connected him, Carl didn't hesitate: "I have some bad news," he told his brother. "The Old Man died early this morning."

A little over two years Carl had re-established contact with his brother and even though they hadn't met they'd had several phone conversations during that time. Joseph had remarried, to an English woman he'd met while studying there. They had a daughter, Wendy, who was ten. Carl had never raised the topic of Joseph's first wife Frances and their first child, Bernadette who would have been twenty-three in July if she were still alive.

A long pause at the other end of the line. What was going through Joseph's mind –did he have the same emotional reaction that Carl had felt just a little over an hour ago? Was he having flashes of his childhood and the later years in Georgetown?

Joseph cleared his throat. "I can't say that it's that much of a surprise," he said. "I received a letter from him last week and he was rambling about so many things I couldn't figure out what he was talking about. I thought that he was surely going downhill. He sounded like a man who was writing his last letter."

So, Joseph had also received a letter. Most likely Thomas would have too. The Old Man must have known that his days were numbered. What had he been seeking –a last hour attempt at reconciliation with his sons?

Carl came straight to the point: "Are you going to make it for the funeral?"

The response was swift and categorical: "No. I can't make it."

Carl couldn't help it –his response was just as swift and firm, with an edge to his voice: "Can't, or won't?"

"Either way it doesn't make a difference," Joseph said. "What did you expect?"

"The man's dead, for Christ sake, don't you think we should at least return for the funeral? After all, he was our father."

"There's nothing we can do for him now, is there? Uncle Jules can take care of the burial. I will pay my portion of the cost."

"Does it always have to come down to money with you? You won't even consider going to pay your last respects? For Christ sake, you're the oldest son! You, most of all should be there."

"Carl, there's nothing more for me in Guyana. I swore I would never return, not after what happened to me in nineteen sixty-four. How else do you expect me to feel?"

"That's over sixteen years ago. You can't live in the past forever. You have to let go, sometime. At least let's go back for the funeral. I have to call Thomas next, though I can't imagine he's going to be able to go back, considering the condition he's in. The Old Man deserves some kind of representation from you and me for the last."

"Count me out. You're right: I don't think Thomas will make it. How about John, are you forgetting him?"

"I haven't heard from John in over sixteen years. I have no idea where he is. Do you?"

"No. He hasn't kept in touch with me."

"Even if we're able to contact him, chances are that he won't even want to attend the funeral," Carl said.

"Not after the way the Old Man treated him over the years."

"So that's it? You wouldn't even think about going back?"

"I'm afraid so." Joseph's response had a touch of finality to it. "To be honest, I don't see why you're going. The country has gone downhill since independence –you will find a far different place from the one you left. Think about it Carl, do you really want to go?"

Carl had visions of his father's coffin being placed in the ground with only Uncle Jules being present and his uncle shaking his head and muttering: *I'm sorry Augusto, my brother, but I tried my best to get your boys here and it doesn't look as if they give a damn about you.*

"Since you won't go and Thomas can't make it, looks like its up to me. We just can't leave everything on Uncle Jules' shoulders. Besides, it's not right that the Old Man is laid to rest with none of his children present."

"The two of you didn't exactly get along in the years before you left, though. Why the pressing need to go, now?"

"I know we didn't get along, a long time ago. I haven't told you this, but I was thinking of returning sometime soon, especially after the letter arrived. I won't live with a clear conscience if I don't go for the funeral."

"Apart from it not being safe anymore, you could find yourself in real trouble with the authorities, and you might not be able to get out. Have you thought of what you're going to do if that happens?"

Carl paused. He had given it a great deal of thought and he realized that there were many reasons why he should not go. However, the idea of his father being placed to rest without any of his children being around to say good-bye was the overwhelming reason why he should go. If both Joseph and Thomas didn't go and John hardly likely to turn up, how could he stay away?

"Yes, I have given that some thought. I'm returning as a Canadian citizen and travelling with a Canadian passport. I don't think there's much of a risk."

"Suit yourself," Joseph said. "I have too many bitter memories of what happened to really have faith in that country. I can't put it behind me, not ever. Besides, you just have to look at the news and you can tell how bad things are down there with very little hope of change, not as long as the Republicans are in government."

Sixteen years and a distance that spanned all the way across the Atlantic to the U.K now separated Carl from his brother. Joseph had turned forty-five last August. How had the years treated him? Carl still had a picture of the oldest of his siblings frozen in his memory. Time and space, and now death, seemed to do that –preserve the last images you had of someone. The picture he had of Joseph was someone who had thick, black, slick hair parted in the middle and combed backwards, someone with a thin moustache that could have been something scrolled on his top lip with a black-ink marker. This had all started when Joseph saw *Down Argentine Way* with Don Ameche in 1946. Don Ameche became a matinee idol and Joseph was sure to see him in every movie in which he played in Georgetown. Joseph later adopted the trademark Don Ameche tux and black bow tie and wore these to any function he attended. Added to his grey eyes and finely chiselled features, he had the look of a wild Latin dancer and was much sought after by women, until he married in 1956. In the months following the disturbances in Wismar in the lower Demerara River, where he lost his wife and daughter, Joseph's appearance had altered: there was a touch of grey in his hair and he no longer trimmed his moustache. Carl had seen recent pictures: Joseph was now bald and tubby, far different from the Don Ameche of old.

"The alternative with the Reform party is not any better," Joseph was saying. "You, most of all should know that with all the connections you had with them over the years."

Joseph had started to tread on a delicate subject –the differences that split the family and the entire country in the struggle for independence. The result was a series of cataclysmic explosions that rent the very fabric of the colony, like lava rising to the surface after a volcanic eruption. He rang off and looked up the phone number for Thomas in his directory.

Thinking about it, Carl understood that even if they had started out from different directions, they had all ended up going down the same path during the disturbances in the sixties. He, to some extent, and Joseph and Thomas to a greater degree, Uncle Jules and his family, all were still around as grim reminders. James was long gone; John had been affected in ways that most of them could never determine since he was somewhere out there, out of touch, and probably trying to adjust his life; and now his father was the most recent casualty. They had all suffered, like so many others on both sides of the divide that opened up in the colony not long after the emergence of nationalism in the fifties and the split in the Reform party – based on racial, philosophical and historical positions, fault lines running across the top of the South American landscape, fissures that were unpredictable and unavoidable from the onset. What had started out as a common goal for independence had fast disintegrated into a fight for supremacy in which divisions were cultivated and exploited to the fullest by all the participants and the powers that be, by the British and Russian governments, and most of all the Americans.

Carl had seen Thomas the previous Christmas when he had flown down to Florida with Natasha, Alexei and Irina for their first visit to Disney World. The last time he'd seen his brother prior to that was back in what was then British Guiana.

He phoned Thomas' home number and no one picked up. He hung up and tried the number for his brother's office that was twenty feet down a flight of stairs in his house. After obtaining his CPA Thomas had gone into private practice and eventually built up a select clientele that enabled him to work from home.

Thomas answered the phone on the first ring and soon as he heard Carl's voice, he said: "It's bad news, isn't it?"

"The only reason I'm calling so early in the morning," Carl said.

"Is it the Old Man?"

"Yes; I heard from Uncle Jules. The Old Man died early this morning in Georgetown hospital. No cause of death is given, as yet, but I suspect it was his heart. He was having severe pains over the weekend."

Thomas was breathing heavily, much more than what Carl typically heard over the phone. Carl pictured his brother, sitting there in his large black leather office chair, the phone resting on its shoulder cradle. He would be staring out of half-singed eyelids, into space, perhaps thinking back to Guyana and the sixties and what had happened to get him to his present condition, something that placed severe limitations on his mobility.

"I can't imagine you're going to be able to make it for the funeral so I'm just calling to let you know," Carl said.

"Yes, I realize that. Thanks Carl. Are you going back?"

"Yes, I've already got a flight out this afternoon."

"What about Joseph –does he know?"

"Yes, I phoned him earlier. He's not returning."

"I didn't think he would. So, that means you're going to be on your own, since I can't imagine John turning up out of nowhere. He probably won't even hear the news about the Old Man's death."

"I'm not sure he would even care," Carl said. "Anyway, Uncle Jules is there. He's already started arrangements for the funeral."

"Good old Uncle Jules –always there when you need him. How about you –do you think you will have any problems down there?"

Carl thought for a while. He said: "Well, it has been sixteen years. If things are in such a mess as everyone keeps saying, I can't imagine that there is any kind of record of what happened, or that anyone will even take the time to follow up."

"I hope so," Thomas said.

Carl rang off.

CHAPTER 2 –On The Way

TORONTO. MONDAY 24 NOVEMBER 1980: PM.

It was raining –one of those pelting downpours laced with occasional bursts of ice-pellets, a taste of what would come later in Toronto when winter's icy grip took hold. Traffic was slow. Carl was glad that he'd left for the airport with plenty of time to spare. He'd spent less than half an hour with Natasha and the kids and said goodbye to them. This hadn't been easy. Since going on his own, he'd found the solitude of his self-imposed exile increasingly difficult.

As he sat in the cab, heading west on The Queensway, he thought of what might be awaiting him on his arrival in Guyana and whether he'd be able to get out after the funeral. If he had problems getting a flight, what would he do? Getting out by sea, assuming he was able to obtain the necessary booking, would take several weeks at best. Travelling overland to the neighbouring countries of Brazil and Venezuela was not an alternative since there was no through-road to those countries, all of which left Suriname –Dutch Guyana, as a resort. He would have to travel by car to the border and cross over the Berbice River, make his way to Paramaribo and board a flight there.

He did a mental check of the list he'd compiled, items he had to take on the trip, things he had to do before he left. His Canadian passport was now safely tucked away in the inside pocket of his jacket along with the BWIA airline ticket. There hadn't been enough time to take any immunization shots before he left but he was reasonably sure that he still had enough built-up protection from whatever it was foreigners picked up while visiting Guyana, since he was originally from there. The suit he was wearing would be used for the funeral. In addition, he had packed enough clothes to last him for a week, and if he had to, he could rotate them. The travellers' cheques he'd bought from the bank were safely hidden in his money belt on the inside of his pants; he could feel the pressure down in his crotch. Based on everything he'd heard and read about the crime situation in Guyana, he didn't think that his precautions were excessive.

The driver had his radio tuned to the Canadian Broadcasting Corporation –CBC, and Carl caught the main item: Prime Minister Pierre Trudeau to proceed with unilateral repatriation of the constitution to Canada.

He saw the driver looking at him in the rear-view mirror.

"Sir, which airline you travelling with?" the man said.

"BWIA –I believe it's terminal one," Carl said.

The man nodded. "Sir, what do you think will happen when Trudeau bring this constitution thing back to Canada?" he said, tilting his head towards the radio. "Do you think it will make a difference for people who come to Canada and can't find a job in their field?"

Carl thought about it. There had been a written constitution when British Guiana gained independence back in 1966. In this new Guyana Constitution, the British government and the British Guiana politicians had prescribed and enshrined all the human rights laid out by the United Nations Charter of Rights. However, it was now expected that The President and his Republican party would rig the upcoming elections to obtain the necessary two-thirds majority needed to amend the constitution and make him President for life.

"I think it's something Trudeau wants to leave as his legacy," Carl said. "I don't know if it will really mean anything to the common man on the street right now, but in the end, it could make a big difference if there are enough safeguards to protect and enforce rights and freedoms." He wanted to add: Unlike back in Guyana where the Constitution turned out to be not even worth the paper it was written on since there was no mechanism for enforcement.

Carl said: "Time will tell. What's your field, by the way?"

"I was a doctor back in the Punjab. The Canadian government tell me they need people like me so I apply and come, bring my whole family over. They tell me I can't practice here unless I go back to school, can't go back to school until I get a job and find the money for the fees. Can't even get a pharmacist job. This is the best I can do right now to keep food on the table –drive a cab!" He laughed, a cynical laugh that came from deep inside his throat. He kept his left hand on the steering wheel and gesticulated frequently with his right as he spoke. He wore a silver bracelet around his right wrist and it was too large for him –it kept slipping down to his elbow and he'd lower his hand and shake his wrist to reposition it.

Carl looked closer at the driver. He seemed to be a modern-day Sikh who had trimmed his hair, replaced the turban with a Blue Jay's cap and discarded his traditional outfit for blue jeans and a plaid shirt, all presumably to adapt to his new country. A doctor back in his homeland – you never know about people!

"Where you going, sir, if you don't mind me asking?"

Carl squirmed in his seat. He really didn't want to share personal information with this man. Over the years he'd grown suspicious of people's motives in asking direct questions and now that he was heading back to Guyana, he was even more cautious.

"You sound like you from the West Indies," the man prompted. "Trinidad or Guyana, but I think more from Guyana?"

The man knew his geography. Carl said: "Yes."

"My next door neighbour in Malton is from Guyana. He's East Indian. He tell me that East Indians and Black people don't get along too good in Guyana. Is this true?"

Carl sighed. "Not as simple as that."

"But, you're not Black or Indian, sir."

"Mostly Portuguese, from way back, with a bit of East Indian, actually."

"I was thinking that only Black and Indian live in Guyana."

Carl shook his head. "Not so. Blacks and East Indians make up the majority of the population. There's some Portuguese, Chinese and White still there, descendants of the original migrants and there's still native Amerindians who live mostly in the outlying areas."

"My neighbour say that there is a election coming up there next month and they might have trouble."

Carl had read about the upcoming election in the *Caribbean Times* that he often picked up from *Ram's Roti And Curry Shop* on Queen Street, so the news was no surprise to him. What would be in store for him with an election coming up?

"My neighbour also say that the government kill a politician early this year. I can't remember his name. But, it was a Black man who form another party."

Carl had also read of this. Back in June, a car bomb killed Walter Rodney in Georgetown. Rodney's brother Donald, who was travelling with him at the time, escaped unhurt. Donald claimed that it was the Republican government who engineered the assassination because his brother's new party would steal votes away from the Black segment of the population, posing a threat to the government's often engineered majority hold on power. Walter Rodney's killer had supposedly fled to nearby Surinam and was still at large. There was even a rumour that the CIA was involved in the plot. Rumours abounded in Guyana these days, especially with the media being tightly controlled by the government.

Carl shook his head. He had followed the career of Guyanese born Rodney, one of the youngest professors at the University of West Indies until he was expelled for his stand against the Jamaican government's lack of progress in alleviating the misery of the poorer class in the country. Rodney returned to Guyana in 1974 and spurned the advances of both mainstream political parties –the Reform and the Republican, forming his own party at the age of thirty-two. He became very popular through his activism in grassroots movements and open opposition to the corruption and dictatorship of the Republican government, becoming a target due to his stand. Another opportunity for change and progress shot down at an early stage, Carl thought.

More news on the radio: Ronald Regan to announce appointments for his cabinet later that day. Iraq invasion of Iran now in full swing; the international community not hopeful of an early resolution. Anastasio Somoza, ousted Nicaragua ruler, and two aides assassinated in Asunción, the capital of Paraguay.

"Do you think things will change in America under Regan?" the driver said. They had left highway 427 and were almost on the ramp to the airport. "Do you think I can get in there?"

Doesn't really matter who was elected, Carl thought. Outsiders would always be involved in the internal affairs of other countries, more cold war power-play politics between the communist and western blocs, more manipulation of elections and governments by the KGB, the CIA and British Military Intelligence. Since the 1950's it had been like that, when Guyana was still a colony and nationalism sparked a fire that was seen throughout most colonial empires. Outside involvement was there in the 1960's, before Guyana's independence, and he had no hope that things would ever change. Somoza: once the protégé of the CIA and supported by the American government despite all his corrupt practices and evil misdeeds, had been assassinated. Had he fallen out with the Americans and was the CIA also involved?

"I don't really know," Carl said.

The rain was still falling as they pulled in to the departure level of the terminal. It could be raining back in Guyana. November was the start of the rainy season and Carl had read of recent floods in the country. That much hadn't changed from when he was growing up back there.

The driver got out and opened the trunk for Carl's baggage. Carl paid him the fare with a generous tip and wished him well in his search for reintegration back into the medical profession.

The flight was scheduled to stop in Antigua and Trinidad before going on to the northern tip of the South American mainland and to Guyana. Looking around at the other passengers waiting to check in, Carl couldn't help wondering: who were the ones going back to Guyana and why were they heading back, when so many were trying to get out? Why would they want to return, knowing the turbulence and uncertainty the country was presently experiencing? How many others were heading back on a bereavement call, reluctantly, out of necessity rather than for pleasure?

Five people were ahead of Carl in the queue. Directly in front of him, a priest dressed in his black cassock, a Guyana passport in his hand was pushing a large blue suitcase on the floor with his foot as the line inched along. Behind Carl was an Indian woman in a long white dress and wearing a white headscarf. The woman wore thick glasses, which tended to magnify her eyes. She kept rifling through the contents of her floral cloth bag as if she were taking inventory. Carl saw a saucepan in the bag; it was one of those carriers used on the sugar estates by workers to take their lunch to work.

The priest turned around and smiled at Carl. "Going on holiday?" he said.

Carl shook his head.

A woman with two large suitcases was arguing with the clerk about having to pay for overweight baggage.

"Things seems slower than usual," the priest said.

Carl smiled. "Island time, I guess, or if you're from Guyana, it would be Guyanese time."

The priest smiled. "You sound as if you're originally from Guyana."

Carl nodded. "Where you headed, Father?"

"Same place."

The priest was a short stub of a man no more than five feet, four inches, sparse brown stumps littering his dome, while short hair curled at the sides and back of his head. He tilted his head downwards when he looked at Carl over his pince-nez glasses perched at the bottom of his nose.

He aroused Carl's curiosity. Carl didn't think there were many Whites still left in the country. "Are you connected with the church in Guyana, then?"

"Yes. I'm Father Ian Martin from the diocese in Georgetown." He sighed and his face assumed a grave look, like someone who'd just received news of the unexpected death of a relative. "I'm also the editor of The Catholic Times."

The Catholic Times –Carl remembered it well. Along with the Graphic and the Chronicle, back in the sixties, it was a thorn in the side of the Reform party when they took power in the first self-government that was expected to lead the country to full independence. The Catholic Times seemed to take extra delight in vilifying Reform, branding their policies as communist, and engaging in personal attacks on the Chairman of the party and members of the cabinet. Almost every edition contained an article on how Reform would nationalize private business and seize properties if they were the party leading the country to nationhood. At times, the attacks in all the newspapers became so venomous that there was little objectivity remaining, even when Reform came out with policies that were based on sound economic practices being implemented in most developing countries, practices meant to break up huge holdings and promote land reform, along with a progressive taxation system based on ability to pay.

"You don't look too enthusiastic about your job, Father."

The priest raised his eyebrows. Red pinpoint spots on his forehead and the top of his head grew larger and his face displayed a deeper shade of scarlet.

"One has to do what one has to do," he said. "The good Lord knows best."

"I remember back in the early sixties, when I was there, The Catholic Times was on the leading edge of criticism against the government," Carl said. "Is it still the same?"

Father Martin nodded.

"The Times can't be too popular with The President and the Republican party," Carl said.

"We're not." The priest looked around and lowered his voice. "My predecessor was assassinated in Georgetown a few years ago. The job was vacant for quite some time and the archdiocese appointed me. Prior to that I was stationed at Lethem in the North West district, working with the native tribes. I knew very little about running a newspaper or getting involved in politics. Saving souls was always my main goal."

"I can see why you'd be reluctant," Carl said.

The clog in the queue had been cleared up. The priest moved on, Carl pushed his suitcase along and followed. He had no problem checking in and he headed through security to the waiting room for his flight.

He took a seat in the waiting area, looking on, trying to figure out who were Guyanese and who were from Antigua or Trinidad. He knew that the East Indians were most likely heading either to Trinidad or Guyana since there was just a scattering in other countries in the region. He could easily pick up the accent and twang of the Trinidadian Indian versus the Guyanese: the former had a sing-song melodic subjugation of syllables, swallowed their R's and sometimes attached *boy* to the end of their sentences. Guyanese, on the other hand had a variation of syntax depending on whether they came from the countryside or the city. With Guyanese country-born Indians, the speech was dominated by partial sentences and broken English, while the city folk spoke grammatically constructed English with truncated words.

An old East Indian man dressed in a bright yellow shirt and sitting across from Carl, was attempting to have a conversation with a teenager who was rocking gently to the music coming through his earphones. The old woman in the white dress and headscarf sat not too far from them, peering through her glasses at everyone passing, perhaps looking for some lost acquaintance or companion.

The man in the yellow shirt sucked his teeth and slapped the boy on his back. As the boy removed the ear phones to determine the reason for the interruption, the man said, "Lock off de radio, boy. Ah don' wan' shout at you all de time."

In the row of seats immediately behind Carl, two women were discussing an acquaintance. "An' how that woman gat plenty brains, I tell yuh," one of the women said. "I don' know where she get all them brains from."

"Yes, she prapah smart," her friend declared. "She does take back all them grips with her back to Guyana, full with all kinds of stuff fuh selling in de market. An' she doesn' pay a single cent in duty. She ask me to travel with one of she grips."

"Me too!" her companion said.

"She mus' be blessed with brains."

"She get all them blessings after she mother dead. By the time she finish, she tekh back no less than ten bags with she, all crammed with goods. She make plenty plenty money selling everything."

Carl wondered if they were talking about the woman who had delayed the queue with her overweight suitcases. She would be sizing up those people travelling with only one suitcase and asking them to take one of hers as the second entitlement. This way, she could bypass customs at the airport and avoid paying duty. He suspected that even if she still had to pay duty she would make a handsome profit in the sale since there was an ongoing shortage of many items in Guyana.

Carl saw Father Martin approaching. The priest spotted him and came over, taking a vacant seat.

"Lots of people travelling back today," Carl said.

"Yes, it looks like a full flight," the priest said. "It's always like this when I travel. BWIA is now the only airline that goes as far as Guyana so there's not much choice."

"How often do you travel, Father?"

"I make about three trips a year to Canada. I have family in Scarborough and I stay with them when I come. They also help to raise funds in the Guyanese community there –it's quite substantial, actually."

"Yes, I know," Carl said. "From my estimation, when you take into account Canada, the US, the UK and some in the Caribbean and Europe, I figure that there must be at least two hundred and fifty to three hundred thousand Guyanese now living out of the country."

"Oh, it's probably much more than that," the priest said, softly. "More like something in the area of half a million people. The population in Guyana itself is close to seven hundred thousand now –it hasn't grown any since independence, there's been too much of a drain over the years."

"The cream of the crop," Carl said. "The best brains and the wealthiest ones."

The priest nodded. "Many Guyanese rely heavily on remittances from overseas –just about one in three families I know has someone abroad. To many, it makes up for no work and no income. Most of them couldn't survive –they would starve without those remittances. There's also a thriving business in sending barrels of used items and foodstuff back home, too."

Carl had sent a barrel twice to Uncle Jules with items for his personal use and to sell in his shop. Just last year he'd sent a hundred dollars Canadian currency back to his father; he'd sent it with a friend who was returning for a visit. The money came back –his father had rejected it outright. Two years prior, he'd also sent a bank draft for two hundred dollars, but this was never acknowledged and the bank confirmed that it was not cashed. Had the envelope been broached at the post office –a practice that he'd been told was prevalent in the country?

Carl said: "A pity isn't it? The President and the Republicans are so entrenched that there is no hope of change in future, is there?"

Father Martin shook his head. "Not as long as we don't have free elections."

"The reason people vote with their feet and leave the country," Carl said. He waved at the crowd.

As departure time neared, it sounded like the gradual build-up of activity in a hive as bees stirred with sunrise. The waiting area was now filled to capacity, with standing room only available and the hum had grown louder within the last ten minutes.

Father Martin nodded in the direction of two people, a man and a woman, both about five feet six, standing by a post at the far end of the waiting area.

"Looking at them tells me that there is always hope," Father Martin said.

The woman was white, slim and blonde, around fifty years old. She was doing most of the listening to the man who was Chinese, and much older than her.

"She's the President of the Canadian Council of Churches. The man is Andrew Chung, head of the newly formed GCRC –Guyana Civil Rights Group. Mister Chung is a retired head master –he ran a private school in Georgetown until he gave it up to start the movement. He is practically a one-man show though, when it comes to human rights issues." The priest sniggered. "The government doesn't know the meaning of the word so Andrew has to tread a very careful line so as not to provoke them. I must say, though, he's learning fast."

The man spotted Father Martin. He said something to the woman, pointed in the direction of the priest who rose to greet them as they came over.

"Hello Andrew," Father Martin said, taking the man's outstretched right hand in both of his and pumping it vigorously. "I see you're heading back."

Chung had a pipe clenched between his teeth. He removed it and held it by the chimney. "Yes, I am," he said.

Chung looked like an eccentric professor: he wore a grey tweed suit that had leather elbow joints, wore no tie, and his thick, fluffy white hair lay in a tangled heap on his head, as if he'd long ago given up on keeping it in order. Carl noticed his shoes –the laces were untied, but still he'd managed to walk without tripping over them.

"This is Heather Johansen," Chung said.

"Hello Father Martin." Heather Johansen offered her hand and Father Martin shook it.

Chung said: "Did you have a successful fund-raising campaign this time?"

Father Martin nodded. "Yes, we're going to be able to buy newsprint for the first time in three months. We'll be up and running before the election next month, God willing. I heard that you're part of an International Team of Observers going down for the election. If it's true, that's good news."

Chung nodded. "Yes, the two of us are members of the team."

"When's the rest of the team going down?" Father Martin said.

"They're already there. About ten others from all over, including a UN representative."

"That was quick work," Father Martin said.

"Should be enough to cover the country, don't you think?"

Father Martin sighed. "I don't know. Sure is a lot of territory for just twelve people to cover all the polling stations. You know the kinds of obstruction that will be placed in your way . . ."

"Well, we're also hiring local staff to help all the members of the team get around. Most of us will be stationed in Georgetown, of course, where about forty percent of the votes will be cast."

"Do you think the Observer Team will make a difference, Father Martin?" Heather Johannsen said. There was a note of expectation in her voice. She sounded like someone who'd long ago received news about a relative lost at sea, but who still lived in eternal hope of the person eventually turning up.

Father Martin took his time before he replied. Carl knew why the priest was hedging. All the priests he'd known in his Catholic upbringing, those from the schools he attended, the ones who heard his confession at weekly mass at Brickdam Cathedral, to the time he stopped going and broke completely with the Church, they rarely gave personal opinions in public or took a stand on any subject. The only exception was when The Catholic Times got involved in the politics of the fifties and sixties, but that was the Church speaking, not an individual priest.

The priest looked around, took in his surroundings, glanced at Carl who was still sitting on the chair, and smiled at him. "Hard to say," he said, looking over his glasses at Chung and Johannsen. "The time is so short to get organized."

Johannsen said, "I mean, the government down there accepted the concept of an observer team to oversee the elections, albeit reluctantly, I admit. Doesn't that point to the desire for change on their part?"

Chung came to Father Martin's rescue. "You've got to realize, Heather, this is a government that's been in power since independence in nineteen sixty-six. For fourteen years they've enjoyed the perks and privileges of office –they're not going to give that up so easily. Some people think that things will not change until the old guard –the President and his cohorts, pass on. Even then, you've got to keep in mind, he's got a hierarchy that will easily slip into place and take over. No, I'm afraid that the only way change will come is for the international community to gain some kind of leverage over the Republicans, and it's going to be economic pressure that eventually brings the party down."

Johannsen opened her eyes wide and frowned. Was she thinking that they were all embarking on a futile mission and it would end up being perceived as endorsing the legitimacy of the Republicans and the dictator, rather than providing a democratically elected government for the first time since the country gained independence?

Carl had his own reservations, as he felt sure that Father Martin would have. How could it be possible in one brief visit, even by well-respected administrators, to dislodge a well-entrenched establishment that had its fingers in every aspect of Guyanese society? They were dealing with an organization that dished out largesse to its supporters, a well-oiled machine that controlled the police and armed forces through perks and privileges, a party that manipulated election results to suit its own ends.

Carl heard the call for boarding and there was a spontaneous surge towards the counter.

The airplane was heading south.

Dinner had been served and the trays had been collected and stowed away. Carl had not eaten much, even though his sensory glands had been stimulated by the fare –dishes of which he had a clear recollection: peas and rice, beef stew which reminded him of the pepper-pot his mother made, fried ripe plantains, a fruit bowl for desert with papaya, mango and pineapple. The Indian woman in thick glasses, seated to his right, declined the airline meal and ate her own food from the container she pulled out of her bag. After a brief prayer, she had shovelled spoons full of rice and curry into her mouth, then pulled out a flask of tea that she poured into a cup and drank. She could well have been an older version of one of the people in his hometown, one of the Muslim population who only ate Halal meat.

After a brief stopover in Antigua and several hours in Trinidad, they were heading for Guyana. The Indian woman had disembarked along with many of the passengers. Carl was dozing off when the stewardess came around and handed out immigration forms to be completed.

The first section of the form was easy enough. Family Name: Dias. First Name: Carl. Middle Name: Charles. Address: 100 Tyndall Avenue, Toronto, Ontario. Date of Birth: 17th July 1945. Place of Birth: Georgetown, Guyana. He came to a section, which asked: *Nationality* and he paused. He'd never officially relinquished his Guyanese citizenship and now, here he was, returning to the country of his birth, travelling with a Canadian passport. What was the protocol in Guyana for a situation like that –how would they look upon him? He wrote: Canadian. The next field asked where he was intending to reside in Guyana –he wrote the address in Repentigny. Then, a section in which he had to declare the amount of money he was taking into the country. He was puzzled –why would they want to know how much money he was taking into the country? Surely they would be more interested in the amount coming out, with the strict foreign exchange controls they had in place?

Carl paused, his pen hovering as he pondered his response to the question. Father Martin, sitting to his left, was also completing his form.

"You should be very careful how you answer that question, my son," the priest said.

Carl's first reaction was one of resentment. He did not see that it really concerned his travelling companion, even if he were a priest.

Then, he felt guilty over his attitude. "I was thinking the same thing, Father."

"Well, I didn't mean to alarm you, but I believe you haven't been back for a very long time?"

"Nearly sixteen years."

The priest raised his brows and looked over his spectacles. "That's a very long time to be away. A lot has happened since you left. So many changes that you cannot even imagine how different things are now. The reason I think you should be cautious, is that while the information you have to give is required by the authorities, you never know how it's going to be used." He squirmed in his seat. "If you declare a large sum, there are stories of the information being passed on to criminals who turn up at the address where you're staying. I'd only be concerned with that section if you plan on returning to Canada with some of the money you're taking in –they won't allow you to take it out unless you've declared that you've brought it in. If not, I'd declare an understated amount."

Carl could imagine how difficult it had been for the priest to offer advice –he'd practically suggested that Carl fabricate his declaration.

"How long are you planning on staying?" the priest said.

"I'm going to be there for about a week, assuming I can get an early flight out. I've heard that it's sometimes very tough to do that."

"Yes, it's very true." The priest returned to his form.

Carl entered $500.00 in the field, satisfied that the six thousand dollars in travellers' cheques and a thousand in cash that he was taking in would be adequate for funeral and other expenses. If there were any left over, he'd turn it over to Uncle Jules. With a side-glance, he observed Father Martin. The priest wrote with a blue fountain pen and he held it almost vertical, his thumb, index and third finger of his right hand wrapped around the stem like someone who suffered from severe arthritis. He wrote in small scribbles, his writing almost indecipherable. Although he was white, Father Martin had the bronze tint of someone who had spent a lifetime in the tropics. Carl was curious: what would motivate someone like him to remain, especially in a country like Guyana, where things were coming apart at the seams and life was nothing but a struggle for survival? Father Martin's hands were all wrinkled, like his face, and he had to be in his late sixties or early seventies. There were some callings where people never really retired and were always dedicated to the ideals of the profession, even unto death, Carl realized. Was there such a thing as a retired priest, even though Father Martin seemed to have long passed the stage where he might have the energy required to be active in his post?

"You said you're not going back on vacation," Father Martin said, without looking up from the form. "Considering the short time you plan on being there, I imagine it must be some kind of a mercy mission. Is someone ill?"

"My father passed away this morning and I'm returning for the funeral."

"Oh. I'm sorry to hear." He seemed to be choosing his words carefully, "Was it from natural causes?"

"Yes it was, but why would you ask?"

"Well, just because there's so much happening in the country, now. With the lack of resources and poverty everywhere, crime is rampant, especially in Georgetown. Many of the innocent are suffering because of this. I didn't mean to startle you. It was very insensitive of me."

"No problem, Father. I think I have a good idea about what's going on, although I believe you're right –after such a long time there's bound to be a shock of some sort. I was brought up a Catholic, by the way."

"I suspected as much. I saw your name on the form. Dias is Portuguese. I imagine you've come from several generations that go back to the last century. Your father would have been Catholic too?"

"Yes. He was a Catholic, all the way down to the end, I believe."

"And you –are you still with the Church?"

Carl shook his head. He'd broken with the Church since back in the sixties, even before he'd become alienated from his father and gravitated towards the socialist principles of the Reform party.

"Not for a long time, Father."

"I'm really sorry to hear that. I hope that you find your way back, one of these days."

A priest never forgets his calling, Carl mused. He thought of his father, Augusto, and his grandfather Alvaro, who were active in the Church. This activism went back to his great grandfather, Carlos Dias who came from Madeira on the brig Zargo in eighteen forty-three as a Colono –indentured immigrant. Once he had served his two-year term and gained his freedom, Carlos opened a store in Georgetown, eventually developing it into a leading establishment. Whether it was to donate for a new church or spend time in the building effort, his ancestors had always contributed generously and they had married Catholic women, until his grandfather Alvaro broke the mould and married an Indian woman, Lilowtie – Grandma Lilly, a Hindu. Grandmother had refused to convert and she remained a staunch Hindu, following in the faith of her parents who came from India as indentured workers.

In his later years, after he'd become successful in business and embarked on his political career, Augusto had stopped attending church, although he'd always kept up his donations. Coming down to the last year, when he'd lost most of his money and was struggling to make ends meet, Carl heard that his father had returned to the fold. Carl thought it was ironic: here was a man who lived somewhat of a dissolute life when he was younger and successful and after he'd grown older and almost lost it all, returned to religion, like a repenting sinner seeking salvation.

"Was your father active in politics?" Father Martin interrupted Carl's thoughts.

The priest must have been racking his brain to come up with something that was lying there, hidden in the inner recesses of knowledge of people he'd met over the years and places he'd been.

"I seem to remember something vaguely about meeting someone by that name. I was in the North West District at that time. The leader of the Conservative party came up along with someone named Dias. I can't remember his first name and they were canvassing for votes for the upcoming election. I believe it was the nineteen sixty-four election, the one that was supposed to lead the country to independence."

"Yes," Carl said. "Augusto Dias: prominent business man, unflinching supporter of the Conservatives." This had been the reason he'd never been able to get along with his father, a long time supporter of the business oriented Conservative party. The Old Man had been opposed to independence under Reform under any condition.

Carl caught the priest looking at him with a frown and he suspected that his intemperate remark had most likely caused the reaction.

The priest said: "I know he didn't run in the North West District. If he had, he would surely have won, since most of the Amerindians there are Catholic and support the Conservatives, even up to this day."

"He ran a couple of times in Georgetown where the Republicans held most of the seats. He was never elected. But, he goes back long before that in government –he was one of the advisers to the Executive Council that was appointed by the Governor to run the country after the constitution was suspended by the British Government in nineteen fifty-three, during the so-called Communist scare, when Reform were kicked out of office."

How does a man go from having a small fortune down to being almost penniless? Blind fanaticism? His father had defended the Conservatives and its policies to the very end, like so many other business men who felt threatened by the socialist leaning principles of Reform. Augusto had remained strong in his support, right up to the time it became clear that the Republicans and the President were using the Conservatives simply to attain power and would later jettison the party and its leader after they'd served their purpose.

"I remember that well," Father Martin said. He smiled. "I can't imagine that you were old enough to know what was going on back then, in nineteen fifty-three, though."

"I was just eight. I do remember my father talking about it with my uncle and older brothers. He was very proud that he was part of that entire process. To him, it was a great accomplishment –suspension of the self-governing constitution and a reversion back to colonial rule under the British."

Something else that Carl remembered from back then: his father's haughty and indignant comments that the colony was far from ready for self-government, much less independence. "What do these locals know about running a country," he often asserted. "They don't even know how to make a safety pin!" All the while, what he was really implying was that he didn't think dark-skinned people were capable of running their own government; that they still needed to be educated and trained, like little children. The same approach he had to raising his children. To Augusto, the British could do no wrong, even with the discovery that there was no communist plot to grab independence. The British troops who were rushed to the colony found that there was no armed insurrection in the streets of Georgetown or in the countryside, where the bulk of the Reform support lay.

Carl believed that his reflections were leading him to thoughts that he'd buried a long time ago and going back down that road would only raise bitterness and a desire for condemnation. He was returning for a funeral and everything that had transpired should be interred with his father's body. If he were lucky, he would be in and out of the country in less than a week.

"I hope everything goes well with the funeral," Father Martin said, "and I wish you all the best."

"Thank you, Father. I hope the newspaper gets back on its feet and you don't have any problems with the government. I imagine it's one of the few dissenting voices not controlled by the Republicans, now."

"Well, there is one other voice, a newspaper printed by the opposition Reform, but I really don't count that since it also prints opposition propaganda. All the dailies rely on government ad-revenue and since almost every big business is now within government control, the newspapers have to toe the line, a not so very subtle kind of pressure. You print only items in favour of the government, or you don't get ad revenue and you go out of business. As for us, we prefer to maintain our independence. I guess you can say that we've become the conscience of the little man."

"I imagine there will come a time when they resort to strong arm tactics?"

"We've always gotten death threats in the mail and phone calls in the night." The priest sighed again and shook his head. "Some ministers are calling for us to be shut down, permanently, even though we're still a weekly."

"So why do you stick it out? Why don't you leave, Father? I would think that you've earned the right to take it easy after so many years. Won't it be a lot safer for you with your relatives in Canada?"

Father Martin chuckled. "My relatives feel the same way. A strange thing at times, you know. Whenever I'm in Guyana, hearing all the problems that surface every day, when I think about the threats and the struggle for survival, I ask myself the same question: Why don't I just pack it all up and leave? Then, the need to go to Canada arises, since we have to raise funds to buy newsprint –the Guyana government will not sell foreign exchange for this purpose. To be honest, it's a real relief to go to Canada where I can be among my relatives. Just the kind of break I need. Strange enough, when I'm there, I can't wait to get back to Guyana. There's something that's always calling me back, something in the blood, I guess."

Father Martin leaned back in his seat for a while –his eyes adopted a glaze that seemed to have transported him far off, to another time and place. Perhaps he was thinking back to when he was a young priest and lived a tranquil life in the savannahs of the sparsely populated Rupununi, providing bible lessons to the aboriginals and counselling them in the ways of the Lord.

"I suppose it would be the easiest thing to do: run and hide," the priest said. He shook his head. "I'm sorry, I didn't mean that as a reflection on all those Guyanese who have chosen to live abroad. Everyone has his own reason for doing what he has to do and the good Lord knows best. My skin might be lighter than many Guyanese, but I am a Guyanese. I was born in Guyana, British Guiana really, and I've lived there all my life and hope to be buried there one day. My grandparents settled in this country, same as most others who now live there. As far as the threats go, we've learnt to live with them. After all, most of the members of the government are still Catholic and that gives me hope."

Carl did not respond. He didn't think there was anything more to add, but he hoped the priest was right. If everything he'd heard so far indicated the state of affairs in the country, it did not bode too well for The Catholic Times, or for his visit.

***

They were about to leave the Atlantic behind. Below, through the haze, Carl could make out the South American coastline. The long slanting rays of the sun bounced off the silver sheen of the 747, pushing an ever-reluctant area of luminosity ahead of it. The plane followed a dirt road running parallel to a wide river. The road was nothing more than a narrow swath of emptiness carved out of the woods. The bright glow raced ahead of the plane; it swerved as it hit a crude wooden bridge, bounced off a cluster of rooftops, disappeared again as it passed over a stretch of trees, reappearing shortly afterwards. The luminous disk hesitated, crept slowly into the nearby river, its mutable bulk undulating with the waves. After it entered it became a fiery omelette, ever changing bands of orange, pink, and maroon, surrounding it.

Going back. Could one ever really go back? Here he was, heading back for his father's funeral. He had not rationalized whether it made sense or not; it just seemed the natural thing to do. One of those rites of living and dying, something automatic. What was it that was drawing him south again? Was it to pay homage to the man who had sired him, raised him and believed he had done his share; was it out of a sense of loyalty to someone who had given him his name; or was it guilt that was really behind it all? Was it as Father Martin had said, something in the blood?

They were now flying through a field of white clouds and his view of the airplane was restricted to what he could see of the wing. With no reference point above or below, it seemed as if they were suspended in mid-air, the silence broken only by the constant hum of the engine and an occasional bump as the plane was buffeted by an air pocket. Wasn't this how it always was in British Guiana during the colonial days: periods of calm when nothing happened and time stood still, and those intervals with events which came along and somehow managed to change their lives forever?

Suddenly, they ran into a rain cloud. Large drops poured down, bounced off the metal skin, cascaded down the flaps and disappeared into the grey void below. Droplets formed on the window, were caught in the backward flow of an air stream created by the movement of the plane, and dispersed into rivulets.

Sixteen years: More than a decade and a half. One hundred and ninety-two months. Not a very long period when considered in the passage of time, but long enough to warp the memory and dull the senses, and like loosely connected parts of a puzzle, the years fell into place once the pieces were joined.

Over the years he'd given little thought to those connections, about the people he had left back home, his relatives he had been separated from geographically and emotionally; about the years immediately before independence and the years after; the good and the bad years, the in-between years.

Sixteen years: They had slipped by so swiftly, the amount of years since he had left Repentigny, a place so small and insignificant that it did not feature in any published map. The area had been very important to him in his early years, his birthplace, the village where he had been nurtured and developed. Repentigny, Middle Walk and the Canal; how could he ever really forget them?

Everything happened around the Canal back in those days. The place where they drifted when school was over for the day; where they spent the greater part of the weekend; their very own preserve where they idled away most of those long, endless school breaks. Sometimes, they played marbles at the Crossroad, waiting for the weekend and a trip to the Paramount cinema. In those clear, warm days, with blue skies and a scorching sun blazing down, there was no thought for tomorrow. Often, in the middle of the afternoon, with white clouds billowing overhead and sunshine rushing in waves along the road, a sudden stillness settled over the surroundings. From as far as they could see, along a road that narrowed until it almost reached the outer fringes of the Backdam, there was a familiar changing pattern as the sky came alive.

First there was a light patter, nothing more than a slight disturbance of the stillness, something more like the gradual awakening at daybreak or the calm that precedes sunset when the parrots bed down in the trees and the Gauldings wing their way to the Botanical gardens. It wasn't something visible, but it was there. You knew it, could smell it, taste it in the air and feel it coming. Like the roll of distant drums gradually growing louder with every passing minute and finally rising to a crescendo, it descended.

If Carl was playing in the Crossroad with his friends, they grabbed their marbles and ran down the Walk, the steady staccato beat at their heels, the sound amplified hundreds of times on corrugated roof tops along the way as they tried to outrun the rain before the eruption. They would be almost home when the swift moving dark cloud overtook them, unloading heavy drops that splattered and stung as it passed over. By the time Carl arrived at his front gate he'd be drenched, his clothes clinging to his body. A few minutes more and he was up the stairs, safely inside, looking through the jalousie window at what was happening. Trees were bending, swaying, heaving and discarding their leaves in the process. The leaves did not even hit the ground; they were caught in a whirlpool. Eddies of leaves and debris moved along in frenzy across the road, around the front yard, up the stairs, on to the landing.

A few minutes is what it lasted, after which the cloud passed as swiftly as it had come, heading for the mouth of the Demerara River. By the time Carl came out on the landing the parched earth was soaking up the moisture like a giant sponge. The sole remaining evidence of the discharge was the mist rising from the road. As Carl sniffed the air he could detect a variety of scents riding the crest of a gentle breeze coming from the north: the unmistakable aroma of dung from the cow pen on Canal Road mixed with the odour of fresh cut grass; the tang of the spice-mango tree in the front yard combined with the pungency of the curry from the family next door.

How exhilarating it all was. In those days, they were always racing with the rain

CHAPTER 3 –In The Deep End

FRIDAY 9ᵀᴴ OCTOBER 1953: statement issued over Radio Demerara by Chief Secretary to the Governor:

Her Majesty's government has decided that the Constitution of British Guiana must be suspended to prevent Communist subversion of the Government and a dangerous crisis both in public order and in economic affairs. The faction in power have shown by their acts and their speeches that they are prepared to go to any lengths, including violence to turn British Guiana into a Communist state. The Governor has therefore been given emergency powers and has removed the portfolios of the Party Ministers. Armed forces have landed to support the police and to prevent any public disorder, which might be fomented by Communist supporters.

It seemed as if The Canal had always been there –long before Carl's father, Augusto Dias built his house, long before the British came.

The Canal had its birth in a time when the Dutch West India Company dominated commerce. The Dutch had carved the Canal out of the backcountry. They had come, lured by tales of the golden city of El Dorado written by Sir Walter Raleigh in his famous *Discoverie of the Large Rich and Bewtiful Empire of Guiana* in the sixteenth century, only to discover that riches were not lying on streets paved with gold and that they would have to work the land to survive.

The Dutch knew that the flat coastland in Guiana would be subject to the vagaries of flooding in Spring Tides, be unmanageable in the rainy season and impossible to irrigate in the dry season. They knew they would always have to fight a relentless battle against the Atlantic to keep their newfound land, something that bitter experience from back home had taught them how to handle. They also knew the reward would be worth it –that they would have some of the most fertile land in the country for their sugar plantations. So, they constructed an irrigation system –a concrete seawall on the coastline to keep the high tide out, a dam to prevent swamp water from encroaching the land, a network of trenches to collect the run-off and punt the cane to the factories. When the trenches swelled during the rainy season, an arrangement of sluices called *kokers* drained the excess water into the Demerara River.

After the colony had been fought over, lost, seized, sacked, negotiated, retaken by the British, French, Dutch, it finally ended up with the British who began the longest uninterrupted period of colonization in the start of the nineteen century.

The Canal was there in the dry season, when people knew how indispensable it was to everyone's existence. It was there in the rainy season when water overflowed its banks and flooded yards right up to the stairs of the houses in the Walk –that was when everyone cursed and swore about what a meaningless ditch of lease water it was and they wondered why it wasn't just filled up with dirt.

More than one hundred and thirty years had passed since the British came. Not a very long time when measured against the span of all eternity but still long enough for change. The colonists had arrived, conquered, occupied, brought slaves from the Dark Continent to work the land and eventually freed them, when, in a period of enlightenment, they felt that no man should be held in bondage. They then lured workers from Portugal and after a short period these replacements found that they could not cope with the harsh land; they flocked to the urban areas, dominating the commercial life of the colony. The colonial masters had turned to workers from China but they too eventually drifted off the land, turning to shop- keeping and cook-shops in the towns and villages. Finally, someone looked at the reservoir of man power available in the Indian colony: here was a solution to all the labour problems on the plantations. Through ways and means designed to entice, cajole, bribe and corrupt the Indian populace, they were brought overseas, far from their mother country, to work a strange, hostile land.

When the Dutch arrived, along with sugar estates, they had established a town on the confluence of the east bank of the Demerara River and the Atlantic Ocean. They named the town Stabroek. When the British took over, they changed the name to Georgetown after their reigning monarch, but they had retained the layout established by the Dutch. As a result, trenches and tree-lined avenues were well placed around the city and its environs.

Just outside Stabroek, the French, in their time, had established a village. Repentigny: just a speck on the horizon – delineated on one side by the Canal and on the other side by the Veldt, where sugar cane stalks grew tall and verdant, swaying in the cool breeze drifting south from the Atlantic. Repentigny: big enough to warrant its own burial ground, not large enough to justify its place on any map.

From his position, twenty feet up in the spice-mango tree in the front yard, Carl felt as if he were on top of the world. For the first time, he had ventured high up in the tree and he'd only done so, coaxed and goaded by Lincoln who kept telling him not to look down to the ground when he was climbing.

Every yard in the Walk had at least one mango tree but the one in Carl's yard was the tallest and the most prolific fruit bearer. The tree had a thick trunk that reached to the sky, anchored by a vast arrangement of roots that ran off in many directions. Spindly limbs branched off from the trunk, interconnected and intertwined at many levels and positions, a display of nature run amok in a green landscape.

Carl surveyed the surrounding area: rooftops and tree-tops, gutters and bridges, rain spouts and rain barrels, stairs and landings. For the first time, in his eight years, it was a perspective that gave him a sense of power and achievement. To the south of the Walk was the Veldt where the sugar cane stalks were in full bloom. To the north, he could see Canal Road running parallel to the Canal. Across the Canal was St. Jamestown: not as many tree tops but many more rooftops crowded a lot closer than those in the Walk. So many people crammed into a warren. He followed the path of the Canal flowing from far up in the unpopulated Backdam to the Cross Road and the Low Bridge leading across to St. Jamestown. Further down to the west there was the High Bridge with cars and trucks crossing over to the city. Next to his house was the Carrington rooftop where Winslow lived with his grandmother. To his right was the Wailee family. Further up the Walk was the old burial ground with the Dutch tombs and south of the Veldt was the Market.

"There, over there," Lincoln pointed. "Is my roof top."

"I don' see it," Carl said.

"Yuh see the cinema? Well, to the left side, the first roof top you see."

Carl saw the sloped rooftop of the cinema –it was the largest roof on both sides of the Canal, heat waves shimmering off the rusted zinc sheets in the afternoon sun. Next to the cinema was Lincoln's house.

The sun was already heading in the direction of the river, and beyond that, to areas of the country that Carl had never seen, regions he only knew existed based on geography class in school and conversations overheard. Over the Demerara River, to the west, was Essequibo, the Cinderella county. Further west were uninhabited areas and the Rupununi savannahs, and Venezuela, where they spoke a different language. He'd never heard anyone speaking Spanish before. His grandmother Lilly occasionally spoke Hindi and his father and uncle still understood and spoke Portuguese, but it was a language his father said was dying a swift death due to a total lack of awareness by the current generation. So many different people, so many different tongues: Mister Chin, the cake shop owner on Plantation Walk spoke Chinese; Mister Ali the butcher spoke Urdu; the Melville family were native Amerindians and they sometimes spoke a strange dialect Carl had never heard.

Activity in the Walk was intensifying: it was coming around to the time when workers were making their way home. Jack the barber came along, his polished wood valise packed with his shears and comb and brush and other tools. Further up the Walk, Milkman was riding his bicycle with the huge aluminum can balanced on the cycle bar. Earlier, he had been to the Backdam to milk his cows. He was now making his rounds, doling out pints of milk with a ladle that hung on the handle of the can. Was it really true, that he watered down the milk to sell more pints?

Lincoln said: "Hey, look Carl, is Pussy coming down de Walk."

Pussy lived in the first house at the Cross Road with the Pastor. He was wearing his usual tattered black jacket, a white shirt below it; a matching black beret on his head and old, blue serge pants hanging loosely around his waist. The area around his crotch swayed to the right and left as he walked, keeping time with the heavy load of his ruptured hernia. Pussy's unkempt, dirty blond hair hung loosely around the beret and meshed with the grizzled beard and moustache, all of which covered his face and gave him an appearance similar to Mister Mike's big dog walking on its hind legs. It was difficult to see his eyes, not only because of his hairy countenance but he always kept them focused on the ground. As he walked, he dragged his feet along in shoes that had worn out their soles.

"Hey Pussy," Lincoln shouted, "Whey yuh goin' with your big t'ing dangling 'tween yur fukkin' legs?"

"Yeah Pussy," Carl repeated, "whey yuh going?"

Pussy continued on his way as if he had heard nothing. Only once did he break his stride, when he came across a cigarette butt lying on the road. He jerked his right foot backwards as if he were trying to relieve a sudden muscle spasm and in the same well-rehearsed, effortless movement, his left hand grabbed the butt and placed it in his jacket pocket.

"Whey yuh left de fukkin' dogs Pussy? How come yuh didn' tekh the dogs with yuh today?" Lincoln shouted from the top of the tree.

"Yeah Pussy, how come yuh didn' tekh de dogs?"

Pussy continued to ignore them.

This only seemed to irritate Lincoln. "Pussy In De Moonlight," he sang, "Pussy In De Moonlight dress in black. Pussy In De Moonlight live in a shack."

Carl shouted: "Pussy live in a shack."

A dray-cart came rumbling along the Walk, a donkey between the shafts, the driver sitting on the left shaft. Langra was returning home from hauling goods to and from the Market.

"Langra," Lincoln called out. "Hey Halffa-foot Langra, limping down de road; going wid de fukkin' dray-cart to pick up another load."

Langra's head turned to the right and left, a wild look on his dark face as he tried to trace the source of the voice. He sucked his teeth. "If I catch you, whoever you is, I goin' show you what I going do with this halffafoot. I goin' kick your ass to kingdom come." Using the end of the rope as a whip, Langra lashed the donkey several times and shouted: "Gwan jackass."

Cromwell passed on his way home, late from school, as usual.

"Hey Antiman Cromwell," Lincoln shouted, "why don' you wear a dress yuh fukkin' Antiman yuh?"

Cromwell raised his chin higher as he passed by the mango tree. Carl thought that he must surely know Lincoln's voice by now, but he said nothing as he sauntered down the road, his hands swinging widely, his hips gyrating. Lincoln never missed an opportunity to tease Cromwell and he often said that Cromwell was different, that he liked to play with girls rather than boys and Lincoln even mentioned that he'd once seen Cromwell wearing a dress. Carl couldn't understand what would cause a boy to act like a girl and wear a dress instead of a pants and shirt and why Cromwell's parents would even allow it to happen, but then, they were hardly ever at home.

Winslow and grandmother Carrington next door were embroiled in their afternoon argument. Winslow had dropped out of school sometime back and now helped out in his grandmother's basket stand in the Market. His grandmother always accused him of shirking his responsibilities when she needed a hand.

The traffic on the Walk dried up. The neighbourhood settled back to the quiet interval that preceded sunset, when mothers were busy preparing the evening meal and fathers were cleaning up after a hard days work. Birds were already flocking towards the Botanical Gardens in the city and somewhere nearby a dog barked. In the far out regions of the Backdam another answered his cry. Lincoln grew bored and started to climb down the mango tree. Carl followed him, his hands encircled around the trunk, his feet grappling for protruding branches and stumps as he negotiated his way down.

"Want to tekh a look at my slinging-shot?" Lincoln asked Carl when they were on the ground again.

Carl took the slingshot and pulled at the rubber strips, feeling the tension as he released them several times.

"I can hit anythin' I want to," Lincoln boasted.

Lincoln knew his way around Carl's yard, the way he knew all the other yards in the neighbourhood. He frequently skipped school, often roamed around, dropping in on his friends.

Lincoln led the way to the side of the house and even before they got there Carl sensed what Lincoln was going to do.

Along the outer wall of his house, high up in the peak, just below the ceiling joists, there was a nest of bats hanging by their claws from the rafters. The bats were huddled together, looking like a mongoose with many heads, dark brown snouts protruding from the congested collection of fur.

Carl had looked at them many times and marvelled how they managed to continue hanging in their upside-down positions without falling to the ground. He'd seen them at sunset, dark streaks across the red tint of the sky as they headed for the Backdam and the fruit trees. Sometimes, they even attacked his mango tree in the front yard, the signs evident in the morning with fruits lying on the ground, skin riddled with holes.

Lincoln selected a stone and placed it in the slingshot, pulled the rubber bands taut, focussed his aim at the peak of the roof and released the missile; it hit dead center in the pile of fur. The bats released their tenuous hold, and with wings outstretched and flapping furiously, they scattered in different directions. Two of them slammed into the wall of the Carrington house, another one headed off to the genip tree, the fourth and fifth flew into the backyard. One of them fell with a *plop* at Carl's feet. He turned the bat over with his big toe and saw the spot where the stone had hit; it was swollen; red where the skin had ruptured, a trace of blood already coming to the surface.

"Gat him," Lincoln said, the triumph sounding in his voice as his eyes opened wide and he licked his lips.

Carl picked up the bat by its large ears; they were soft, fragile, as if they could come apart in his hands with just a slight tug. The nostrils of the bat projected outwards, and they were round, a hint of burgundy with a tint of black, like a ripe twin-cherry ready for picking. As he stared at the breast of the creature, he could see the tiny convulsions of its heart still throbbing and pulsing within its small body. He felt his own heartbeat starting to race. He looked at the bat's eyes, large, brown and bulging; they stared back at him without flinching. The eyes had a transparent look about them, as if he could look deep into them and see way beyond the sockets, into the very heart of the little creature.

Lincoln took the bat from Carl. He held it by both wings and stretched them out wide. The wings were paper thin, tiny capillaries running up and down like a spider's web seen against a beam of sunlight and when he released his pressure on them they collapsed like the broken umbrella lying in Carl's bottom-house.

"Blood sucker," Lincoln said, "dis is one motherfukker not goin' to suck any body or eat any more mangoes." He held the creature by one wing, swung it several times in the air and threw it over the paling-fence into the Carrington yard.

A palm-fly flew past, its wings fluttering furiously as it settled on one of the hibiscus trees by the fence, its black body framed against the red flower. Lincoln held his right index finger to his lips and motioned to Carl to be silent, then, he crept up to the fence. Moving very slowly, he grabbed the fly. The fly flapped its wings, trying to get away, as it continued to move its long tail up and down.

"Wonder if it can fly with one wing only," Lincoln said. "Leh we see, nuh?"

Lincoln applied pressure on the thin, transparent right wing of the fly and in a few seconds he had separated the wing from the body. He let go of the insect and Carl watched as it flew away clumsily, hopping from one branch to the other, its body leaning to the left like an airplane that's lost a wing.

As it hopped across the hibiscus tree, the fly startled a lizard. Lincoln saw the lizard. He dropped the wing, reached down and pulled out a long stalk from the tall para-grass in the yard. Placing the stalk in his mouth, he nipped off the top portion where the grains grew and quickly formed a loop with it. He held it in front of the lizard. When he touched the lizard's tail it scooted into the loop and Lincoln tightened the noose around its neck. Carl watched as the lizard's eyes bulged, to the point where he thought they might pop out of the lizard's head.

"Dis lizard jus' like you Carl. Look at it," and Lincoln turned the lizard over to show its underside. "Dark 'pon top and light underneath. How come you stay like that Carl?"

Carl thought for a moment. True, in many ways he was brown like his grandmother Lilly but when he took off his clothes he was as fair as any of the Portuguese people he knew.

"I don't know," Carl said. "I guess I mus' tekh after my father in some places and my grandmother in others."

"Them say that de lizard tail does grow back, yuh know. I wonder if this is a true-true t'ing." Lincoln pulled out his penknife from his pants pocket and turned it over to Carl. "Open it," he said.

Carl took the knife, holding it by the handle and turning it over on both sides to look at it. The pearl handles gleamed in the sunlight, the long blade safely sheathed between the dividers. The knife was heavier and longer than he'd imagined.

"Why yuh tekhing so fukkin' long, boy? Dis lizard not going to wait all fukkin' day yuh know."

Carl grabbed hold of the blade with his index finger and thumb and tried to pry it out. It came out part of the way, then, snapped back in.

"Here boy, hold this," Lincoln handed over the lizard, still held firmly in the noose of the blade of grass. "Leh me do it."

Lincoln pried the blade from between the dividers, took the lizard from Carl and placed it on the lower cross-runner of the fence.

Lincoln held the lizard and sliced off its tail with the penknife.

"We goin' leave it here an' see what happen later, if the tail grow back," Lincoln said, as he placed a rock on the end of the snare. "Come on Carl, leh we go shoot some birds by de rum shop," Lincoln said.

On the way out, just before Lincoln opened the gate, he stopped by the bougainvillea tree, picked up a stick from the ground and whacked the branches of the tree several times.

"Fukkin' hairy worms, they eating out the whole tree," Lincoln said.

The ground was littered with caterpillars cast off by the severe mauling to the tree. Some of them were squirming and inching along in different directions, but many of them lay prostrated, green skin ruptured, innards oozing out and forming a slimy mass on the dry ground.

"I not allowed to go by the rum shop," Carl said, as he leaned over to survey the carnage.

Everything has a purpose in life, the Pastor had said in one of his Sunday school classes. Carl remembered what his father said about caterpillars, though. All they did was eat leaves, making their way inch by inch until the entire tree was stripped bare. After that, they moved to another tree and then another. They were like Communists, preying on people and taking everything away until the cupboard was bare. Carl had seen caterpillars turn into cocoons and a swarm of butterflies in the backyard not too long after. Was there anything as colourful and graceful as a butterfly? This had to be worth something, he thought.

"Okay, then, we can go as far as Mister Mike," Lincoln said.

"Well, if it's that close." Carl pulled the gate behind him and followed Lincoln down the road.

They passed the Carrington house, the front paling leaning precariously over the gutter and ready to collapse any day. The Robertson house was next –it was where Reds lived. They passed the Melville and Das house and then came to the Raymond house where the twins lived. Underneath the mango tree in the front yard one of Mister Raymond's two donkeys stood, eyes half closed, his tail flicking back and forth, large ears flapping in the wind as flies swarmed around him. Next to Mister Raymond was Mister Mike's yard.

Mister Mike had no fence around his yard; two dogs were standing under the mango tree in front.

The two dogs were locked in a copulatory tie, attached in the rear and facing opposite directions like Siamese twins. They stood there in the shade of the tree, moving back and forth in nervous spurts, a cowering, simpering look on their faces as if they had been caught doing something they were not allowed to, and now all the evidence was stacked against them. What else could they do except wait for the right moment when their passions would subside and they could disengage themselves without too much pain or effort?

Lincoln grinned. His mouth opened wide, his incisors protruded from the corners. "Fukkin' dogs," he said.

Lincoln took out his slingshot and reached into his pocket for a missile. The dogs whimpered, tugged and pulled frantically at their unyielding bond, as if they knew what was in store for them, but they couldn't agree on which direction to head. They ended up tugging against each other. Lincoln took aim and released the stone from the slingshot. The stone hit Mister Mike's black and white dog in the left leg and it yelped and howled. The brown dog, a much larger one belonging to someone up the Walk, sensed what was coming and intensified its efforts to get away.

Lincoln laughed. He took out another stone and aimed. The two dogs continued to run in opposite directions, first one, then the other taking the lead. Lincoln released the stone; it hit the brown one on his rump and this was his cue to exert all his power to force the smaller black and white to head up the Walk. Lincoln sensed they were about to slip from his grasp. The slingshot was taking too long to load and shoot; he picked up bricks from the unpaved road and hurled them at the dogs. Carl, caught in the excitement, picked up stones and joined the chase. They pursued the dogs as far as the Crossroad, scoring several glancing hits, but, at this point Lincoln could contain himself no more; he stopped, laughed loudly and pointed at the retreating animals.

"Look how they run," he said, holding his stomach with his hands. "Is like how we start racing when the rain coming down."

Carl laughed. The afternoon had been very exciting so far. First, the thrill of climbing all the way to the top of the mango tree, shooting at the bats in the roof, the encounter with the lizard, scattering the hairy worms on the tree, then, the experience with the dogs.

Lincoln turned off at the Crossroad and headed towards his house in St. Jamestown. He would have to cross the Low Bridge over the Canal to get to his house. Carl hesitated and Lincoln turned back and looked at him.

"You coming with me?" Lincoln said.

Carl shook his head. He had no intention of crossing over the Low Bridge –the memory of what had happened last year was still fresh in his mind...

***

Lincoln had stopped in at Carl's house that afternoon.

"Leh we go down by the Canal," Lincoln had suggested.

"No, I can't go," Carl said. "I'm at home, sick. I have to stay in the yard."

Lincoln laughed. "You only start back school last month and you sick already?"

"I had a fever last night. My mother said that I have ague, or something like that."

"I get fukkin' sick too all de time. But, I still go all over de place."

"I don't know," Carl said.

"We won' take too long. You can see de punts coming from the Backdam with de cane and molasses. I can get some molasses for you from one of de punts, I know how to do it."

Carl was convinced –he followed Lincoln up the Walk and turned into the Crossroad.

School was over for the day and kids were heading home. Boys were dressed in khaki pants and shirts, shoes gleaming with a thick coat of whitening; girls in their navy blue armless dress with white blouse. Some kids were barefooted, threading their way carefully over the exposed, jagged stones on the surface of Canal Road.

Carl's oldest brother, Joseph was bundling his pants and shirt and about to lay them on the grass-corner when Lincoln and Carl arrived. Next to Joseph stood his other brothers James and Thomas who were stripped down to their underwear.

"What yuh doin' here Carl?" Joseph said, a frown creasing his forehead. "Lincoln, did you bring Carl here?"

"Not me," Lincoln said, "he come all by 'imself." Lincoln had already stripped off his clothes. He dropped everything where he stood and plunged from the wooden parapet into the water.

"You know yuh not supposed to be here," James said. "You will get a good walloping if father finds out."

"We will all get in big trouble," Thomas added.

"He's already here, he might as well stay," Joseph said. "He can sit right here on the grass-corner and keep an eye on our clothes."

Carl nodded eagerly. The Canal had quickly turned into a huge swimming pool. He had never seen so many boys together at the same time, except perhaps at the Playground on Sundays. As far as he could see, up and down the Canal, in the shimmering rays of the afternoon sun, light bounced off the cocoa-brown surface of the water and outlined heads bobbing up and down. There were still more kids crossing the Low Bridge, joining the crowd in the Canal.

Low Bridge was made of a sturdy cut of Greenheart lumber about two and a half feet wide, thirty feet long and connected to crossbars attached to huge wooden piles on both sides of the Canal. During the rainy season, when the water level rose, the bridge dangled about eight feet above the water, with just enough room for a convoy of punts to pass underneath.

From where Carl sat, the water looked very warm and inviting, beams of sunlight dancing on the surface. Every time someone jumped into the water from Low Bridge, Carl felt the spray, the drops fresh on his face, the smell so earthy and welcoming. He could see Lincoln frolicking in the water, ripples pulsing outwards from his body in ever widening circles until they flapped against the parapet. The Canal was so crowded that the momentum of scores of children sent wavelets surging over the top of the wood barrier. Joseph was swimming towards the other side, parting the water effortlessly with long hands outstretched. He was such a good swimmer, like a fish in water, everyone said.

Kids were using the Low Bridge to plunge into the Canal. Carl decided to see the view from on top of the bridge.

He climbed the five steps from the road and took a seat on the bridge. From there he could see all the way up the Backdam. Kids were coming alongside him and every time someone jumped he found himself heaving up and down, his small frame sometimes hanging precariously over the edge. He could taste the water on his lips. From here he felt as if he were the one diving into the water. He could almost experience the excitement of the jump, the thrill of taking a plunge.

It might have been when two or more kids jumped off the bridge together, or a point in time when he looked down and felt giddy over the sensation of seeing the churning, brown water below him, but before he knew it, he hit the water with a resounding splash and he went down, into the deep, murky, swirling depths of the Canal, into regions he'd only imagined existed.

Rainy seasons always brought floods to the Walk, especially when it coincided with high tides in the Demerara River. High tides meant that the *kokers* couldn't be opened to ease the rising water level, for fear of creating a reverse flow that would make matters worse. During the floods, when gutters overflowed, roads were covered and water crept up to the very front steps of the houses in the Walk. Wood bridges became detached and floated away. People had to wade through knee-deep water to get into and out of the Walk and everything came to a standstill. When the *kokers* were finally opened to reduce the water level, Carl had seen the Walk turn into a swirling cauldron with water flashing by on the way to the Demerara River. Leaves, branches, pieces of wood, all caught in the flow, were sent cascading down the gutters. Standing by the mouth of the large underground sluice which ran under the Walk and drained the water from one gutter to the other, Carl had looked at a whirlpool, thrown twigs into it and seen them swirl around and around rapidly into an eddy, finally disappearing. Where would they end up? Was it as Lincoln had said: into the mouth of the Demerara River and then out to the Atlantic, never to be seen again, perhaps swallowed by a great whale, like Jonah? Or, maybe washed up one day in some area in the countryside where no one ever ventured?

Panic seized Carl. His movements became spasmodic, completely uncoordinated. He groped around the depths like someone locked in a dark room, unable to see except for slivers of light created by his memory of what it was like to wake up early in the morning and see sunlight seeping through the cracks of the wallboards. His main thought was to get out in whatever way he could, as swiftly as he could. But, he could find nothing firm. All around him, everything was awash in liquid brown. Why didn't someone come for him? What was taking them so long? Surely they remembered that he couldn't swim?

He came to the surface once, his hands still thrashing, trying to grab hold of something. If only he could make it to the parapet at the side of the Canal, but it was so close and yet so far. He had no idea what to do to keep afloat. As he started on his way down for the second time, there were only blurs, images and bodies in motion clouding his vision and confusing his mind. He felt like a kid lost in the Backdam, not knowing whether to wait for someone to find him or to continue his desperate act of wandering.

As he sank to the bottom of the Canal again, Carl's feet touched mud and silt that added to the murkiness. He knew his movements were slowing down. He held his lips tight to avoid swallowing more water and he opened his eyes wide, trying to peer through the brown liquid but he could see nothing beyond his hands, hear nothing but the gurgling water rushing past his ears. He gasped and choked and didn't know whether he should breathe through his mouth or his nostrils. Was he already on the way to the Demerara River? Would he ever see his mother and father again?

Suddenly, just when he thought there was no end to it, when he'd given up hope, he felt something take hold of his right hand and tug him as if he were a punt being hauled by a large mule. He clung to it with all his might, the first firm object he'd felt for what seemed an eternity. He felt the movement, saw the rush of water going past him again, but this time he was moving upwards, faster and faster, to an area where there was light showing in all its glory. Light, like the break of day, light dazzling and brilliant like he'd never known existed. In the blur of coming to the surface he caught flashes of Joseph hauling him up to the parapet and laying him on the grass. Then, he was lying there, looking up at faces blocking the sunlight and staring anxiously at him. He gasped, choked and sputtered like he'd seen the cat do when she'd eaten the praying mantis in the back yard. He felt sick to his stomach, the portion of the Canal he had drunk coming up the same way it had entered, but the relief of being on firm ground again, there was nothing compared to it.

Familiar faces: how wonderful it was to see them again; Joseph, water running off his nose and beading on his moustache and small goatee, his curly black hair all soggy. There were James and Thomas, both of them looking scared –were they really concerned for him or anxious over father's wrath that would have descended on them if he'd drowned? Lincoln: had he been crying or were his eyes red from the water? How wonderful it was to see them all again.

"You okay?" Joseph said.

Carl nodded. "I t'ink so."

"You don' want to mention this to the Old Man," James said. 'You know how mad he will get if he knows what happened."

"Okay," Carl sputtered. His relief at being rescued from a watery grave and the thought that his punishment might have been worse than the near drowning experience was enough to keep him silent. That summer would always remain in his memory.

***

"You coming with me?" Lincoln said, as he started up the Walk towards the Crossroad.

Carl shook his head. Though he had the urge to stick around with Lincoln, he wanted to be nowhere close to the Canal. The memory of the previous year's incident was still vivid –he had flashes of it every time the water level in the gutters rose after a heavy rainfall and for the first few days after the incident, he'd even had a problem entering the bathroom to have a shower. When he finally did, he had to make the sign of the cross, something that he felt would protect him.

Lincoln was backing away. "Come with me, nuh . . ." he urged.

Lincoln stopped and leaned to the right. Something down the Walk had caught his attention. Carl turned around to see what it was. Far off, half a mile or so, there were people heading in their direction, the images becoming clearer and larger with every passing second.

"Look, is soldiers coming," Lincoln said. He ran off. Carl followed.

In a few minutes they had caught up with the soldiers and joined the stream of kids following them. Carl saw Wilfred and Cyril, his friends from school, and many other kids were trailing behind, some of whom he knew from the Walk.

Carl counted: twelve, all white men dressed in military uniforms, helmets and boots. He'd heard his father talking about British soldiers on patrol but this was the first time he'd seen them in the Walk. He remembered his father in conversation with Uncle Jules: *It was the best thing that ever happened to the colony since all this damn nonsense about self-government and independence started. I'm glad they'll be able to stop the Communists from taking control. Business can go on as usual.*

The soldiers walked slowly, in two columns, on opposite sides, rifles held in front. The one bringing up the rear was young, not much older than Joseph; he looked as if he was not too long out of high school. He turned around, looked at Carl, smiled and winked with his right eye, the eye blue as the cloudless afternoon sky, his white face splattered with red blotches, as red as the flowers of the hibiscus tree in full bloom.

"Hey kid," the young soldier said. "Got any sisters at home?"

The soldier laughed and his mates joined in. Many of the kids in the Walk had sisters, some of them older than Carl, most of them younger, but Carl couldn't understand why the soldier would be interested in any of them. Carl's only sister, Vivian had died of Gastro, years before he was born, he was told.

The soldiers kept going, unhesitant, on a mission it seemed. Only, Carl wasn't sure what the mission was. It was a rare event for them to even see a police man in the neighbourhood, and police, wearing thick black serge outfits and black boots, never carried guns. For the first time in his life, Carl was seeing British soldiers with rifles. The soldier at the head of the column carried a revolver at his side. The only other time Carl had seen a sidearm was in the movies –just last week he'd seen the western *Shane* at the Paramount, the sound of gunfire booming through the audience when Alan Ladd and Jack Palance shot it out in the final confrontation in the saloon.

The soldiers were Royal Welsh Fusiliers who'd arrived on the cruiser Superb and the frigates Bigbury Bay and Burghead Bay direct from Bermuda. News about the arrival of the soldiers had been widely publicized. Carl had heard it over Radio Demerara and read it in The Daily Graphic that was delivered to his father at home.

"Yeah kid," a second soldier said, "tell us if you have any sisters. We need something to ease the fookin' boredom."

"Does anyone know what the fook we're doing here?" a third one said.

The Chief Secretary and Governor Sir Alfred Savage had delivered speeches over the radio. They had said that the British government had suspended the constitution. The House of Assembly and the State House had been dissolved and troops were being rushed in to put down an expected Communist takeover.

"Yeah," another soldier said, "where's all the fookin' action they promised us. Where's all the Communists?"

"Where is the fookin' emergency they were talking about?" another said.

Police and British soldiers had raided the homes of government ministers, including the Chairman, looking for arms and what they called subversive literature. Many of the ministers and even the Chairman were now being held in detention behind barbed wire at Atkinson Air Force Base down the Demerara River. Carl had never heard the word subversive before and he'd looked it up in the dictionary. *Subvert: overturn, upset, effect destruction or overthrow of (religion, monarchy, the constitution, principles, morality); so subversion.*

So, what did it all mean? Reform had won the last election with a clear majority, despite vocal opposition mounted in the media by the labour movement and religious groups who had all attacked them for having Communist connections with the USSR. The Catholic and Anglican Church leaders had even hinted about the leader of Reform's wife being Jewish, and what this had to do with anything, Carl had no idea. He recalled reading after the last May Day celebrations, that members of Reform had carried banners of Stalin, the leader of the USSR, and they had declared that they would now open the country to literature and writings from all sources, including Russia. The Governor had now overturned this and the police and army were searching for subversive literature that had been brought into the colony.

The soldier at the head of the squad shouted: "Shut your fookin' yap and keep your eyes open."

The only other person that Carl had heard curse as much as the soldiers was Lincoln –*Cussbird Lincoln* he was called. Carl's mother had often warned him that if she ever heard him cursing like Lincoln, she would wash out his mouth with soap and water.

The squad went down the Walk, kicking up dust and heading in the direction of the Backdam. Carl had been in the Backdam a few times with his brothers. There wasn't much out there –only wild bush, tall trees that towered over the landscape, black-water trenches and cane-fields, and alligators and piranha. His father had told them around the supper table just last week that guns were buried in the Backdam and subversive literature had been found in the home of Carl's two friends: Wilfred and Cyril.

The patrol soon passed Carl's house. Carl stopped and stood on his bridge, watching them and Lincoln along with the other kids still trailing behind them. They passed the Lee house next to his, then the Mohamed, the Ledman, and the James residence. In another few minutes they were approaching the Crossroad and then heading towards the Backdam. Carl stood there and watched them until they were dots on the horizon and only when they had disappeared completely from view did he re-enter his front yard. What would they find, if anything at all?

CHAPTER 4 – Arrival

MONDAY 24TH NOVEMBER 1980

Father Martin was saying something.

"I'm sorry, Father, I was not paying attention," Carl said.

"I was just saying that we're coming in for landing. Look over there. You can see the lights at Timehri Airport."

Carl looked through the window. Far off, in the distance, he saw a small cluster of twinkling lights, like candles burning on a windowsill for a lonely wanderer trying to find his way home. He craned his neck to take in the surrounding landscape but there was nothing else visible. He felt as if the plane was beginning its descent into some remote jungle outpost in the heart of the interior, rather than the capital.

The priest must have read his thoughts. He said: "Not very welcoming, is it? We're actually flying over Georgetown but you wouldn't know it. We have blackouts sometimes. Seems like donkey years that this been going on and yet there's no sign of change coming." He turned his head towards Carl and in that instant when the cabin light bounced off the lens of his large glasses, Carl thought he detected a flash of anger in the priest's eyes.

Looking out the window, Carl thought it wouldn't take much for the surrounding darkness to overwhelm the lights. It was probably something like this when the first Europeans carved a settlement out of the wilderness –an ongoing battle against the encroaching jungle and an endless quest for survival. Had things changed much since then?

"Some people use their own generator, that is, if and when they can buy the fuel," the priest continued. "Things not so bad in Georgetown where the current comes on and off most times; it's much worse in the countryside where there is none."

Carl shrugged. "I grew up in Repentigny and in the early years we had no electricity. After many years we finally got road lights, but I can remember when I was a boy, looking out the window and seeing skies lit only by the vastness of the Milky Way and the occasional full moon. I didn't mind it so much back then. I thought it was exciting and awesome. After you get accustomed to something, it's hard to do without it, though. Looking out the window, makes me feel as if I am going back to that time."

The priest laughed. "Yes, sometimes, I feel that we now living far behind God's back."

Carl smiled –he hadn't heard the term in a long time. People often used it to depict the remoteness of the area in which they lived.

Father Martin had the type of laugh that lit up his entire face and relaxed his hazel eyes. His glasses slipped down the length of his long nose only to be pushed back up with an index finger. He grew serious again. He subjected his fingers to close scrutiny, examining the joints, picking at the cuticles, probing the fingertips and twirling the gold band on his ring finger. His fingers were long and slender, fingernails blending almost completely with his pink hands.

"I suppose you can say that time's stood still after independence. Many people think it's actually gone backwards. As much as twenty years. The time this government been in power."

"There can't be much of a nightlife," Carl said.

"You're right –the streets are almost empty after nightfall. Although daytime can be just as bad in Georgetown." He paused, then, he added, almost inaudibly in his soft voice, "My son, you must keep a watchful eye out when you're in Georgetown. A lot changed since you left. You're going to see so much change that you will start to think that your mind's playing tricks on you. The streets can now be a very dangerous place."

Things really haven't changed much since he left, Carl thought. He did a swift mental calculation and tried to figure out the markings in time: Fourteen years since independence; sixteen since the racial conflict and the eighty day general strike; eighteen since the disturbances in Georgetown when the downtown area was looted and burnt to the ground. Looking back, these were all years of conflict and strife and he shivered when he thought of the incidents he had witnessed and read about, the people close to him who had been hurt, the growing racial tension both in the cities and countryside, and the potential for civil war. Throughout it all, he'd managed to survive. Now, Father Martin was telling him that the streets were still not safe.

"I don't think I'm going to be here that long. A few things to settle up, then I'm out the end of the week," Carl said.

The priest passed his right hand along his bald dome, caressed his light brown hair at the side and moved his fingers along his forehead. He traced the red pimples that dotted the landscape of his forehead, as if they held the code to a message he was trying to decipher.

"Nevertheless," the priest said, "you keep a sharp eye out. You never know who is looking on and what they're planning. Things have a way of happening, things that you have no control over."

Carl knew what Father Martin was talking about. During the disturbances, roving mobs of youths accosted innocent people in the streets, harassing them at first, then growing bolder when police failed to take strong action to disperse them. Harassment soon turned to organized banditry: victims were beaten and robbed of their valuables; some killed, a few dumped in trenches and left for dead.

"If I do have to go around, I am planning on blending in with the crowd."

The priest smiled. "Easier said than done. First of all, we don't have too many fair-skin people around anymore. Most of the Portuguese left a long time ago –they were among the very first wave to leave the colony, even before the official handing over ceremony to the new government. Next, went most of the rich Chinese and Indians with business. Lately, even the middle class and poor Indians are heading out in droves, to America, Canada, the West Indies, anywhere they can get to. There're people even heading over to Suriname and Venezuela. They can't speak Dutch or Spanish but they try to adapt. These days, most people feel that anywhere is better than Guyana."

"It all sounds very bad!" Carl said.

The priest nodded. "All the embassies are packed every day with people trying to get a visa. But, you know, even if you happen to pick up a fast tan, you will still stand out. It's just a combination of different things. From the moment you open your mouth to say the first word, they will know the change in accent. Even, if you don't say a word, it's the way you look, the way you dress, the way you carry yourself." He chuckled. "They will spot you even from the way you smell – mark my words."

The movement from cloud cover to the ground was almost unnoticed.

A screech of tires as the aircraft hit pavement, a jarring sound, lights being switched on and the single terminal of the airport emerged slowly from a low lying mist. Some people were standing up even as the aircraft taxied closer to the terminal, despite being told to remain seated.

Carl could tell who were the ones who had been away for a long time. Like him, they were staring out the window, looking for signs of something familiar, something with which they could identify or connect. An old Chinese woman had her face pressed to the window –was she returning to visit relatives after living in Toronto with her son or daughter? Something that many Guyanese in Toronto did these days:

grandmother took care of the children while both parents worked during the day. An East Indian woman had a small girl with her. Was she bringing the child for her parents to take care of until she was older? Families were being split this way too: children being sent back for relatives to look after while parents worked at several jobs in Toronto, all of which didn't contribute to a stable family life, but people were more concerned with survival than nurture.

Father Martin was up and extracting his suitcase from the overhead compartment. A stewardess was trying to assist a woman up front with her baby.

As he joined the queue behind Father Martin, Carl said: "I'm not sure if my uncle has made arrangements for a funeral service. Could I call on you to do it, if he hasn't, Father Martin?"

Father Martin nodded. "Of course. I'd be happy to. You will also find that not much gets done in the country anymore, without a contact to speed things up. If I can help in any way, call on me. You can reach me in Georgetown, at the diocese."

Carl hardly heard the goodbye or took notice of the smiling cabin attendant as he started down the stairs. He was more intent on looking at the terminal that was still partly shrouded, clouds of mist floating across it. He stepped on to the tarmac. Was the weakness in his legs from the inactivity of the long flight or being back on soil with which he had such a strong emotional attachment? His breathing was now coming in deep gasps. He steadied himself and started towards the terminal.

Every now and then the mist cleared. The terminal was a squat building, zinc sheets on a sloped roof, a glass enclosed viewing area to the right with people waiting for arrivals. He made out the vague outline of figures, a kerchief fluttering, hands waving, someone jumping up and down. He hoped Uncle Jules was one of the people in the viewing area. He followed a group of people to the entrance of the building past a sign that said *Welcome to Timehri Airport*.

Carl found himself caught in a stream of arrivals going down a long corridor enclosed on all sides by walls dabbed with the traditional government coat of cream paint. The corridor opened out suddenly into a large area and he saw that there were already four long lines of people in the centre of the room. Carl paused, lowered his carryon on the rough concrete floor and tried to decipher the intent of the signs hanging over the dais at the head of every line. Three of four signs were labeled *Guyanese Nationals* and the fourth had *Foreigners* in bold, black letters. A fifth line was for *VIPs*. Carl was an expatriate Guyanese. Which of the four lines should he be joining?

Father Martin was way off to the left, at the rear of the line, talking to one of the guards with whom he appeared to be on friendly terms. The Chinese man Carl had seen at Pearson was in the second line. The old East Indian man and his son –earphones still inserted in his ears, were moving up in the third queue. Carl decided on the line that had already accumulated ten Foreigners.

The hall was now packed and even more stragglers were pouring in through the entrance to join the queues. Two cabin attendants passed Carl and made their way through the crowd, pulling their small bags on wheels as an Immigration officer waved them through.

Huge, colourful cloth banners with slogans hung on the four walls. On the rear wall was a large flag, the Golden Arrowhead, its red, black, yellow and white representing the country's nationalities, triangles superimposed on a green background. Below the flag was a larger banner with the words *Welcome to the Peoples Co-Operative Republic of Guyana*. Directly above Carl, loomed a huge portrait of the President. The President was taking the salute as head of the armed forces and he was dressed in full military khaki uniform: medals, decorations, badges, ribbons, ceremonial cord, polished brass buttons adorning both sides of his tunic. His stern gaze was focused on the milling throng, as if they needed a reminder of who was in charge.

The queue started to move again. Carl was now number nine from the front. At the head of the line to the extreme left of the room a commotion broke out and activity ceased for a moment. Immigration officers stopped their processing and looked on; people waiting in the lines turned to see what was happening.

"I don' understand. What is the problem?" an East Indian man said, in an emotionally charged voice.

"Aint no problem," the Black immigration officer said firmly. "I'm telling you to go with this officer." He pointed to a security guard.

"Why? Why do you want me to go with him?"

"Some more questions we need to ask and I don' want to hold up de line."

"This is nonsense. Is all my papers in order? Tell me this."

The interviewing officer shrugged. "I telling you once and for all, you go with the officer if you want to get out of here soon."

The officer handed the passport to the guard who started to leave the room, the East Indian trailing behind him. They both disappeared around the bend. Five more guards had taken up positions along the wall, waiting to be summoned.

Carl stood behind the faded yellow line, waiting his turn, wondering what it was all about.

Attached to the front of the dais, facing Carl, same as with every other one in the room, was the Guyana coat of arms: a leopard on the left, a cheetah on the right, and an Amerindian headdress on top. The motto on the coat of arms was *One People, One Nation, One Destiny*. Great words, Carl thought. He looked around: every official that he saw was Black, with no sign of any other of the five nationalities that inhabited the country –not a single East Indian, no Chinese, no Portuguese or White, no Amerindian Native, not even a mixed race person like him. How was it that none of the other races was represented in the Immigration department?

Was it the same for all the other departments in the civil-service? Was it as he'd heard, that the only way to gain entry to government jobs, was through a party card, and since mainly Blacks joined the governing party, they were the only ones in the civil-service these days?

Over the coat of arms was a sign: *Visitors must wait behind the yellow line until called.* Carl waited and he watched, wondering what could possibly be going on as he saw the scene repeated several times, more men led out of the room by a security guard, although there was very little opposition now from those being escorted out.

Finally, Carl's turn came and he moved up to meet the officer.

The officer stood with his elbows on the slanted surface of the wood stand, his torso slightly bent over at an angle that suggested either tiredness or boredom. A name tag on his chest labelled him as Johnson. He reached out and took Carl's passport without a word and started to flip through the pages in the passport, slowly, methodically, checking the personal details and looking Carl up and down.

"Purpose of visit?"

"I'm here for a funeral," Carl said.

"Is who dead?" Johnson asked.

"My father."

"How long you plan on spending in de country?" Johnson said, with no emotion in his voice.

"I have a return flight the following Sunday...as you can see from this," Carl said, holding out his plane ticket for scrutiny. He added, as an afterthought, "I'm only here as long as it's necessary for the funeral and make some other arrangements, then I'm leaving." He couldn't help wondering: why was it necessary for him to justify a return to the country where he was born and had spent his early years? But, could he still consider it his country, with all that had happened and the many changes before and after independence?

The officer ignored him –he was examining the entry and exit stamps, rifling through every page in the passport. "You born right here in Guyana, right? How long ago since you left?"

"I left sixteen years ago."

"Is this de first time you coming back?"

"Yes, the first time I'm returning."

"You coming from where in Canada?

"Toronto –that's where I live, now."

Johnson's eyes opened wide as he came across something in one of the pages. He shook his head to clear it, like a man suffering from a horrible hangover.

"Says here you have a visa for Cuba," Johnson held the passport open to the page with the stamp. It was almost a statement of triumph, as if he'd found something incriminating, something that would place him in the good graces of his superiors.

Carl did not hesitate. "Yes, I do have a visa for Cuba, for business visits."

"You been there to Cuba?"

"Yes, I've been there. All part of my job."

Johnson scribbled something on a piece of paper and inserted the paper in the passport. "Just follow de guard," he said and motioned to one of the men waiting against the wall.

The room suddenly grew silent. All through the interview Carl had been aware of the activity around him: the whirring sound of the overhead fans, the flapping of paper as people fanned themselves to relieve the oppressive heat. A baby had been crying, its mother trying to console it. Someone had a coughing fit. Johnson's words echoed in Carl's ears and he was unsure of the implication for him.

Johnson handed the passport over to the guard and said, "Next," with a curt dismissal.

"Could you tell me what the problem is?" Carl said. "Where am I going?"

"No problem, man. Just routine. Follow de guard and he will show you where to go."

"If there's no problem, why am I not going on my way?"

The officer shrugged.

"Look, I've told you, I'm just here for a funeral. I'll be out by the weekend."

The presence of the guard loomed next to Carl. The guard was just inches away –Carl could feel the man's hot breath on his face. Johnson motioned to the person at the head of the line to come forward.

Carl followed the guard, the man looking back furtively every now and then to ensure that he had not lost his charge. They went along the same narrow corridor so many people had passed through, a corridor with bleak cream walls faded and peeled, and around the same bend people had disappeared. Carl had been curious about where they were heading. He was about to find out.

They came to a large chamber and Carl was not surprised to see familiar faces from his flight. A loud hum emanated from the area as people congregated in small groups, no doubt discussing, exploring, speculating on what the delay could be all about. He recognized the East Indian man and his son, the boy with the earphones still on his head. The Chinese man hoping for a cheap holiday was there. At the end of the room was Father Martin, chatting with a guard who stood in front of a closed door.

"Wait here," the guard escorting Carl said. "Somebody going call yur name soon."

The guard handed Carl's passport to a woman sitting behind a desk. She entered details of the passport in a logbook and then added it to a pile in a tray. Every now and then, another clerk picked a passport from the bottom of the pile, called the name of the owner and ushered the person into one of the rooms.

Carl slung his bag over his shoulder and inched his way through the gathering, heading for a small clearing to the right of the room.

"I don' know why the kiss-me-ass people keeping we here for," the East Indian man was saying, to no one in particular, since his son was still shaking to the rhythm of a calypso which could be heard through the earphones.

"Jesus Christ," the Chinese man said, "Is what is the problem here, man." He looked at his watch and seemed to be calculating the number of hours that the delay was eroding into his cheap vacation.

Carl passed a group of East Indian men. He overheard snatches of conversation.

"Man, things don' change here at all you know. Is the same thing over and over again."

"You would think that things would work better after independence, but they jus' seem to get worser and worser every day."

"You notice not a single East Indian working here. What does that tell you?"

"Yeah, and look around. Do you see any Black people in this crowd being detained for more questions?"

"Look how they treating us here today, as if we was common criminals. Is who they really after anyhow?"

"How long more we got to wait here before they clear up this mess!"

"I hear somebody saying that some group or the other in Toronto planning to overthrow the government."

Carl took a seat on a chair, one of many braced against the wall. Most of the people in the room seemed to prefer standing, as if they expected that they would be out in a matter of minutes. Carl counted twenty heads. At a minimum of fifteen minutes per person, it would take five hours for all the interviews. There appeared to be five interview rooms: if there were five officers conducting interviews, it might take around an hour to finalize everyone in the room, but there could be less than five officers and there might still be more people diverted for interviews from the flight; all potentially adding up to a very long wait.

Waiting: it was not something that Carl did well. His hands and feet had a will of their own, always demanding movement and activity. He leaned forward on the chair, his hands supporting his head, elbows propped up on his legs, feet shaking. His hair was long and hung over his forehead, partially obscuring his vision. He'd been meaning to have a haircut and a manicure over the weekend, but then, the phone call had disrupted his plans. That's all it took at times: one simple phone call with bad, or good tidings, depending on whose perspective it was.

Carl was at work one day when he received a phone call from Natasha; she told him she was pregnant, for the first time. He'd been at a complete loss for words. Having children at this early stage in his career hadn't featured in his plans and while they had discussed it a few times, he'd never really factored it into his life. She'd gone ahead and stopped her birth control pills without his knowledge, yet another plan she'd made on her own without consulting him. He found it infuriating at times –the way she went about things and he couldn't help wondering if it had anything to do with her upbringing in the Soviet Union, where decisions were made by a hierarchy and expected to be implemented by those on the lower rungs of the ladder, without discussion and without thinking about it. Over the years it was one of the factors that had made him question whether she was really the right partner for him and the issue had continued to fester and loom as an obstacle in their relationship.

Carl remembered the waiting room of the hospital in Toronto. Natasha had already been in labour for ten hours with Alexei and he was outside pacing the floor, waiting for the ordeal to be over. She had asked him to be there with her during the delivery and after thinking about it for a long time, he'd decided against it. When he thought of the pain and the agonizing hours leading up to the delivery, it was not something that appealed to him. He had a vision of him fainting and making things worse. Two years later, when Irina came along, Natasha had not repeated the request for him to be present at the birth and he remembered how relieved he was. For the second time he'd found himself waiting outside the delivery room while she went through the ordeal, again. The guilt surfaced every time he looked at the pictures of his two children as babies. If Natasha ever thought of it, she'd never brought it up in conversation.

Progress was being made with the interviews: he saw people coming out of the rooms, heading for the baggage area to claim and process their suitcases through Customs. When would his turn come? What did the immigration people know about him, about his past life and his associations that could possibly influence their attitude towards him? He knew that he'd never really done anything against the current government, at least nothing that they could hold against him, though there was a time in the distant past when he'd been a loyal member of the RYM –the Reform Youth Movement, the youth arm of the Reform party who were in power before independence. In the current political situation, where party membership was being used as a yardstick to measure fidelity to the government, how would they interpret his past loyalty? Would he be perceived as a threat if he entered the country?

There was something that he'd almost gotten involved in, foolishly in hindsight, back in Mississauga just over two years ago. A long time ago, it seemed, but government officials had a long memory, and with the almost paranoid state of affairs in the country, with the added interviews that were being conducted, he couldn't help thinking that it might be used against him if it came out.

During Natasha's last pregnancy he'd received a phone call out of the blue. He could remember most of the conversation.

"Carl, this is Cyril. Cyril Ramdass –one of the three musketeers."

Carl had been elated to hear the voice from the past. He had a lot in common with Cyril and hearing the man's voice evoked the memory of a third person: Wilfred Ledman. The three of them were born and raised in Repentigny, attended the same high school, graduated the same time. They'd grown to share the same values and ideals, cultivated around a time when the country was experiencing radical social and economic upheaval. They'd also joined the RYM, together.

"Cyril, my God. Is it really you? How long has it been? Has to be around ten years!" Carl said.

"More like twelve," Cyril said.

"How have you been keeping?"

"You know how it is: could always be better."

"What about Wilfred? Have you kept in touch with him?"

Cyril said: "Wilfred's back in Guyana. He's now the head of the Repentigny wing of the party. Still doing the same thing, in the same old way." Did Carl detect some disappointment in Cyril's tone?

Cyril came straight to the point –he'd never been one for much preamble when he addressed an issue. "The reason I'm calling: we've formed a political party with people on both sides of the border, to do something about this dictatorship back in Guyana. RDG –Restoration of Democracy in Guyana party. I'm on the executive council. We plan on running candidates in the next election in Guyana and need all the support we can get."

"I don't know, Cyril. I've been out of that for a long time. I have no interest in what's going on back there. Besides, you know how entrenched the two parties are –there's very little hope of change."

Cyril was always the most passionate and aggressive of the three. "You can't abandon the country to those people. Guyana's now run by a fascist and it's obvious that we can't rely on the opposition Reform to do something –they're always boycotting the legislature. On top of that, the Chairman of Reform lost his voice and his will to do something about the dictatorship. We need fresh blood." Cyril was like that – always hoping to be an agent of change, even when it was impractical and bordering on the impossible.

"You're chasing a hopeless cause," Carl said.

"You were always someone who wanted to change things. Here's your chance to make a difference."

"That was a long time ago, Cyril –a different time and a different place. Things are not the same now."

"There are some very influential Guyanese behind the movement and we have the backing of some members of Congress and senators in the US, who want to see a return to democracy in Guyana. Look, you don't have to commit to anything right now. Just keep an open mind and see what it's all about. No harm in that, is there? You never know, it might awaken some of that old fire you had when you wanted to change the world. The executive of the new party is having the next meeting tomorrow night. I've told them about you and our past connections. Why don't you at least come and see what it's all about? I'll pick you up. It'll be like old times, again."

Carl had given in to Cyril's persuasive arguments and agreed to attend the next meeting. Cyril had driven them to an Industrial park off Highway 10 in Mississauga, the headquarters of the new party. The executive of the party consisted of ten Guyanese, all East Indians, wealthy business men who had fled the country. The members of the group had one thing in common –an unquenchable thirst to get rid of the current dictatorship in Guyana. They talked about their growing membership and the extensive network of people they were linked to, in America, Canada, the UK, the Caribbean, and in the rural areas of Guyana where the bulk of the East Indians resided.

Carl soon realized from the ensuing discussions, that, while the group was called the Restoration of Democracy in Guyana, the members were prepared to use any means necessary to remove the current government. Carl was alarmed that they would even discuss an approach that involved an armed uprising –it would start in the country areas where the East Indians were predominant and eventually spread to the cities where support for the government was entrenched. The executive claimed they were going to get financial support from the American government and that the CIA was backing their plans, even to the extent of providing arms for the venture.

That was the first and last meeting of the RDG that Carl had attended. Over the phone, Carl had told his old friend that he was not interested in supporting the movement since, while he might share their desire for a change in government in Guyana, he did not believe in their armed approach. Cyril hadn't given up –he'd continued to phone and make entreaties for Carl to support them. In one phone call, Carl had found out, to his irritation, that Cyril had paid for Carl's first year membership in the group.

There seemed to be no apparent method to the way names were being called for the interview. At first Carl had thought it was alphabetical but then Father Martin was summoned after an East Indian man named Singh. Carl thought that perhaps the travellers with Guyanese passports were being called first, until another man he'd seen in the Foreign Passport Holders line was called ahead of him.

Carl stood up. His keys and coins were hot against his legs and he started to move them around in his pockets. The jingle and jangle, the twirling and constant movement up and down succeeded in restoring a sense of calm in him. He started to walk around the outer perimeter of the room.

Carl had been timing the interviews. The longest so far had been twenty minutes with the East Indian man who had kicked up a fuss over being pulled aside for further questioning. Were they punishing him? Surely they wouldn't stoop so low, to seek retribution on someone, a citizen at that, for asking a simple question! There were civil and human rights enshrined in the Guyana constitution, meant to protect freedom of religion and speech, among a multitude of other things, all of which appeared to be now meaningless.

Carl was one of two people remaining. He looked at his watch: Nine o'clock. One hour and thirty minutes since they had landed and he was only now closer to the point where he might be getting out of the airport. Ninety minutes: in his early years at the bank he'd been able to process several personal-loan applications in the same time. Less than half a day's work –the amount of time in which he could have done two business reviews and made his decision on whether to approve or decline the venture. What a waste!

A door opened and Father Martin came out. The clerk at the desk picked up a slip of paper and called for Mister Persaud. The second man jumped up quickly from his seat and hurried to the door.

Father Martin came over to Carl, mopping his head and brow with a white handkerchief that was now crumpled and stained with perspiration.

Carl stood up. He said: "They kept you a lot longer than everyone else, Father. Are you okay?"

The priest sighed. His face was flushed, looking much more enflamed than when Carl first saw him. He placed his overnight bag on the floor and rested his overcoat on it, took off his glasses and wiped his face.

Father Martin looked behind him, at the guard who was now leaning against the wall, his chin resting on his chest. "Well, it's not too comfortable in there. I suppose they looked at this as an ideal opportunity to send another message to me about how dissatisfied they are over my editorials in *The Catholic Times*."

"Do you really think it has to be about your editorials, Father, with all these people being questioned?"

"They're mainly interviewing people who either live in the Toronto area or have travelled to New York over the last few weeks or so."

Carl passed his right hand lightly over his head and flipped his hair back in place. With his left hand in his pants pocket, he could feel the coins –they were now much warmer and seemed ready to burn holes in his pocket.

"Could turn out to be the whole plane. What are they after?" Carl said.

The priest looked back at the guard who had not changed his position. "From what I understand, it seems that there was a plot being hatched by some Guyanese living in New York and Toronto. Earlier, one of the guards told me that these people were buying arms and planning an armed invasion in the countryside, the idea being to overthrow the government."

Carl thought for a moment. "All so crazy. They hold up a whole planeload of people for that! Customs will find out what you're bringing in when they check your baggage. Besides, how could you ever bring arms through Toronto International Airport?"

Father Martin placed his right hand on Carl's shoulder. "They're not after arms, at this stage. They're looking for the ringleaders, or anyone who might have anything to do with the plot. Be careful what you say, my son. Seems as if the RCMP and the FBI found out about the plot and are investigating a number of people on both sides of the border. The government here is trying to get more information." He smiled and looked back at the interview room. "You can well imagine how paranoid they must feel. The first time anything like this has happened since the Rupununi uprising back in sixty-eight."

Carl was not in Guyana in 1968 but he'd read of the plot by a group in Lethem in the North West District. Local ranchers, supporters of the Conservatives, now opposed to the Republican government, concocted a plot to secede from Guyana and align the district with Venezuela. The conspirators had declared their intention and seized the government offices in the area, placing trucks on the runway to prevent planes from landing. The plot had been put down by soldiers of the newly formed Guyana Defence Force, flown into a nearby district, making their way by foot through the jungle passes.

The priest moved his coat from his right arm to his left and eased the strap of his overnight bag on his right shoulder. "Be prepared. They're either going to be very tired and give you an easy time, or they could be going through their second wind and really throw a lot of questions at you. Would you like me to wait for you? I can hang around a little longer, in case you need me."

The door to the interview room opened. Carl heard his name called. Had they been saving the best for last or was it all coincidence that he was the last person from the flight?

"No, Father. You've had a very long day yourself. I am sure everything will be fine. Can you do me a favour? My uncle –his name is Jules, is most likely waiting for me outside. Can you seek him out and let him know that I'll be a while longer?"

"Okay. Don't forget to look me up in Georgetown."

Two officials stood at the far end of the room when the guard opened the door and ushered Carl in. One of them was tall and lanky, close to six feet and he had a well-trimmed goatee. With his thick glasses and formal attire, he could well have been a professor. He wore a tie and blue blazer, while the other, a short, squat man, about five feet three, wore a white shirt-jacket which was a compromise between a shirt and a jacket, an open collar, tieless apparel introduced after independence, something meant to sever the ties to the country's colonial past. The squat man had a cigarette clutched in his right hand. If the first one was the intellectual of the two, the second could well be an enforcer, Carl thought.

"Mister Dias, please sit down," the man with the goatee said. "I am very sorry you had to wait so long, but it has been a very long night." He stifled a yawn and took a seat. "My name is John Ross and this is Malcolm Brackett."

"We are with the Ministry of Home Affairs, Special Branch." Ross waved Carl to one of the two vacant chairs on the opposite side of the table. "We're just trying to confirm the information that you gave the immigration officer on arrival. Hopefully, we will not have to keep you too long." He spoke with the accent of someone who had spent many years abroad, probably in the UK.

The room was sparsely furnished. A large wooden table with metal legs for support, four chairs, all of which could have been picked up at a used furniture sale. A picture of the President hung on one of the walls; it was identical to the one that was in the arrival area, right down to the brass buttons on his military jacket loaded with medals. A watercolour painting completed the décor: it was of Kaieteur Falls in the interior.

"From your passport I can see that you live in Toronto. How long have you lived there?" Ross said.

"Almost a year. Prior to that in Mississauga, just outside the city, for many years."

"Where in Toronto do you live?" Ross passed his hand down his left cheek, across his chin and then up his right cheek, a fluid, swift movement, but Carl could hear the rustle of a day-old beard.

"Tyndall Avenue, the King and Dufferin area."

Ross smiled. "Ah, King and Dufferin. Is there still a supermarket there? A Dominion, if I remember correctly. Also, a bank, a Canadian Imperial Bank Of Commerce across from it I think." He was a fast talker, someone who had an impressive command of the language and showed no hesitation in displaying it.

"The supermarket is long gone –now replaced by a Mac-Donald's. The CIBC you're referring to is right next to the MacDonald's on the same side of the street. The bank across the road is actually a Bank Of Montreal."

"Ah, yes. Been a long time." Ross slumped back on his chair, crossing his right leg over the left, his knee angled against the table. He picked up the passport lying in front of him and opened it. "I see you have a visa for travel to Cuba. What's the nature of your travel there?"

"I work for the Canadian Business Bank at the head office in Toronto. We're funding a number of projects in Cuba."

"You a Communist?" Brackett interrupted. The man took a long drag on his cigarette and glared at Carl with large, bulbous eyes that never seemed to waver.

Carl turned and addressed Ross. "The answer is no, but I don't see what my political leaning has to do with anything,"

Ross was about to speak when Brackett continued. "If you're a Communist, it is our business. How many times you been to Cuba?"

"I've been there three times this year."

"How long you spend there each time?"

"No more than three days at a time. Except, a week the very first time to get to know our clients."

"How come you doing business in Cuba if you not a Communist?"

Carl looked at Brackett. The man had a way of pushing his head forward, like an ostrich. He appeared to be the junior officer, but he was certainly more aggressive. He was probably someone who belonged to the lower scale in the ladder when independence came and managed to be elevated due to his party membership. It wouldn't pay to antagonize him, but Carl refused to be bullied when there was no reason for it.

Carl turned to Ross. "The Canadian government's policy is to deal with any country that wants to trade. Prime Minister Trudeau has made several trips to Cuba to meet Castro and there are several Canadian companies now setting up shop there, mainly in mining. Our bank is financing a number of projects. That's all there is to it."

Brackett glared at Carl. He obviously did not like being bypassed.

"Why you?" Brackett said. "Why they choose you to go there? What so special about you?"

This sounded like an attempt to antagonize him, Carl thought. What was the man aiming at? Was he hoping that Carl would lose his temper and give him an excuse to detain him longer?

Carl shrugged. "I happen to speak Spanish fairly well." He looked at Brackett. "Habla Espanol? No? I know the country, a bit more than the average Canadian does right now. Add to that, my background in Economics and banking experience – I'm one of the most senior members of the advisory board, the person responsible for expansion into the Caribbean. The reason I was chosen." Carl wanted to add: *For my expertise, not because I have a party card*, but he stopped short.

"Where you learn to speak Spanish?" Brackett said.

Carl sighed and turned to Ross. "Mister Ross, I'm guessing that you're the officer in charge here. I'm not sure where this is heading or what relevance it all has to do with my visit here for a funeral."

"You a member of Reform? Is that why you spend all that time in Cuba?" Brackett persisted. He was like a pit bull, Carl thought. The man would never let go if he managed to get his jaws on him.

"Look, I don't know what is the issue here," Carl said. "I haven't hidden the fact that I've been to Cuba. What's the big deal about that? The Canadian government wants to open up trade and other relations with Cuba, even though it's an obvious irritant to the Americans. The government wants to lay the groundwork for breaking those strong economic ties with the Americans. Why, Trudeau was even the first western leader to go to China and he's certainly not considered a communist!"

Carl thought for a moment, and turned to Ross: "As a matter-of-fact, your President has been to Cuba a few times and the Guyana government is trading with the Cubans all the time. You sell them rice and timber. Why is it so abnormal that I have been there on business?"

"How long have you been in banking?" Ross asked Carl.

Carl was happy that Ross seemed to be attempting to reclaim control of the interview.

"Ten years at the end of this year," Carl said.

"You have been abroad for how long?"

"'I've been living in Canada since 1968."

"I was in Toronto in the late seventies, not too long after I left England. There were many Guyanese in the King Dufferin area back then. I felt at home. I don't imagine much has changed since then?"

"Very much the same place. Different faces though."

Ross started to doodle in his writing pad. He paused after he had filled the page with circles and bordered them with squares, then filled the squares with triangles, activity that indicated he was desperately trying to keep awake.

"Yes," Ross said. "The area was always a transit point for new immigrants. After the Guyanese and West Indians passed through on their way to the suburbs the Vietnamese boat people came in. Then, the refugees from the Sri Lanka civil war took over. Do you remember those times?" He appeared to be a man reliving memories of a time long gone. He was probably one of those Guyanese who had answered the call to return home and help build the country, someone who had been enticed with an offer of a high paying job and perks that included a house allowance and tax-free benefits, only to discover that the system had a built in bias against anyone who was not a dedicated party loyalist. Was he unhappy about the move he'd made in returning, or was he trying to gain Carl's confidence to admit to something that might incriminate him?

Carl nodded. "As you said, many Guyanese and West Indians passed through there."

"There were quite a number of Guyanese groups back then too. Is it still like that?"

"I am not sure what you mean by groups."

Ross passed his hand across his face again. The rustle from his cheeks and chin seemed to be louder every time he did it, as if his stubble was growing exponentially. After this, he would open his mouth wide and clench his jaw after the movement. "You know. I mean organizations, or associations. Immigrants are always forming groups and associations. That's the first thing they do when they go to another country –part of the desire to connect, if you want to put it that way, or perhaps just a nostalgic journey to the homeland. I saw it in London and it happened in Toronto again."

"I suppose so," Carl said.

"Are you a member of any group like that?"

"No, I am not currently a member of any group." Carl was not lying –he'd rescinded his membership with the RDG.

"Have you ever heard of a group called the Restoration of Democracy in Guyana, known as RDG?"

"Can you tell me what this is all about? What does this have to do with me and my visit here for my father's funeral?"

"Dias," Brackett said, placing heavy emphasis on Carl's name. "Just keep in mind, we ask the questions here, not you."

Carl turned to face him. "Surely you can give me an idea what's happening and what it has to do with me?"

"We don' have to give you no idea about nothing," Brackett said. His cigarette had burnt down to a stub and he had lit another one.

"How can I honestly answer your questions when I have no idea what you're talking about?" Carl said.

"You don' have to understand. Just answer them, if you want to get outta here tonight," Brackett said.

Carl frowned. "Do I detect a threat?"

"You can detect anythin' you want. Keep in mind you not in Canada, now. You back in Guyana an' we in control."

Yes, you are, Carl mused. After obtaining power in a coalition government with the Conservatives, the Republicans had rigged the first election in a post independent Guyana, obtaining a majority that enabled them to govern without the support of the Conservatives. His father would have been shaking his head in consternation when this happened, Carl thought. Had it changed his father's opinion in any way about the need to exclude the Reform party from power, at any cost? Carl doubted it.

Ross cleared his throat. "Mister Dias. There is no threat. Please…just answer the questions so you can get out of here." He looked at his watch. "We have another flight to deal with. We have a long night ahead of us and you have a funeral to go to." He locked his fingers together and twisted and contorted his hands to the left and right. "Do you know of the RDG?"

"I am not sure. As you say, there are so many groups and associations soliciting your involvement in Canada that it's almost impossible to keep track of who is who anymore. I might have read about them in the Caribbean newspaper, sometime. I really can't recall."

"Have you ever joined any group in Toronto?"

"Look, let me make this very clear: I am not an active member of any Guyanese group. I am not actively involved in any political organization, either in Canada or Guyana." Carl glanced over to Brackett. "Or even in Cuba, where I happen to go only for business purposes. I pick up the occasional Guyana Times or Caribbean Camera when I am in a West Indian shop on King Street or Queen Street, to keep abreast of what's going on and that's about it. I'm here for a funeral and will be out of here soon as things are cleared up."

Ross was about to say something when the door opened and a man with a large head appeared in the doorway.

The man said, "Ross, you have an extra pen to spare?" with a slight slur in his speech. He had a scar that started in the middle of his right cheek, coursed through the top lip and ended up just below the bottom lip. Someone had done a bad job of patching him up: the stitches were centipede like and had left a permanent split in both lips.

The man added: "De ink just run out on mine," as if he felt the need for an explanation to justify the interruption

"Sure, Winslow," Ross said. He reached into his jacket pocket and pulled out a pen.

Winslow entered the room. He had the body of a stevedore and it was a perfect complement for his head; huge, round shoulders that curved and drooped, as if they were tired of carrying the head and massive arms over the years. He glanced in Carl's direction, through eyes that were as black and large as two fruits from the Jamoon tree that once grew in Carl's yard in the Walk. For an instant Carl saw a flicker of recognition in the man's eyes. The man had changed over the years but if there was any doubt about the scar, it was the walk that confirmed it for Carl. Winslow's left leg was shorter than his right: just about a quarter of an inch, enough to affect the fluid flow of his movement across the room. He came to Ross' desk, to about five feet from where Carl sat, picked up the pen, turned around and retreated without another glance at Carl.

Carl looked at Winslow as he left the room and closed the door. How many years had it been? Sixteen years since Carl left the country. How many years prior had he seen the man? He had lost track of Winslow even before he left Guyana to go abroad. He couldn't remember if Winslow had even completed high school. Now, here he was, an official working for a Ministry. Was he another card-carrying member of the party who had worked his way up the bureaucracy, like Brackett, perhaps?

"I t'ink you a Communist!" Brackett said.

Carl sighed. He was feeling more tired with every passing minute and the air in the room had grown stale. The overhead fan did nothing to improve things; it merely circulated the musty air.

Carl said. "You would hardly think that I could have Communist sympathies and be working for a bank in Canada, would you?"

"Good enough for me." Ross said. He opened the passport to a blank page, picked up one of the rubber stamps from the top of an ink pad and slammed it on the passport. "I'm giving you seven days to complete your business in Guyana, that's about all you should need. Good night Mister Dias. I hope everything goes well with your father's funeral."

Brackett had to have the last word, it seemed. "Jus' keep in mind we can check you out easily."

Carl picked up his overnight bag and exited the room. Brackett was still glaring at him. Ross was leaning back in his chair, his hands behind his head, perhaps trying to obtain a few minutes respite before the next set of interviews. Carl was reasonably sure that he would be out of the country before they found anything that was contrary to what he had disclosed in his interview.

A fresh batch of people was entering the waiting room as Carl came out. He followed the sign on the wall: *Baggage Claim and Customs*. He joined people waiting for their luggage.

Carl's suitcase finally came into view on a carousel that creaked and groaned and made its way ponderously around the pickup area. He claimed his suitcase and headed across the large room where people were standing in lines for customs clearance. Here, there was no distinction: everyone joined a line regardless of nationality. When his turn came, he approached the customs station and heaved his suitcase on top of the counter.

"Only one grip you come with?" The officer said. His name tag hung lopsided on the left side of his white shirt jacket and it had the name *Smith* in faded black letters. His stomach hung over the counter, and he stood there, both hands resting on his protuberance with a calmness that contrasted with the bedlam in the rest of the room. Here was obviously someone who was not suffering from food shortages for which the country had grown notorious. He probably never had to wait around for food vouchers or join a line to buy bread and he appeared to be in no hurry to go anywhere or do anything much. After all, he was at work, supposedly doing what he did best, exercising the authority vested in him by the Republic.

"Yes," Carl said.

"Open the grip."

Carl rotated the three cylinders of the combination and opened the lock. He flipped the lid of the suitcase and looked at Smith.

"What yuh bringing into the country wid you?" Smith said.

"Everything's right here," Carl pointed at the open suitcase. "Personal items: some clothes, an extra pair of shoes, underwear."

"Anyt'ing to sell?" Smith seemed to be disappointed. He poked around the open suitcase, looked at the bottom, in between the clothes and pulled at the inside flaps. "No presents for yur people!"

"No. Nothing. I'm just here for a few days for a funeral."

"So, yuh got nothin' that you leaving behind when you leave the country?"

"No. Nothing."

"How 'bout the carryon bag. Open it."

Carl unzipped the shoulder bag and pushed it towards Smith who started to pull out the contents. Toothpaste, toothbrush, soap, a roll of toilet paper, all found their way on the counter.

Smith came across the camera. "You got to pay some duty on this camera here." He picked up the camera case and opened the flap.

The camera was a top of the line SLR that Carl had bought when Alexei was born. He'd intended to chronicle his son's progression over the years and had started out with the best of intentions, diligently taking pictures of Alexei as a child, until he was two years old. The camera was capable of producing pictures of a quality that was admired by everyone who saw them in the album. The pace of picture taking had slowed to a trickle and eventually ceased as the demands of his job had increased. After another burst of activity for a few months when Irina was born in 1978, the camera had fallen into limbo, a half-used roll of film still in it; yet another project fallen by the wayside.

Carl raised his eyebrows. "Why is that? This is my personal camera. It's not new, if that's what you're wondering about."

"Never mind. Yuh still got to pay some duty."

Carl looked around. At the second station across from him, the officer was subjecting two suitcases of an East Indian to a close examination. The suitcases were crammed with canned goods, shirts that had shed their outer wrapping but had not lost their brand new look, and white cotton underwear neatly folded in rolls. The Indian man was looking on with an emotionless expression on his face –as if it was something he'd been through many times in the past.

Carl knew that the shortest route out of the terminal was to pay the duty. Did he really want to prolong the agony of a long day and get into a protracted dispute over the payment of a few dollars? It was the principle that mattered, though, and the long flight and the unnecessary interview had added to his irritability.

Carl shook his head. "I don't intend to pay duty on something that's for personal use."

Smith shrugged. "The way it is, man. Pay the duty or leave the camera here. Besides, is not much duty, you know. What you making all this fuss about?"

"Look, I'm not importing this for resale. I should not have to pay duty on a personal possession that's going back out with me, regardless of the amount."

"Come on man, you holding up the line. Pay ten dollars US and you can go. That's all. Ten dollars."

A blatant attempt to extort money from him. Carl had been up since the phone call from Uncle Jules and he'd been without food since the meal on the plane. Four hours had passed. His hunger was making him cranky and obstreperous.

"I want to see your supervisor," Carl said.

The officer pointed to the office at the end of the room. "He over there in that room but he goin' tell you the same t'ing I telling you."

"You'd better call him over because I am not paying duty on something of a personal nature."

Smith mumbled: *personal nature*. The implication of the words seemed to elude him –was there something in writing in some chapter, section and paragraph of the Customs Act that governed the levy of duty on items brought in for personal use? He'd probably done this a thousand times over the years and thought very little of it and now here was someone challenging his interpretation of the Act!

The officer sucked his teeth and rolled his eyes upwards. His hands were no longer resting on his large stomach but were waving around in wild gesticulation. "God damn people like you still t'ink you running this country," he muttered.

After he had sucked his teeth again, he said, "Okay, jus' zip up de grip and get outta here, man."

Carl zipped up the suitcase and lifted it off the counter. As he rolled it away, he saw the officer in the next queue relieving the East Indian man's suitcase of a number of items, no doubt his unofficial levy on the importation of the goods, along with the duty that the man would have to pay.

The Exit sign was on the wall to the right of the large room and Carl followed the other passengers. As he stood behind the small crowd laden with suitcases, handbags and children, he looked back at the throng in the large room. The scene presented a sight of bedlam, with people opening and closing suitcases and goods strewn over counter tops. He shook his head and thought of the crass and blatant extortion being practiced on people bringing in items that were probably not available in the country due to a lack of foreign exchange to permit importation.

An abrupt left turn and he found himself in a short, narrow passage, the outer wall of which was constructed of concrete blocks with a cavity in the centre of each, something that permitted a partial view on both sides of the wall. A sea of humanity was on the other side of the wall, with faces pressed against the concrete blocks. Eyes, noses, mouths, cheeks, all of different shapes, sizes and colours filled every cavity of every block, all appearing to be disconnected, so much that it startled him and broke his concentration.

Two security guards stood at the end of the passage: short Black men in khaki uniforms that were two sizes bigger for both of them.

"Tikket." The one who was much darker than the other, said.

Carl was still staring at the different parts of facial make up on the other side of the wall. He turned back to face the guard. Was this yet another step in the bloated bureaucracy to ensure that he would leave the country when the time came? He fumbled around in his overnight bag for his airline ticket, found it and handed it to the guard.

"Not that. The other tikket," the guard repeated.

Carl was about to enquire what ticket the guard was asking for when he thought of the baggage claim that was in the envelope with his itinerary. He extracted it and gave it to the guard.

The guard compared the number on the baggage claim with the tag on the suitcase, glancing at each part of the puzzle to ensure it was accurate. He mumbled each digit slowly, like someone who'd dropped out of school in grade one would have to do. How many people had he caught trying to smuggle someone else's suitcase outside the terminal? The guard handed the ticket back to Carl after he was satisfied that there was no violation of the airport's security policy. As Carl left the passage he found himself surrounded by the people waiting outside.

"Want a taxi, boss?" someone asked.

"Goin' to Georgetown, chief?" another asked.

"Want someplace to stay in GT Mister?"

"Gat any US dollars to change, Sir?"

"Bring back anything yuh want to sell?"

"I know a cheap hotel yuh can stay."

"Lehme help you wid yur grip boss," another said.

"No, thank you," Carl said, holding his suitcase firmly.

The man grabbed the suitcase, attempting to wrest it from Carl.

Carl made sure that the tone in his voice was clear and compelling.

"Back off," Carl said, and the man retreated.

At the rear of the crowd, someone stood out: a tall man with a brown hat and thick glasses. Carl elbowed his way towards the man.

"Hello Uncle Jules," Carl said as he put down his suitcase and embraced the man.

Uncle Jules pushed him away gently and scrutinized him closely. "Cal. Is really you?"

"Yes, Uncle Jules, it's really me. Thanks for waiting for me."

"But, what happen to you in there? A priest come out and tell me that they asking people all sorts of questions."

"I did have a bit of a problem. I'll tell you more about it later."

"Earl did say he see you from the viewing room but he never meet you before so I weren't sure. I think after a while that you change your mind."

"Oh no, I didn't change my mind. I'm here."

Uncle Jules pointed to a man who was standing next to him. "This here is Earl. He's driving us down to the house."

CHAPTER 5 – A New Era

Memorandum.

From: Director of Bureau of Intelligence Research.

To: Deputy Under Secretary of State for Political Affairs.

Washington, October 17, 1961.

SUBJECT: US Policy in British Guiana

In reviewing materials recently on The Chairman and his associates, we have multiplied our doubts about the feasibility of the policy adopted for British Guiana. Our position is set out below.

The current US program for British Guiana is based upon general agreements with the UK for a coordinated effort to get along with The Chairman. At the same time resources are to be built up to enable a harder line to be put into effect if, after a reasonable time (but before British Guiana becomes independent), it is clear that British Guiana is going the way of Castro Cuba.

There is the possibility, if not the probability, that strong direct ties with Moscow will emerge as British Guiana achieves independence.

The UK, which remains the responsible power in British Guiana, is not willing to take a hard line. If as we suspect, the UK policy cannot be successful in the short time that remains before independence, then US planning should be directed to converting the UK to a program of direct anti-government action.

> *In the final analysis we should plan for the possibility that we will have no reasonable alternative but to work for The Chairman's political downfall, which would have to precede the granting of independence. To bring about such a result will require an extensive and carefully coordinated effort, for which much planning has already been done.*
>
> *It is, therefore, proposed that the present policy for British Guiana be reviewed immediately following the visit of The Chairman to Washington.*

The cafeteria at North Georgetown College was always packed at lunch, especially on Fridays, when students seemed keen to escape from a home-cooked meal or sandwich. Carl and his two friends –Wilfred Ledman and Cyril Ramdass occupied a table at the far end of the large room.

"Here comes Miss Georgetown and Miss British Guiana," Wilfred said, just loud enough that the two students coming their way would hear him.

The two girls were East Indian: long hair dangling in plaits at the back, dark tan complexion glowing. They looked like first formers, prim and demure, attractive enough to compete in any beauty competition.

Wilfred smacked his lips as the girls passed. "Hey senoritas," Wilfred said, "¿Querría usted a salió conmigo esta noche?"

The girls giggled and looked away.

"You're lucky they don't understand what you're saying," Cyril said, "or you'd be in deep trouble if they report you to the principal."

"Who, Pinhead? He can't do anything to me," Wilfred said.

"What makes you think that one of them would go out with you tonight?" Cyril said.

"Of course they want to go out with me." Wilfred pulled out his pocket comb and passed it through his hair, "Both of them, badly. Only, they don't know it yet."

"They just started high school, Wilfred." Carl looked up from his newspaper. "Give them a break."

The three of them had just finished lunch. Carl had the *Sun* spread out on the table, and both Wilfred and Cyril were trying their best to break his concentration. The fact that it was just half a day more to go for the end of the week's classes seemed to increase their frivolous activities. Cyril compressed the leftover foil from his sandwich into a ball and tossed it at Wilfred, hitting him smack bang in the middle of his head. Wilfred rolled up a section of the Sun and slapped Cyril across his head.

"Hey, man, don't mess around with the hair," Wilfred said, as he used his comb to reset his hair.

Wilfred had a head of thick, black hair that started in a high muff in front and cascaded to the back in several waves. He was now patterning his hair Elvis Presley style, from the movie Blue Hawaii that he'd seen last weekend. He was the class-clown and rarely took anything seriously, except when it came to his carefully groomed coiffure and his school uniform. His hair was his Achilles Heel –touching his head was certain to invoke an angry response. Cyril, on the other hand was not very particular about his appearance. His hair was in a constant state of disarray and most times his white shirttails hung loose out of his pants.

The large clock on the wall was showing 12:40. In twenty minutes students would have to return to their homerooms. The noise level increased: shrieks and laughter rang out, one student was chasing another around the room, someone fell backwards on his chair; tables were repositioned and relocated.

"What's so exciting in the news anyway?" Cyril said, as he reached over and attempted to flip Carl's long hair from his forehead.

Carl anticipated the move and leaned backwards. "The Chairman is heading to Washington to meet with President Kennedy. He's hoping to get aid for his development plan. From there, he's heading to Ottawa to meet Prime Minister Diefenbaker –he's thinking that the Canadians will have more sympathy for our cause."

"Good luck to him," Cyril said, sarcasm dripping in his voice. "Fowl cock will grow teeth before the Americans give us aid. The Canadians are just going to follow what the Americans do –pressure will be applied, just you watch and see."

"Yeah, the Canadians might sympathize, but sympathy don't build bridges and roads and feed people," Wilfred said.

"Did you guys know that Kingsley is no longer a Republican?" Carl pointed to an article in the newspaper. "He's calling for a partition of the country. Berbice county for East Indians, Demerara for Blacks."

Kingsley was a former member of Reform. When Reform split along two mainly racial factions –the deputy leader left and took the Black segment with him to form the Republican party. Kingsley had opted to side with the new faction. The man was supposed to be notorious for his radical views on non-accommodation among the races.

"Where would somebody like you and all the other Puttagees go, Carl?" Wilfred said.

Carl looked up and shrugged. He was accustomed to Wilfred's label –his friend often referred to him with the shortened version of Carl's Portuguese heritage. "I suppose, Essequibo County, along with the Chinese, Amerindian Natives and all other."

"Partition will never happen," Cyril said. "That's the reason Kingsley is no longer in the Republican party. They must have expelled him."

"Makes sense," Carl said. "The Republican party is trying to get backing from the Americans before the election. They can hardly get American support if they have racists in the party hierarchy."

"Don't make no difference now," Cyril said. He jumped up and shouted: "Reform in power again. We're now the government; we will be the first party to lead British Guiana into independence."

Students from the nearby tables looked around, but for the greater part, most of the cafeteria took no notice due to the noise level.

Reform had won the last election in August, gaining twenty of the thirty-five seats. The main opposition party, the Republican, had won eleven and the Conservatives four. Even if the two opposition parties were to merge, they still wouldn't have enough seats to form a government under the existing First Past The Post system, where seats were won based on a majority of votes in each riding. Unless, of course, the system was changed to allocate seats on a population basis, which is what the two opposition parties were now demanding.

"The British can still insist on another election before independence," Carl said.

Cyril sat down. He looked as deflated as a punctured balloon. "Yes, that's what the Chairman said might happen."

"Even worse than that," Carl said, "the British might agree to change the election method to a Proportional Representation system, which is what the opposition wants."

"Hey Carl," Cyril winked at Wilfred, "does your father, the great Augusto Dias know that you canvassed for Reform instead of the Conservatives during the election?" He had a smug look on his face, as if he was privy to a secret that no one else knew.

Carl looked up. He sighed and shook his head, slowly.

Cyril laughed. "What he going to do to you if he find out?"

Wilfred reached across and slapped Cyril on his shoulder. It was a touchy subject: both of them were well aware of the political conviction of Carl's father –he was vocally and fiercely anti-Reform.

There was much more to the story. Cyril's father was a Reform member since the party was created when The Chairman returned from America to start the first independence movement. Wilfred's father was also a long-time member. Both parents had been incarcerated back in nineteen fifty-three when the constitution had been suspended by the British in the Communist scare that never materialized. British troops had been shipped in, houses had been searched for subversive literature, Reform members had been rounded up all over the country. The fact that it was Augusto Dias who turned the two men in, had left Carl with a feeling of guilt and remorse over his father's action against the parents of his two best friends.

When Reform returned to power, one of the first pieces of legislation they had introduced was the repeal of the Sedition Act and books of all political conviction had flooded into the colony. Carl had read his fill of the new literature at the house of his two friends –this had been his introduction to Marxism and before long, he was a member of the youth arm of Reform. Carl's father, on the other hand, was a card-carrying member of the Conservatives, the party deemed by most as the only logical choice for all the Portuguese in the colony, since many of them belonged to the commercial and business sector.

Augusto Dias was proud of his heritage, and never failed to give his children history lessons of their descendants and how far the family had travelled to achieve their success. Augusto's great grandfather, Carlos Dias, after whom Carl was named, came from Madeira to British Guiana in 1843 as an indentured sugar plantation worker. Carlos arrived on the brig Zargo, travelling across the Atlantic along with one hundred and sixty-two boxes of potatoes, one thousand crates of onions and fourteen other Colonos, or labourers. He was one of many escaping the economic hardship of their homeland and seeking a better life in the new world. Brazil was the choice of many of the Portuguese back then –but Carlos had chosen British Guiana, much closer to Europe and his homeland, where he'd planned to return one day after amassing his fortune, to build a house on a hill overlooking the sea and enjoying the rest of his days in comfort. Carlos never made it –he died in the fields.

By the time the third generation came along, Salvador Dias, Carl's grandfather had established himself in business and Augusto followed in his footsteps, opening a store in Georgetown, running an import-export business and eventually starting his own winery. The store and winery had grown fast and Augusto was now a wealthy man. With his wealth had come power. In nineteen fifty-three, he had been nominated by the Chamber of Commerce to sit on the governor's Executive Council, the body that would go on to run the country by decree, without the benefit of consulting Reform, the party that had won the election and was out of office for its strong socialist leanings. Augusto could not have asked for anything more: he was totally against independence for the colony. *How can you give independence to a place where the people don't know the meaning of the word? They can't even clothe and feed themselves,* he often said. Deep down, Carl couldn't help feeling that it all came down to the question of colour –his father was referring to the non-Portuguese, non European descendants, the darker elements of the population that he felt were not intelligent enough to run the country.

Carl could imagine his father's reaction if he knew that his fourth son was involved in the youth arm of Reform. Augusto was someone who preached about the evils of Communism and what it would do to the entire business class if Reform ever came to power in an independent British Guiana. His father would tilt his head to the right, and with the fingers of his right hand wagging –the way he often did when he was confronted with something that was opposite to his way of thinking, he'd say: *No son of mine is going to be a member of a Communist party –do you know what it would do to my standing in the community if this ever came out?* He'd pull out his watch from the vest of his three piece suit, wind it, look at it –time was always money to him, and he would add: *Why can't you be more like your older brothers? Get more involved in the business like James. Get a career like Joseph and Thomas. Do something useful with your life.* Wanting to avoid a scene similar to this, Carl had decided to campaign away from his neighbourhood of Repentigny.

"Don't matter if they want another election –we going to win again," Wilfred said. "They can have any amount of elections they want, we will always win. East Indians will always be more than Blacks and we will always get more seats."

Carl looked up from the newspaper. "Wilfred, Indians only make up about forty-two percent of the population. If seats are based on percentage of population, instead of ridings, the two opposition parties can form a government leading up to independence."

"Reform will never agree to changing the system from what it is now," Cyril said. "No other country in the West Indies has it, so why should British Guiana? Besides, how can the British do this when they themselves don't have it?"

Cyril was the incurable optimist of the three. He thought that power would always lie in the hands of Reform and the party would go on to introduce and cement its brand of socialism in future.

"Everybody knows that the Republicans and the Conservatives don't get along," Wilfred said. "Their's would be a marriage made in hell. Even if they get married, divorce won't be too long down the road."

"The Americans might put pressure on the British and both parties here to do it –call it a marriage of convenience, if you want," Carl said. "Keep in mind: Kennedy and the White House are not exactly in love with the Chairman and Reform right now."

"Yeah, remember what the Chairman said in the meeting at Liberty House," Wilfred said. "He didn't think that Kennedy would extend help to us."

Wilfred was referring to a meeting that they had attended at the headquarters of Reform, not long after the last election. The Chairman had gone on a rant, criticizing the

Americans for actively engaging in schemes to undermine Reform. He talked about the U.S. Information Services arm of the Consulate moving its film-shows to street corners with anti-Castro, anti-Cuba and anti Reform propaganda. He raged about the Christian Social Council and the Defenders of Christian Freedom, the Sword Of The Spirit, the Anti Communist Crusade, all American based organizations openly campaigning against Reform's proposal to end Church run schools, something that was needed to make education a national priority. He lashed out at newspapers owned by opposition members, and The Catholic Times, for spreading propaganda that an independent Guiana under Reform would mean a denial of freedom, the suppression of the free press, mass arrests and the destruction of trade unions, when he had stated time and again, that Reform had no such intention. The irony: the Chairman had said that Reform was being accused of threats against trade unions, when, he had received reports that the Americans were funnelling funds to the local unions to mount campaigns in opposition to his government. The Americans were even smuggling arms into the country to destabilize his government.

The Chairman had cautioned party members to be alert to clandestine means that would be used by the opposition, in league with the British and the Americans. He had referred to information he'd received about a CIA attempt to penetrate Reform and seek information that the Chairman and his government were part of an international communist conspiracy to overthrow elected western governments.

"We don't need money from the Americans," Cyril said. "The new budget will raise all the money we need."

The government was drafting a new budget. They had consulted widely and held informal talks with many sections of the population to gain a consensus, as far as was possible to do with so many disparate parties in the colony. A Hungarian economist who had provided assistance to the British Government in its fiscal reforms, had been brought in by Reform and he was the man behind the changes expected in British Guiana. The budget proposed new taxes on capital gains, a gift and wealth tax and a minimum business tax, all measures designed to balance the disequilibrium in a tax system that penalized the poor and favoured expatriates, big business and wealthy landowners. If Reform failed to obtain aid from abroad, it was determined to push ahead with the new budget. The Chairman expected that those opposing the measures would stop at nothing to bring down his government. Already, the Conservative party and its leader had started to mount a campaign to vilify the Chairman and the members of his government as being communist ideologues who were anti-business.

Carl had witnessed his father's reaction. Augusto was steadfastly opposed to the budget proposals –he'd even gone as far as to call the measures anti-Portuguese, even when Reform had taken pains to explain in its document that the budget would have an impact on all the East Indian business in the country the same way. His father was like that: someone who donned blinders and refused to see clearly, where Reform was concerned.

Wilfred smirked. "Hey, this is what I see happening. Reform wins the election. The government comes out in the open and starts to clamp down on big business. The Americans invade us. We become an American state. Money starts to flow in. Everybody lives happily ever after."

"The Americans are chicken shit," Cyril sneered. "They can't invade us. Look what happened to them at the Bay Of Pigs this year –they got their asses kicked well and proper by Castro and the Cubans."

"The Bay Of Pigs invasion is why Kennedy must be now under pressure," Carl said. "Don't forget: Venezuela is right next door to us, with all the billions of dollars in American investment and its oil supply that the Americans rely on. Big business must be really tightening the screws on Kennedy to make sure the same thing doesn't happen in British Guiana that happened in Cuba."

"Talk about being paranoid," Wilfred said.

Carl shrugged. "If they think that Reform is communist they might be afraid that an independent British Guiana would be used as a base to attack and overthrow other South American governments: their domino theory in practice."

Wilfred laughed. "Little old British Guiana, all its –how much? Six hundred thousand people? No army, no air force, no navy! We're going to invade other countries in the area?"

The two first-year students were making their way back from the washroom. Wilfred pulled out his comb again, made several passes through his hair and watched as the girls approached. They were starting to giggle.

"Which one of them you want Carl?" Wilfred whispered. "I seen the tall one looking at you –I think she likes you. I can get her for you if you want. The short one's for me." He tossed a crumpled napkin at Cyril. "None for Brer Rabbit though –he's too ugly with those two buckteeth sticking out in front."

The girls came closer.

"Hey senoritas," Wilfred said. "Usted mira tan agradable en mini –como las chicas en la Calle de Agua."

Carl thought the two students might like the compliment about the way they looked in short skirts, if they understood Spanish. Minis were the current rage of all the girls in the school, but Carl doubted if they would react favourably to being compared to the prostitutes who plied their trade in the red light district on Water Street. That was Wilfred –he tended to mix the good with the bad, without much thought sometimes about the impact of his words.

The two girls giggled. The taller one turned around as they passed and she said: "You can see all you want but you too ugly to touch."

Wilfred looked dumfounded at the rebuff –he was left with his mouth agape.

The clock on the wall showed one o'clock; time to return to classes. The three friends joined the stream of students making their way out of the cafeteria.

The first session after lunch for the trio was a Spanish class, one of Carl's favourite subjects. Lately, he was developing a knack for the language and he was now competing with Wilfred for the number one position in the class. He could see himself pursuing it to the Advance Level if his high marks continued.

The Spanish master, Mister Jordan, entered the room and headed for the desk in front. He placed the yellow jacket textbook on the desk and turned to address the class.

"Hable conmigo en español," was the first thing he said, as he usually did at the start of every class. He didn't tolerate English being spoken by his students.

Jordan was short and thin and was renowned for two reasons. One was the bushy black moustache that he grew and was constantly twirling around with his fingers, like a Latin lover in the movies. The two edges of the moustache were honed into sharp points while the portion directly under the base of his nose was thick and bushy. The other notable feature about Jordan was his green trousers –he never wore any other colour. The talk in the class was whether it was the same pants Jordan wore all the time or whether he had several of the same make. The fact that the pleats on his trouser legs were always well creased made Carl come to the conclusion that the Spanish Master must have several pants like it.

"Buenas tardes, el Profesor," the class cried out.

"El Señor de buenas tardes Bigote Negro," Wilfred whispered to Carl. *Mister Black Moustache* was Wilfred's nickname for the Spanish Master.

"Abra su texto a la primera página cien y veinte," Jordan said. "Hoy hablaremos de uso de gramática en español."

Almost in unison, students opened their text to page one hundred and twenty that dealt with grammar –it would be their subject for the afternoon.

Jordan was about to continue when the door opened and he turned to see who it was. The principal walked in, accompanied by a stranger. The two men who entered the class were a study in contrasts: brown and white, short and tall, frail looking and well built, a balding dome and a full head of hair.

The students turned to see who it was. "Mutt and Jeff," Wilfred whispered. "What does Pinhead want now? Who is this guy with him?"

Carl shook his head. "No idea, but it must be important if he's bringing the guy around during class."

"Sorry to interrupt your class, Mister Jordan," the principal said. "I want you to meet Hal Perough."

Jordan and Perough shook hands.

The principal continued: "Mister Perough is coming to us under the *Training for Underdeveloped Countries* program funded partly by the American Development Bank. We're lucky to be able to participate in this program."

Perough was dressed casually: a light green suede jacket and a black pants, white shirt and a plain blue tie. The man was built like an athlete: just over six feet tall, broad shoulders and a barrel chest. His tie was hanging loose around his neck and lying off to one side, as if it were an encumbrance that he could well do without.

Perough stood with his back to the blackboard, his hands supported by the extension holding the eraser, as he listened to the principal and took in the entire classroom and the students. He had spectacles, but they were not on his head – they dangled in his left hand and every now and then he would twirl the frame around several times.

"Mister Perough is taking up the new role of Career Counsel and will be contacting students individually, to give them guidance in their choice of careers," the principal said. "He has a great deal of experience in his field. I'm sure he will be an asset to us."

Jordan nodded.

"Who is he kidding –the man can't even fix his tie properly," Wilfred whispered. "Why wear one if you can't tie it the right way! Remember Lee Marvin –*Crow*, in Commancheros? This is who this man look like."

Carl and his friends had recently seen the new Western with John Wayne at the Astor cinema. He knew that Perough would be referred to as Crow from now on, as sure as the Pinhead label that had been attached to the principal after they had seen Armoured Command where there was a similarly named character. Indeed, Perough had a striking resemblance to the character actor Lee Marvin, right down to the way his lower jaw hung open and his steely eyes took in the entire class. It was vintage Wilfred –he was the buff in the group and saw every new movie that was screened in Georgetown, sometimes more than once if nothing else was being released. He could quote whole lines from the dialogue of the movies he'd seen and often associated people he met with characters, some of them famous, others not so well known. Wilfred was most fond of quoting the villains of the piece. Carl often wondered how his friend ever found the time to study and keep up his high grades, but over the years he'd come to accept that Wilfred was one of those who had a natural talent to pick up and retain information and lectures without much effort, something that Carl couldn't help but envy at times.

"Pinhead and Crow –what a pair," Wilfred whispered. "Remember when Crow says: I got one rule: never go to bed without makin' a profit? Could just be Pinhead talking, you know."

Added to his role in the college, the principal was involved in several business ventures. He owned a hotel and held shares in a large department store. He was also head of the Consolidated Trade Unions. Carl couldn't help thinking of the Chairman's speech at Liberty House. He'd openly criticized the principal for his alignment with the American trade union movement and for entering into an agreement that saw leaders of the most fervent anti-communist unions in America being brought to British Guiana, ostensibly to develop the trade union movement in the country, but covertly to provide assistance in agitating against Reform and the government.

So, was Mister Perough really there as a new member of the staff, or was there something else on his and the principal's agenda, Carl couldn't help wondering.

CHAPTER 6 – Repentigny

MONDAY 24ᵀᴴ NOVEMBER 1980, PM.

Carl and his Uncle were now in the thick of the crowd that overflowed from the entrance of the terminal to the parking lot, making slow progress to the car. The taxi driver led the way out with Carl's suitcase and carryon bag in his hands.

Carl noticed the hesitation in his uncle when they came to the edge of the sidewalk –there was a six-inch drop to the pitch surface of the parking lot.

"Here, let me give you a hand, Uncle Jules." Carl said as he reached out for his uncle.

"Thank you," his uncle said. "My eyes're not as good as they used to be. Night time I really have a problem." He laughed, and added, "But, everything else still in good working order, you know."

Carl was amazed at the firmness in his uncle's arm as he guided him through the dark parking lot. The man was two years younger than Augusto, which would make him sixty-eight, but hard work over the years on his copra plantation at Madeira on the East Coast of Demerara seemed to have cemented his arm muscles into a sturdy appendage.

The driver had already tucked away the suitcase into the trunk and closed the lid when Carl and Jules came up. The car protruded about two feet beyond the other cars parked on both sides and was much wider than any other vehicle around. The logo of a once proud Chrysler product was still affixed firmly on the rear lid –it was an old De Soto Diplomat. In the beam of the overhead light standard, there was a sheen on the bright, red finish and the chrome trim, unmatched by any other car in the lot.

"I will rest a while in the back seat," Uncle Jules said. "You can ride up front with Earl."

Carl assisted his uncle into the back seat and took the front, next to the driver. The interior of the De Soto was in a similar spotless fashion as the outside.

A fine mist was rolling in as the car pulled out, moving along with a stream of cars heading in the same direction, the beams from their headlights piercing the mist and the darkness and spotlighting the sides of the road as they went around bends and straightened out again. By the time they left the airport compound all the cars exiting had already pulled ahead of the slow moving De Soto and then, they were on their own. In the stillness of the countryside, there was no indication that the De Soto was still travelling in space and time, except for the car's headlights –two bright beams penetrating the blackness of the night and pulling them forward, yard by yard. They might well have been travelling in a vacuum, were it not for the creaking of the car's suspension system and the wheezing of Jules in the backseat.

"Cal," Uncle Jules said, "what kind of problem you had in the airport?"

Carl hesitated. He didn't want to alarm his uncle.

"Some mix-up over baggage and stuff being brought into the country, Uncle Jules."

"They didn't take any of your stuff, did they? They always doing that at the airport, you know."

"No, everything worked out okay."

Carl stroked the dashboard and the chrome trim on the door of the De Soto.

"There can't be too many of these around, anymore," Carl said, to Earl.

Earl looked at Carl for a moment, then, returned his attention to the road. He slowed the car, swerved to the right to avoid a pothole and straightened up again. He nodded. He looked like a man who had to give careful thought to everything he did, or said, lest he offended someone.

"I can see that you take good care of the car," Carl said. "It's Earl, right?"

Again, Earl nodded.

The mist had brought a fine drizzle with it, and now, the rhythm of the wiper-blades added to the sounds breaking the silence of the night: the consistent tempo of crapoud croaking and calling for rain, the unbroken chirping of crickets, the rustle of the breeze through the trees. November was typically the start of the rainy season.

What would it take to get Earl to open up? Carl was curious –where was he from, what did he do, what was his connection with Uncle Jules? How did he lay his hands on the De Soto?

"What year is it? Can't be easy to keep it going, to get parts and make repairs," Carl said.

Earl shook his head and there was a slight relaxation in his facial features. "The car's a nineteen sixty-one –the last year the model was built for export."

After a while, Earl added: "Might even have been made in Canada, I'm not sure, but it's the only one in this country and maybe even the whole of the West Indies. A dentist in GT was the first owner."

GT –had to be Georgetown, Carl figured. He'd never heard it referred to as that in all the years he lived there. Was this a way of breaking with the past, to sever ties with the historical attachment to a monarch back in the nineteenth century when it was founded, someone who'd never visited his only colony on the South American mainland? What other names had they changed, what other organizations connected to all things British had been reconfigured to delete association with times gone by? He expected that there would now be an indoctrination process in place in schools and government institutions to expound on provocative periods in the history of the country: colonialism, slavery of the Blacks, indentureship of the East Indians and Chinese and Portuguese.

"And you're right," Earl continued, "parts are no longer available for it. I have to improvise most of the time and do my own repairs."

"Cal," his uncle said from the rear seat, "is you alone coming for the funeral?"

"Yes, Uncle Jules, I'm the only one."

Uncle Jules had already heard that piece of news when he phoned Natasha. Had he forgotten, or simply found it incredible to accept?

"But, is why the others can't make it for their father's funeral?" Disappointment filled his voice. "Is the last time they ever going see him before he get buried six foot down below, you know."

Carl thought for a while before he responded. "I don't know what to tell you, Uncle Jules. Thomas can't come because he's still not too well. I tried my best to get Joseph to come, but you should know how he feels about Guyana, after what happened to his family at Wismar. As for John, well, you probably know more about John and his whereabouts than me."

"Well, I'm glad that you managed to come. Is not right that a man is buried without his sons around for it."

Earl slowed down to a crawl and negotiated into and out of a crater -there was no escaping this one: it ran the entire width of the road. The springs on the De Soto groaned and moaned like a woman in the throes of labour.

"Is just not right, I tell you," Uncle Jules continued. "I hope something like that never happens to me when it's my turn to go down in the ground," and then, he lapsed into silence.

They passed the first village, a few houses scattered along the roadside, the outlines silhouetted against the car's headlights as they came around a bend in the road. A dim light bulb shone in the gallery of a house and East Indian music blared through an open window. After that, they were plunged into darkness and silence, again.

"Not very much light out this way, is there?" Carl asked Earl, as they left the village behind them.

"Something we don't think about much, any more. Just a part of everyday routine –life goes on. Even when the electricity comes on, we still don't have lights. Most of the bulbs have burnt out and we don't have replacements."

Uncle Jules seemed to come awake in the rear seat. The opportunity to inject something about the everyday malaise affecting the country did not escape him. "Boy, Cal, they thief anything and everything they can get their hand on," he said. "Nothing you have is safe. You have to lock up everything. They will thief the clothes you leave outside for drying on the line, or the telephone and electric lines for the copper to sell on the black market. They even thief burnt-out bulbs, these days."

"Some stupid people have been electrocuted thieving the wires off the lantern posts," Earl added.

Carl shook his head. "Why would people steal burnt-out bulbs?"

Earl laughed. "You'd be surprised; it's a thriving secondary business –burnt out bulbs, used engine parts, you name it. They buy these things cheap, steal good ones, replace them with the bad ones and the owners are none the wiser –they think the parts just burn out natural like. Everything has a price on the black-market these days."

Carl passed his hands along the dashboard. "How did you manage to get your hands on the De Soto? The body is in excellent condition. Will the engine hold out?"

"It's doing good so far," Earl said. "When the dentist left for Toronto, he left the car with his father. The Old Man never drove it –he kept it under cover. He'd have the oil changed and turn it over now and then. I was giving one of the grandchildren after-school lessons and since the dentist wasn't coming back and the Old Man didn't have any use for the car, he offered it to me instead of money."

"That happens a lot, Cal," Uncle Jules said. "Very little money circulating in the open these days. Everything is done under the table. I give you something and you give me something in return."

A car approached from the opposite direction, the beams of its headlights growing progressively brighter as it reached and lit up the interior of the De Soto. Carl studied Earl in the minute that lapsed before the car passed on. What he saw was someone younger than him, by maybe five years or so, someone whose sharp nose, high cheeks, wide forehead were all marked by a fair complexion. Carl was curious.

"I'm sorry, Earl, I didn't get your last name."

Earl looked over at Carl. "...Singh," he said.

Earl Singh –he had to be mixed, Carl thought. What part of his background was Portuguese or some other European strain? Somewhere in there was an East Indian link.

"Earl and his mother, Sumintra, they staying at the house in the Walk, Cal," Uncle Jules said. "I put them in there to help out your father when he get sick and needed to go to the hospital for treatment. Patricia –Patsy, you remember her? She and her son Jimmy also living there, now."

Carl remembered Patsy, the wife of his brother James. Patsy was Black. Her son, James Junior –Jimmy, was born shortly after James died back in nineteen sixty-four. Carl was not here for Jimmy's birth, but he'd heard of it, and Augusto's reaction. As far as Augusto was concerned, in the events leading up to and involving his son's death, colour far outweighed blood, enough for him to dissociate himself from Patsy and her son.

"When your father take in sick, I couldn't come down to GT for too long," Uncle Jules said. "You know what would happen –they would steal everything at my place by the time I get back."

Carl thought it would be interesting to know how Uncle Jules had managed to change his brother's perspective. Or, had it simply been the repentance and last wish of a dying man? Whatever it was, James' wife and son were now living in the family house in the Walk, something that Augusto had been adamantly opposed to.

"The ride appears to be much longer than I remember," Carl said. "I'm not sure if it's got something to do with the darkness, or the eagerness to get closer to the city, but I remember cars dashing down this road at a much faster pace. As a matter-of-fact..." They came onto a huge billboard as they approached another village. "I recall that speed was such a big issue and there had been so many people killed in accidents that the traffic department put up that large sign."

Earl said: "You mean the sign that says *Speed Thrills And Kills*? Nobody pays any attention to that anymore –it's become a piece of the scenery. Besides, the police don't worry too much about cars speeding these days. For one thing, you don't have too many cars on the road since you can't find parts to repair them when they break down. For another thing, the holes in the road are sure to slow you down or else you ruin what little shocks you have left and end up breaking your car chassis."

Carl heard the rustle of cloth as Earl moved his right hand to his mouth, folded his fist, cupped it front of his mouth and breathed in and out slowly. Almost as if it were an afterthought, Earl reached into his shirt pocket, pulled out a pack of cigarettes and offered the pack to Carl.

Carl said: "No thank you. I don't smoke."

Earl shook the pack, placed a cigarette in his mouth and continued to drive.

The drizzle had stopped and the interior of the car had turned humid. Earl rolled down his window and Carl did the same on his side.

In the darkness and silence beyond the car, Carl could hear water lapping against a dam or wharf off to the left; a loud, yet sonorous, almost soothing sound.

"Is that the sound of water in the Demerara River I'm hearing?" Carl said. He thought it incredible that he could hear it even above the hum of the engine and the cacophony from the insects in the thick bushes that surrounded them.

"Yes, it's over there." Earl pointed to his left, even as the direction of the road took a sharp turn away from the river.

Far ahead, there was a cluster of lights that shone like a vivid display of the Milky Way in a dark, cloudless night. The cluster grew increasingly brighter as they approached, revealing itself to be spotlights attached to the roof of several houses, lighting up the entire yard of every house. Carl counted five houses as the car passed. In the background he could hear the loud hum of generators.

"Strange place for houses, almost in the middle of nowhere," Carl said.

Earl still hadn't lit his cigarette which dangled between his lips as he spoke. "Yes, the East Indian people who live there had to run from a Black neighbourhood during the last disturbances. In the next village you will likely find some Blacks who had to run from an East Indian village. There's many situations like that around. I guess after what they went through, some people very particular about where they live, especially if it's not one of their own kind."

Carl felt a tap on his shoulder.

"Cal, Earl is a teacher, you know," Jules said.

"I gathered as much, Uncle Jules. Where do you teach, Earl?"

Earl puckered up his lips, moved the cigarette in and out and sighed. Was he a smoker who was trying to quit?

"I'm now teaching at St. Stephen's Primary in GT."

A question was left hanging in the air and Carl asked it: "So, driving a taxi is a part-time job?"

Earl moved the cigarette from his mouth and placed it in his top pocket. "Yes, it is. The teaching profession in Guyana has gone to the dogs. This government doesn't really care about education any more. We haven't had a salary increase in years and years. There is no school supplies; roofs leaking, desks broken, children falling through rotting floors. The students with no textbooks. Many children have to go to work to supplement the family income and those that do come to school, can't concentrate because they haven't had a proper meal. A real mess, I tell you. You will see for yourself, things not getting any better."

Earl extracted the cigarette from his shirt pocket and placed it between his lips, again. He started to chew on the filtered tip. Carl picked up whiffs of nicotine on his breath when he spoke.

"Teachers leaving the profession in droves, if you can call it a profession, anymore. A cane-cutter makes more, these days. Can you imagine that? You go to Teachers' Training College and you end up cutting cane in the fields just to keep your family fed and clothed, and a roof over your head."

Carl sensed the frustration in Earl's voice. If this man, fairly well educated, a teacher at that, was so disenchanted, what about the next generation? Were they resourceful enough to cope with the situation, or was the government facing a tinderbox that was waiting to ignite at the slightest provocation? Could the party that his old friend, Cyril Ramdass started back in Toronto, have a chance of sparking a revolution in the countryside? Or, was the government satisfied that Guyanese would always remain compliant?

"What keeps you in the profession?" Carl said.

Earl reached into his shirt pocket and extracted a lighter. He looked at it for a few seconds, then, replaced it in his pocket, along with the cigarette. He shrugged.

"I've been asking myself the same question a lot, recently. Truth is –I'm not sure. I'd like to believe that it's because of some noble reason, perhaps to contribute something to the future of children growing up. Heaven knows that they need something to look forward to, if we're ever going to be a progressive country one day. The way things are going nowadays, I could very well change my mind and focus more on making money, the way other teachers are going."

Around the next bend in the road, the headlights spotlighted four people. Carl was shocked to see them standing there off the road, on the parapet. They looked like apparitions. As the car passed he turned his head and saw them stepping back onto the road to continue their journey.

"Kind of dangerous to be walking on the road where you can't be seen by drivers, isn't it?" Carl said.

"Hire-car drivers won't stop for passengers in a stretch of road like this, especially at this time of night. Many cars have been hijacked in this area and drivers have been murdered; a growing trend, these days."

"Where could they be going to at this time of night?"

"They could be going to the cinema in the next village."

Carl shook his head in amazement. "As you said, life goes on, eh?"

"Yes, people still go to the cinema, even if the movie is shown in spurts and bursts at times due to lack of consistent electricity. It can be funny at times. People just sit there and wait for the current to come back on. They play cards or dominoes or have a drink, in the meanwhile. They turn it into one big party."

"Boy, Cal," Jules said, "you have to have patience to live in a country like this. Everything move slowly or don't work at all."

Carl sighed. He suspected that the next few days would demand a tremendous adjustment in his attitude, either that or he could see himself facing complete frustration over the way things work in the country. He knew, with frustration could come hostility and anger, which he could least afford to entertain if he wanted to get out of the country on time and in one piece.

As they got further away from the airport, they passed more villages and houses scattered in-between, an occasional lamp or candle burning, the silhouette of someone keeping watch at the window behind blinds. People: an old lady in a rocking chair, a boy standing on the landing, a woman shouting at someone to fetch some water. Dogs barked along the way, running out of yards with fences hanging precariously on crooked posts and no gates to keep them in. People moved swiftly in pairs or groups, always pausing to take notice of the distinctive features of the De Soto, or to see who was travelling in the car.

They passed through Diamond –a village built on sugar and its interconnected alcohol products. In the centre of the village was a cinema –the Deluxe, its name spelled in large, faded letters on the top of a wood facade illuminated by light bulbs on both sides.

The time was after 11pm and the double bill was over. There were groups of people milling around and vendors plying their snacks and confectionary: a woman under an umbrella selling fruits –mangoes, bananas, a red fruit that Carl vaguely recalled as Cashew; a man chopping water-coconuts for customers; a cake and soft drink vendor. A billboard next to the entrance of the cinema had posters that heralded a double bill: *The Rise And Fall Of Idi Amin* and *Tom Horn*. Shops were located on the same side of the road as the cinema and people were coming and going, crossing wood bridges on foot or pushing bicycles. On the other side of the road, across a trench, was a cane field where green stalks were silhouetted against a silvery moon.

Ironic, Carl thought. People were going to see a movie about Idi Amin –one of the most notorious despots in recent times. Would anyone try to strike a comparison with the leadership in Guyana after they saw the movie? In some circles and most recently by Ebony magazine in the U.S., the President of Guyana was considered to be one of the richest Black men in the Caribbean. What part of this was true and what part fiction, was anyone's guess. What was universally known though, was that the country was near bankruptcy: investment had ceased after international companies had been nationalized and foreign exchange was no longer available for drugs, machinery and equipment and foodstuff from abroad. At work at the Industrial Bank in Toronto, Carl had come across several files where Canadian corporations were hoping to invest in Guyana to take advantage of low costs and he'd had no alternative but to decline the loans needed for start-up financing. He wouldn't recommend a change in his bank's policy as long as the present government refused to open up to private sector investment and repatriation of profits.

"There doesn't appear to be a shortage of customers here, even for a Monday and at this time of night," Carl said. "Where's all the money coming from?"

"Is like this all the time," Uncle Jules said. "Everybody trying their best to hustle and make a living. Except them people who don't want to work and want what you work hard for. They just like carrion crow –vultures waiting to pick the flesh off your bones." Bitterness dripped from his voice. This was something that Carl's father would have said, and after Uncle Jules' experience on his estate, Carl could understand why he felt the way he did.

Earl was doing that breathing in and out activity with his fingers folded against his mouth, again. "Helluva lot of money coming from outside," he said. "From Canada, America and England. Guyanese living outside the country sending money and goods to relatives. The ones who don't have a job and no relatives abroad suffer most. There's no real support system in place to help them out."

They passed through the busy section of the village and reached the outskirts where an imposing structure stood a few hundred yards from the road, its chimneys belching columns of smoke, bright lights illuminating the parking lot and surrounding area. Large diesel generators hummed and whined somewhere in the background. The building housed the factory of the Diamond Sugar Estate. The cane field in the surrounding area seemed to stretch for miles and miles, as they drove by, until they finally left it behind.

Faded road-signs appeared with more frequency at the entrance to every village, and caught in the glare of the head-lamps, were names on those signs: Agricola, Eccles, and Ruimveldt. After another hour, they left the main road and crossed into Middle Walk with the market on one side and more cane fields on the right. They were now in Repentigny and this was the first time he was returning in sixteen years. The sinking feeling he was experiencing deep in his stomach –was it because he was this close to his birth place or coming face to face with the reality of his father's demise?

Carl looked at the clock on the dashboard –its luminous dials showed it to be close to midnight. A long day for him and it still wasn't over.

Middle Walk –the Walk, as Carl had known it, was the longest road in the town. Houses were dark shadows against the night sky, fast moving rain clouds seemed precipitous and ominous and an eerie silence pervaded the surroundings. Instinct gave him clues to their whereabouts and memories of locations and names of places and people came flashing back. At the Junction used to be the Cake Shop and opposite that the Rum Shop. Up the road from there would be the High Bridge across the Canal and beyond that was St. Jamestown, the gateway to Georgetown.

The drive down the Walk was slow –the road was not any better than the one leading out of the airport. More houses: Mister Mike's with the dog that he and Lincoln had pelted with stones; Ramdass' house: where Cyril lived, one of the Musketeers and a high-school friend; Melville, the sole Amerindian family so far away from their natural habitat in the hinterland; Robertson and his son Reds who scalped tickets at the Paramount cinema. Further up the Walk would be Wilfred Ledman's house. Did these people still live there? Were they even alive?

Carl had seen a bright glow up the road, even as they'd turned into the Walk. He knew the spot –it was where his father's house was located. They were being drawn there, inexorably, like an insect to a light bulb.

They came to the bridge over the gutter and Earl stopped the car. People were standing on the bridge and milling around the parapet, some of them with beer bottles in hand, a few holding plastic or foam cups. Earl honked several times. In the couple of minutes that it took for the people to clear the bridge and for Earl to gain access, Carl took in the surroundings. A tall fence now secured the front yard, and zinc sheets had been bolted onto the wrought-iron fence that once stood proudly in front. Razor-sharp wire was strung over the top of the fence and floodlights were positioned on tall posts. The glow he had noticed was coming from these lights. As they entered the driveway that led to the left side of the house and the garage, he saw that tall zinc sheets were even bolted to the double steel gates. The right and left side of the property, as far as he could see, were enclosed in a protective mantle of the same type of zinc sheets that were used on roofs.

The driveway curved around the left side of the property and they made slow progress, wrenching inch by inch from people reluctant to cede space or willing to yield only after they'd looked through the windows of the De Soto. A tarpaulin hung from the balcony in front of the house and was supported by makeshift posts. Light bulbs dangled from cords hanging in the dome of the tarp, shedding areas of light that captured the faces of people transfixed in wonderment or awe, and casting shadows where people lurked in silence. Tables and benches were laid out under the tarp and there were people sitting and playing games or drinking and talking. There must have been over a hundred people there, a large number for so late into the night. Were they all neighbours, friends of his father, relatives, or just curiosity seekers? There were a few faces that were vaguely recognizable, but Carl couldn't be sure, this late into the night, and being as tired as he was.

Earl let them out of the De Soto before he drove the car into the garage. Augusto's car: a Morris Oxford loaded with options when it was bought, was not in the garage. It was probably one of the first things that had gone when Augusto fell into hard times. What else would his father have had to dispose to carry on just his everyday existence in the new Republic?

Soon as he came out of the car, Carl found himself besieged by a crowd of people shaking his hand, patting him on the shoulders and extending sympathy for his loss.

"I'm so sorry about your father," a Portuguese man said. "He was a good man –he helped me to find a job many years ago."

"Your father buy all the equipment for the Playground," another man said.

"Your father was like a brother to me," a third said. "He was always there to give me advice when I started up my business."

Carl was tired –he wanted to find someplace where he could collapse and block everything from his consciousness. But, these were all people who were there out of respect for his father and to comfort the family. How could he deny them this moment?

He was steered to a table under the tarpaulin and he took a seat on a bench with a table where two men sat next to him and four men across from him.

The people at the wake seemed to readily consider him as one of them. A white enamel cup filled with steaming black coffee was placed in front of him, along with a plate of salt biscuits and several slices of cheese. To his left was a group of men playing cards and to the right another set playing dominoes. One table had a large bottle of rum in the centre and at another a case of beer. Men were sipping or standing with enamel cups or beer bottles or plastic cups in their hands. Many of them smoked. At every table and for every group of people, the scene was repeated, looking more like a celebration of a man's life rather than a time for mourning. Things hadn't changed much in all the years he'd been away.

He wondered about the stories being exchanged about his father, tales he'd never heard before. He knew of his father's early history and that of the entire family when they came to British Guiana from Madeira. How much more had happened, how many more events had transpired in his father's life of which he was not aware after leaving British Guiana in 1964? There had been an ocean separating them even before his departure.

Carl saw traces of features in people he knew many years ago: older, greyer, stouter or sometimes leaner versions of people who lived in the Walk. Mister Lall –the beer and alcohol would have been bought from his rum shop; he was now porting a large distended stomach and appeared to have shrunken in height. Mister Lee, the next-door neighbour was there, looking much less Chinese and much more Black than Carl remembered. He'd lost most of his curly hair, though. At the entrance to the house, Carl saw Earl talking to a woman. She was a couple of inches shorter than Earl, was just as fair and had the same profile. Was it Earl's mother? What was the name that Jules had told him –Sumintra? They seemed to be having an argument over something, taking the occasional glance, the woman pointing a few times in Carl's direction. Was he the subject of their dispute? And, why?

Carl looked around: so many people, most of them strangers to him; so much outpouring of sympathy for the passing of his father. Was this all genuine or just another reason for a get-together and have a good time? Here it was – he was the only son present for the funeral. He resented that Joseph hadn't even expressed an interest in returning. How about John, would he turn up, would he crawl out of whatever hole he had dug for himself? A passing glance at a table far off on the outside of the tarpaulin and he saw a boy playing cards with three men. There was something hauntingly familiar about the boy –he was around sixteen, wore a short sleeve tee shirt that he appeared to have outgrown, his muscles now bulging out of the sleeves, and he was smiling. He was obviously pleased with the hand he'd been dealt. The smile did it, but also the way he tilted his head and pursed his lips. My God, Carl thought: it was James, a much younger version, the one he grew up with, but nevertheless, it was his brother James. If the boy's features were that close to his brother, then it had to be Jimmy: James and Patsy's son.

The cup of coffee sufficed to keep him going for forty-five minutes and then, the effects of the long day and evening started to take a toll. When he looked at his watch, it showed that time already moved over into the next day: it was Tuesday. He'd had enough. Today was going to be even rougher, with the funeral to attend and more people to greet. He got up from the bench and headed into the house, blissfully unaware of anyone extending greetings and well wishes. He felt giddy –had they spiked the coffee with rum, as he'd known people to do in the past?

Nothing much had changed in the layout of the house or the furniture and it was an easy path that took him up the circular stairway, making a left turn at the head of the stairs, then, entering his father's bedroom down the hall. No one had mentioned anything about sleeping arrangements but he thought it was the most appropriate place for him, at least for now. He stripped off his clothes, got down to his underwear and dropped on the bed.

CHAPTER 7 –Black Friday

MEMO:

From: Department of State

To: Embassy in United Kingdom

Washington, February 16, 1962, 5:16pm.

SUBJECT: MEMORANDA ON BRITISH GUIANA TO STATE AND CIA

For Ambassador from Secretary. Please deliver following message as soon as possible:

You know from our correspondence in August of last year of my acute concern over the prospects of an independent British Guiana under the current leadership of the Reform party. Subsequent to its victory in the August elections we agreed to try your policy of fostering an effective association between British Guiana and the West and an Anglo-American working party developed an appropriate program. At our request safeguards, including consultations about new elections, were included in case matter went awry. In pursuance of this program the President received The Chairman on his visit to this country in October.

I must tell you now that I have reached the conclusion that it is not possible for us to put up with an independent British Guiana under The Chairman. We have had no real success in establishing a basis for understanding with him due in part to his grandiose expectations of economic aid. We have continued to receive disturbing reports of Communist connections on the part of The Chairman and persons closely associated with him. Partly reflective of ever growing concern over Cuba, public and Congressional opinion here is incensed at the thought of our dealing with The Chairman. The Marxist-Leninist policy he professes parallels that of Castro. Current happenings in Brit-

ish Guiana indicate The Chairman is not master of the situation at home without your support. There is some resemblance to the events of 1953. Thus, the continuation of The Chairman in power is leading us to disaster in terms of the colony itself, strains on Anglo American relations and difficulties for the Inter-American system.

These consultations, I believe, make it mandatory that we concert our remedial steps...seems to me clear that new elections should now be scheduled, and I hope we can agree that The Chairman should not accede to power again."

From a balcony on the top floor of the Legislature, Carl could see the swelling number of demonstrators, the largest crowd seen in the city within recent times. Traffic had grounded to a halt in all directions.

The media had preordained it earlier that morning:

From: The Daily News: Friday 16 February 1962

Headline: Mass Protest Rally Planned Today

Supporters of the two main opposition parties are expected to cripple the city this morning as they continue their protest against the Government's budget proposals. A rally, supported by the leaders of the Republicans and the Conservatives, will be held at Parade Ground. The rally will end up in a march to Parliament Building where the Budget is being debated without the opposition who continue to boycott the proceedings. This paper has learnt that the two leaders will meet outside the legislature where they will shake hands, in a rare, historic show of solidarity and an attempt to disrupt the work of the legislature.

Carl, Wilfred and Cyril and the hapless volunteers had left the domed room of the Legislative Assembly where the Chairman and his cabinet were still engaged in speaking about the Budget proposals, even though there were no opposition members there to conduct a meaningful debate.

Outside, two sets of protesters, hundreds of people making up each group, were converged outside the building, where a wrought-iron fence and gate were expected to keep them out of the compound. What if they breached the gate and came into the compound? Carl looked around at the others gathered with him. They were at most, a hundred government supporters. What could they possibly do under the circumstances?

What was he doing there in the first place!

Carl had been at a meeting at Liberty House late the previous night, along with Wilfred and Cyril. The party secretary had told them that the government was determined to pass the Budget Bill the next day and wanted as many members to turn up to support it. Wilfred and Cyril had been among those who were indignant that the government's bill was not receiving the hearing it needed in the Legislature and they were determined to provide support. Carl had been caught up in their enthusiasm.

He wasn't sure he'd made the right decision.

The leaders of the Republican and Conservative opposition parties, approached, shook hands and clapped each other on the shoulders. Shouts of approval rang through the crowd, made up mainly of Blacks and Portuguese, a sprinkling of other races, all blended into a solid mass of humanity united with one goal in mind: they would accept nothing other than the collapse of the Reform government.

The other government supporters –how were they feeling? Were they like Carl, crippled by a growing sense of impotence, that there was nothing they could do if the situation got out of hand? With its rural base, Reform had limited support in the Capital, and the Chairman had made it clear that he was unwilling to bring in supporters from the outside and run the risk of a confrontation that had the potential of leaving many injured on both sides.

A squad of riot police waited on the grounds of the Legislature, shields and batons ready. Carl hoped that the police would prevent the situation from deteriorating. The city police was made up mainly of opposition supporters, though. Would they act and do what was needed when the time came? Carl was praying they would.

The throng around the Legislature was now forty or fifty deep and still growing. People blocked the sidewalk and entrance to the Legislature. They took up positions under palm trees and hung out of windows in the surrounding buildings; they sat on the hood and trunk of cars parked on the street; they waved banners and pickets in the air and sang songs of solidarity. Then, what Carl could only describe as a menacing silence, descended, as the Republican leader waved his hands in the air for silence.

Someone had provided an empty wooden packing case used for shipping soft drinks to cake-shops and the Republican leader was standing on it, higher than anyone else in the crowd.

"Brothers and sisters...," the leader said, through his megaphone. He was a man noted for speeches of such eloquence that his fame had spread throughout the British West Indies and beyond. He knew how to move a crowd. "History is in the making today. We're all united with one purpose, to slay the evil demon of Communism that has reared its ugly head in our fair and beautiful British Guiana. This government is determined to pass a budget that is aimed at stripping away the freedom of the working class and undermining the democracy that we now enjoy. They want to take away everything that you've worked for all your life. We will not let this happen, not in my lifetime, not while I breathe and live and lead you. We will show them, you and me, that they cannot trifle with these freedoms that we enjoy."

The crowd roared. Chants of "Down with the government," arose. A loudspeaker blared a song by Ray Charles and the Raylettes. The people joined the chorus. *Hit the road Jack and don't you come back no more.* The blind singer's popularity had skyrocketed overnight in British Guiana.

Jack Hall was the special adviser to the Chairman of the governing party. He was the man who, along with a Hungarian economist had drafted the Budget and drawn the ire and wrath of the opposition parties down on his head. They would not be satisfied until Hall was fired and the Hungarian expelled from the country. The media had also joined the attack recently: the airwaves rang with the song played many times every hour in advertisements funded by the opposition parties. The release of the song and its treacly appeal had been timely. Even Carl, to his consternation, had found himself humming it, at times.

"*Hit the road Jack,*" the crowd continued.

The demonstrators continued to wave their pickets and placards: THIS IS A CHOKE AND ROB BUDGET and SLAVERY IF REFORM GETS INDEPENDENCE were the most widely toted ones in various sizes and colours, but there were others with much more inflammatory language: DOWN WITH THE GOVERNMENT; DEATH RATHER THAN COMMUNISM; GIVE US FREEDOM OR GIVE US DEATH; NO INDEPENDENCE UNDER THIS GOVERNMENT.

The entire street in front of the Legislature, stretching from High Street in the east to the area of D'Aguiar Imperial House to the west, was now packed with people. The opposition members of the Legislature were prominently positioned in front of the crowd.

The Republican leader was still addressing the crowd. "Comrades, friends," he said, "we have to do more than wave pickets and flash placards. Merely waving pickets will not get rid of this inept and dictatorial government. We have to take control of the situation. We have to show them that we have the power. We have to take action. We have to strike while the iron is hot. This is the hour. There will never be a better time than now."

"He's actually telling them to start a riot," Carl said.

"Not looking too good," Cyril said, a slight tremor in his voice.

"I know, man, these people up to no good," Wilfred said. "Look like a scene straight out of El Cid –the Moors attacking the castle!"

Cyril pointed: "Carl, it look like your father in front."

Carl followed his friend's direction and sure enough, his father was there. In the sea of faces, it was not difficult to pick out Augusto's –he was up front, prominent, active, boisterous, waving his placard, his mouth opening and closing in a seemingly endless display of hostile denouncement of the government. Augusto was wearing his blue pin stripe three-piece suit and carried a picket with the words: AXE THE TAX. As a prominent supporter of the Conservatives, Augusto was making his presence known. He had already failed on his first attempt to win a seat in the Legislature and this time it seemed as if he wanted to ensure the party was fully aware of his dedication to its philosophy and cause.

The irony that he and his father were now on opposite sides of the fence did not escape Carl. The chasm that separated their two philosophies on politics and how best to gain independence for the colony had been widening for some time, even though it hadn't come out in the open. Carl realized, though, that Augusto would eventually become aware of it and this would create an unfathomable gap between them.

The situation was deteriorating by the minute. From the street, a barrage of missiles came flying onto the grounds of the Legislature. The police raised their shields and took up defensive positions. The assault was kept up: an unrelenting fusillade of bricks and bottles. It was no coincidence, Carl thought, that he had seen bulges in the pockets of many in the crowd, including the two opposition leaders. They had all come prepared!

The missile assault continued. The riot police pulled back to the entrance of the Legislature. The crowd pressed on. Something else was happening. As the crowd advanced, the two opposition leaders and their shadow cabinet members withdrew to the rear, and before long, they had disappeared from view. So had Augusto.

They're leaving the scene of the crime, Carl thought, so no one could ever blame them for subsequent acts committed by their supporters. He had to agree with Cyril: the outcome of today's events didn't look promising.

Three days prior, the President of the Consolidated Trade Unions, the powerful association of all trade unions in the country, had called a general strike against the government's budget. They were demanding that the government drop the controversial aspects of the budget.

Two days prior, prompted by the government, the police had banned all demonstrations in front of the Legislature to guarantee access to and from the building. In an effort to head off a confrontation, the government had offered to negotiate on the budget. The opposition, sensing a weakness in the government's position had done a complete about turn and was now demanding that the government resign since it could not stand by its own budget proposals. There was no recognition that the government had come to power in a free and fair election.

Today: The combined opposition campaign in front of the Legislature was one of planned disobedience against the restriction on mass assembly, one intended to show the government that it had no control over the capital and supporters of the opposition parties.

A black car pulled out of the parking lot inside the compound and stopped at the front entrance of the building. Riot police quickly formed a cordon around it. The Chairman and two of his bodyguards climbed into the back seat and the car made its way slowly to the gate, police trotting on both sides. As the gate was opened the crowd surged forward and separated the police from the car. They started to rock the car back and forth, even while it was in motion. Hands clawed at door handles, fists banged on the roof, pickets were slammed on the sides.

"Ooh, ooh, it don't look too good," Wilfred said. "The Moors trying to get hold of El Cid!"

"Why are the police standing by and doing nothing about it," Cyril fumed. "Why don't they do something?"

The riot police had been completely cut off from the car. Or, had they? The police were standing aside and allowing the situation to take its course. Gone was any pretence of aiding the head of government that they had taken an oath to protect. The Chairman and his bodyguards were on their own.

As the car inched through the crowd the protesters became bolder and more aggressive. Stones were hurled at the windows; the headlights were smashed; the windshield wipers were broken off. People jumped on the hood and the trunk.

"They're trying to get to the Chairman," Cyril said. He was almost hysterical.

When it seemed that the car was sure to be breached, a window was lowered, and a hand with a gun appeared. The crowd around the window backed away. Two shots went off in quick succession in the air and pandemonium broke out. The crowd scattered in all directions, people piling up on one another in their haste to get out of harm's way. In the commotion that followed, and before the crowd could recover, the Chairman's car sped away.

"Thank God he's safe," Cyril said.

"That was a close call," Wilfred sighed. "El Cid lives to fight another day."

The crowd surged down the street, chasing after the Chairman's car, throwing missiles and tossing pickets.

"The perfect time for us to leave," Carl said.

***

From: Radio Demerara. Friday 16 February 1962.

6 pm newscast:

Here's an update on the situation in the city's downtown core this evening.

The Georgetown Fire Brigade continues in its attempt to bring the fires under control. The riot police are still trying to clear the area of looters. It is reported that the Chairman has called on the Governor to bring in British troops to aid in the effort. There is no word on that as yet.

As we reported earlier, several incidents seem to lead up to this evening's disturbances.

The situation started to heat up this morning, when a peaceful demonstration outside the Electricity Corporation turned violent. Stones and bottles were thrown at employees entering the building. The riot squad was called out, and in their attempt to restore order with the use of tear-gas, several demonstrators were hurt. A riot broke out when word spread through the crowd that a woman and her child were affected, with the woman subsequently dying in the fracas. At this time, we are still unable to confirm whether this is true or not.

Meanwhile, the mass rally at Parade Ground, attended by several thousand supporters of the Republican and Conservative parties, ended up outside Parliament Building where it resulted in a confrontation with riot police. Following that, roving bands struck at stores on Water Street, smashing glass cases and looting merchandise. We don't know exactly when the first fire started, but it is known that several major stores have suffered seriously from the arson.

Stay tuned. We understand that the Chairman and the two leaders of the opposition will make an address to the nation.

The Dias' house, two stories of concrete construction, was the most prominent on the Walk. Standing on the rooftop, Carl and his brothers had a vantage point where they could see far into the city, into the downtown commercial district where fires were raging, columns of dark, acrid smoke spiralling over the city into the evening, long after the setting sun had left its glow on the horizon.

Carl had read of so called Great Fires in the past, several conflagrations in the nineteenth and early twentieth century that had spread rapidly through the wood buildings of the colonial city and razed entire blocks by the time they were brought under control. Those had all been accidental: a careless cigarette smoker, an unattended stove, or an electrical malfunction. This present event, however, was marked by several precedents: the first fire that resulted from riots and the first time that the entire commercial district, spread over several miles, was on fire. Everything had conspired to make the event one of historic proportions: the strike at the Water Works that stopped water flowing through the mains; fire men refusing to man the hoses even when the power came back on; police standing by idly; looters emptying stores and then torching them.

"Things will never be the same again," Joseph whispered. He was standing behind Carl, and he spoke so softly that Carl thought it was the wind murmuring in his ear.

Carl looked at his oldest brother. Joseph had caught the first boat early that morning and travelled to the city to start a three-day leave from his job at the Demerara Bauxite Company at McKenzie. He'd said that rumours had abounded in the mining community about trouble brewing all over the opposition dominated areas and he'd decided to play it safe and bring his wife and daughter to Georgetown to be with the family.

"What do you mean?" Carl said.

Joseph said: "The first time I'm seeing something like this. The breakdown of law and order will start a trend. Once the genie's out of the bottle, you can't get it back in."

A parade of people living far down the Walk and beyond in the housing scheme had continued in a steady stream into the afternoon after Carl arrived home following the incident at the Legislature, and it was now reduced to a trickle. Carl had seen people perform feats of strength that would have taxed all their resources. A man carrying a fridge on his back; another with a twin-sized mattress; a woman toting a kerosene-oil stove. Looters passed with items of every type and description, carried along by any means possible: furniture, electronic equipment, booty stuffed in garbage bags, cartons and stacks of various plunder precariously balanced on their head. Dray carts were laden with the stolen items, bicycle carriers were piled up –everything that had wheels was enlisted in the process of carting off the booty.

"I wonder how much of that stuff belongs to the Old Man's store," Joseph said.

In typical British tradition, the colonial office had never armed the police –the result was the creation of a force unable or incapable of contending with the growing disorder. The Volunteer Force, an armed local militia, was the next line of defence but they hadn't been called in –Carl doubted if they would be, since the force was composed mainly of opposition members and had very little or no training in handling civil disobedience.

"Over the radio, I heard that British troops are coming in," Thomas said.

"About time," Carl said. He couldn't mask the bitterness in his voice. "Since last night the Minister of Home Affairs and the Chairman have been asking the Governor to bring in troops from the base at Atkinson, but the Governor refused – he said that it was an internal matter to maintain law and order, something that had to be dealt with by the police. If needed, he said, troops were just a stone's throw away –they can be brought in at the push of a button."

"I guess they're learning that unarmed police can't cope with a situation like this," Joseph said.

"How can the overthrow of an elected government in a British colony where peace and order still lie with the Governor, be an internal matter?" Carl said.

"People will never have any respect for the police force anymore." Joseph said. "Mark my words, officers will have to carry guns from now on."

"Even if the police were armed," Carl said, "do you really think they will fire on their own people? There's no doubt in my mind that they're under orders from the opposition not to take any action during the riots and arson."

"It's all so stupid and insane," Thomas said. "If the government had dropped the budget in the first place, this would never have happened."

Thomas was spouting their father's line. Of all Carl's siblings, Thomas was the closest to their father in word and deed and followed the Old Man's approach in almost everything. Joseph, on the other hand, had his own family and his ambition was to leave the country and go abroad; he didn't think there was much of a future in the colony, so it didn't really matter to him what direction the government took. James, the second oldest, even though he worked for the Old Man at the store, always managed to keep his distance and maintain his independence. Unknown to Augusto, James was seeing a Black girl and talked about marrying her soon – whether Augusto approved or not. In the end, there was little hope of him gaining their father's approval for dating someone outside of the Portuguese community, much less marrying her.

"I wonder what's happened to Dad, and James," John said.

All afternoon, John had been asking about their father and brother, anxiety in his voice. Carl was concerned: what else was going through the mind of the youngest member of the family –how did this all appear to a boy just turned nine? Total blackout in the suburbs, fires raging on the horizon, the sound of gunfire in the air –John might have looked at it all as the world coming to a premature and calamitous end. At his young age, was it the unbearable thought of losing their father and brother that was affecting him?

"Perhaps we should go down to the store and see if they're okay?" John added.

Just as he'd done every other time that evening, Joseph put an arm around him and said: "We can't do that –there's a curfew on. I'm sure they're okay."

"Don't worry, it will take more than something like this to stop that Old Man." Carl reached out and hugged John. "James is with him, so they will watch out for each other."

Carl couldn't help wondering about his father's whereabouts. The last time Carl had seen him was outside the Legislature. Carl assumed that his father had made his way back to the store after the demonstration and he would have been there during the looting on Water Street. When the arson started, he would have joined the battle to save the store, as many storeowners were reported to have done. Carl hoped that the fire hadn't spread further, and his father's building had been saved in the ensuing inferno.

Around midnight, Augusto and James finally came home. The Old Man collapsed on the sofa in the living room.

"Está tudo acabado," was the first thing his father said, tears swelling in his eyes. "Eu estou acabado, dizimado."

His father did that: revert to his ancestral language whenever he was faced with a crisis, but his usage had diminished over the years and grown to a trickle when he became active in politics. The few words that Carl had picked up were enough for him to know that the Old Man was saying that *everything was gone and he was wiped out*.

"How did you manage to get home?" Joseph said.

Augusto seemed surprised to see his oldest son. He reached out and took his son's hands. "I'm glad you came down," he said. "I'm hearing that terrible things will happen down river."

"What kind of things are you talking about?" Joseph said.

Augusto ignored him and repeated: "Está tudo acabado."

"Luckily the army was escorting store owners," James said. "We managed to get a ride from them."

"There's nothing left," Augusto said. "All gone, wiped out." He retreated back onto the sofa and seemed to dig himself deeper into the cushions, as if it was the only place he could find sanctuary.

"Terrible, terrible" James said. "You wouldn't believe it. I closed up the store early in the afternoon after I heard about the looting, but they came soon afterwards, broke all the showcases, stripped them, entered the store and take off with anything that was not bolted down to the floor. All we could do was stand by and watch, helpless."

Carl's father believed in carrying a large inventory: *Give the people a choice and they will come back again*, he always said. The value of the inventory in the store was slowly being rebuilt to a peak after the hectic Christmas season and now it was all gone: several hundred thousand dollars worth of merchandise carted off in a wholesale theft that defied imagination and logic.

The Old Man sobbed. "They looted everything on the floor, then they moved to the warehouse and stripped it bare. They even carted away the fixtures before they set fire to the store. Why did they have to set fire to it? I can't understand them. Why set fire and destroy everything that I've built up? I've always been good to them –why did they do it?"

"You can recover everything from the insurance company, can't you?" Thomas said.

Augusto shook his head and looked at his son. *You don't know much*, was what his eyes seemed to suggest. He said: "Você está louco. You're crazy. Our policy doesn't cover riots and acts of civil unrest and insurrection. None of the owners will be able to recover from their insurance policies. We're all going to go broke."

Carl had never seen his father break down in an emotional outburst like this. The picture he'd always had of the man was one of steely disposition and determination in everything he pursued. Carl had even faced up to the fact that he looked upon his father with a mixture of reverence and awe over his achievements, though he could never forget that his father had succeeded with very little social awareness for those who were less fortunate around him. Now, his father was postulating about how good he'd been to the people who had looted and set fire to his store, while failing to understand that he had placed the same people into the separate category of *them*. It was still *Them* versus *Us* and this would never change.

The monster was loose, Carl thought. Frankenstein, Mary Shelley's classic macabre creation was ravishing the city, beyond the control of his master. Did any of the architects of the declared peaceful but vocal revolution against the current government ever give serious thought to the possibility that their plan would backfire? Or, had it all been planned to exploit the use of the criminal elements in the city to bring the government down to its knees and create such an atmosphere of instability that the British government would have no choice but to suspend the constitution, again, and impose home rule? Ironically, it was the business sector, perhaps the most unrelenting and unforgiving in its criticism of the government's budget, that would now suffer the most.

"I tried to stop them, I tried, but no one would listen. I told them, we're all in this together. *I'm Conservative, you're Republican*, I kept telling them, but no one would listen," Augusto said.

The day's events were so well orchestrated, so well executed, that they had all the makings of an attempted coup. How much of what had occurred was at the instigation of foreign influence? Carl remembered an interview at school one day, just two weeks prior...

Carl had been summoned to the Principal's office through the broadcast system.

"Looks like you're in trouble again," Wilfred had joked. "Some girl complain about you, I bet."

Carl had puzzled over the reason behind the summons as he headed for the office. His school fees were paid up, he was reaching high A's in all his subjects, his attendance was perfect and despite what Wilfred had said, he couldn't recall singling out any particular girl for undue attention.

He'd found Hal Perough waiting for him in the office when he entered.

"Carl," the man said, "come on in. Take a seat. I've been wanting to meet you for some time."

"As you perhaps know," Perough continued, after Carl had settled in a chair across the desk from him, "I'm conducting career counselling in the school. I understand you're one of the top students in your class and I've been wondering how I could help you reach your goals."

Carl was puzzled. He thought that the American student adviser would have been more focussed on the final year students instead of the fourth formers. Carl still had another year to complete high school.

"Can you tell me what you want to do when you leave high school?" Perough said.

"I'm not very sure at this stage of the game. Of course, I'd like to go off to university, perhaps the University of the West Indies or somewhere else abroad."

"That's great," Perough said. He spoke with a drawl, his jaw hanging loose and his eyes never leaving Carl's face. "Do you know what you want to do?"

"I'm thinking about journalism, or something connected with it."

Perough nodded. "A noble profession. We can't have enough journalists in the world, I always say. Have you thought of going to the States to study?"

Carl was taken aback. "No, not really."

"I think you'd do well there. If you keep up with your high grades you'd have no problem getting into the university of your choice. There might even be a scholarship in the offering when you finish next year. I can help."

Carl raised his eyebrows. *Why me?* "Sounds great," Carl said, and he wanted to add, *What do I have to do in return?* He waited.

"I see that you're a very popular guy around and about." Perough pulled a document from a file that was laid out in front of him. "Head of the debating team, member of the society to promote intercultural and interracial harmony, in the school's top eleven cricket team."

"I try," Carl said.

Perough closed the file. "The principal and faculty think very highly of you, both academically and personality wise. Everyone says that you will go very far."

Perough got up and came across the room. He took up a position in front of Carl's chair. He picked up a paperweight that was lying on top of a stack of documents in the IN tray. Carl could see the logo on the paperweight: CTU –Consolidated Trade Unions of British Guiana.

Perough juggled the paperweight between his hands, and replaced it on the stack of papers. He smiled. "I understand that you, along with some of your friends, are also in the youth arm of the Reform party. Sounds very exciting."

Carl raised his eyebrows.

Perough nodded. "I think it's very important for youth to get involved today in politics. They're the future leaders of tomorrow. They call it the RYM –don't they? Reform Youth Movement?"

Carl nodded.

"I'm curious about how this organization functions. I'd like to do some research on it. You know, find out how they motivate the young membership, where they get their ideas. I'm sure this can be of help to me in my job here in counselling the students. I'm wondering if you'd be willing to help me?"

Carl sat up and took a deep breath. It was clear to him what Perough was after, but he wasn't sure how to respond.

On the one hand he was disgusted that the man would even approach him, and on the other hand, he was reluctant to antagonize him. Perough obviously was working on behalf of the principal and Carl's academic future lay in both their hands.

"I'd very much like to talk directly to the members of the organization. Can you give me a list of their names? Better yet, can you introduce me to them?"

"I'll think about it," Carl said. "I only recently joined the group, so I know very little about how they operate, and I've only gone to one meeting, so far."

"You plan on continuing, don't you?"

Carl shrugged. "I'm not so sure. I have a great deal on my plate. I'll keep it in mind."

Perough stood up. He reached over and took Carl's hand, holding on to it for a few seconds. His hand was huge, cold and clammy; it encircled Carl's hand completely. "Great. We should talk again soon. I hope this is the start of a great friendship. I'd very much like to help you, in any way I can. Keep that scholarship in mind."

***

"Não há nada mais," Augusto said. "Não há nada mais."

Carl shook his head. He wanted to scream at his father: *Of course there's nothing left. You should have thought of that before your party joined forces with the Republicans.* But, even with his disdain for his father's actions, he couldn't help but feel that his father was paying a high and unwarranted price for his party's unholy alliance with the devil.

The Old Man often boasted about how his father, Salvador, had started out as a humble merchant –a Josie, a Portuguese shopkeeper, was what the community called him. He was someone who walked around his shop with leather *alpargatas* and he'd pulled himself up and succeeded after many years. Augusto would have to go down the same road.

Augusto said: "Se Deus quiser! God Willing, we will rebuild and start all over. We have no choice."

Carl had to admit, it was a quality that his father always possessed: the tenacity to pursue business goals. However, this would take more than energy and resolution to do it. A lot would depend on the colony's ability to overcome the economic collapse that was sure to come.

From: The Daily News: Friday 16 February 1962 Late Late Night Edition

Headline: British Troops On Patrol. Order Restored.

The 1st Battalion, Royal Hampshire Regiment was finally called in from Atkinson Air Base and arrived late this afternoon. At the time of writing, order had been restored, but at what price?

Seven square blocks of prime commercial real estate were razed to the ground, representing some of the largest and most noteworthy business establishments in Georgetown, including, J.P. Santos, Bettencourt's, Sandbach Parker and Dias And Sons. Banks were not immune: Barclays Bank was levelled and several other financial institutions were torched and burnt.

Fire fighters were severely hindered in the initial hours of the disturbances by striking employees who had walked off the job at the Water Works. Water mains couldn't function and ambulances and police failed to arrive due to lack of petrol.

Several looters and arsonists were shot, many incarcerated. Two platoons of soldiers were assigned the task of guarding the Chairman's Residence and key installations, including the Water Works and the Electricity Corporation and other government buildings. Two other platoons were assigned the task of clearing the streets of Georgetown of the rioters and arsonists.

The 1st Battalion, East Anglian Regiment will arrive soon to augment the troops already here.

CHAPTER 8 – The Canal

TUESDAY 25TH NOVEMBER 1980

He was falling, slowly, helplessly, down, down, down and there was nothing he could do about it.

Carl could see the swirling waters of the Canal below, the Low Bridge above, where he'd been standing just seconds before. He wasn't sure how it happened: whether he'd jumped or been pushed, but he knew that he was falling, his arms flailing helplessly, his body catapulting relentlessly into the brown, murky water that would propel him towards the koker, out to the gaping mouth of the Demerara River. From there he'd be sucked into the Atlantic, to wash up on some unknown beach or sink to the bottom of the ocean. He opened his mouth to shout for help but he had no control over his vocal cords –try as desperately as he could, no words came out. If only he could grab hold of something to break his fall, but there was nothing –just the bridge above, the water below. He was terrified. Why didn't someone help him? There were people walking on the bridge, which he could clearly see and hear and yet, no one paid him attention. They seemed to deliberately ignore him, dooming him to his fate.

Just as he was about to hit the water, he woke up. His underwear was wet, his body dripping in perspiration. Good God, he thought, this hasn't happened to me in so many years, not since I left the country to go abroad. For a long time, after he nearly drowned in the Canal, his sleep had been broken by a dream –reliving every terrifying moment of his fall from the bridge into the water. At times, he couldn't decide which was more horrific, the near drowning incident or the nightmare. As he'd grown older and started out to high school, the nightmare had reduced in frequency and stopped completely. Here it was, back with a vengeance.

Rain was falling: a steady downpour that sent heavy drops crashing against the zinc sheets on the roof. He could also hear a steady patter on the veranda in front of the house. The branches on the mango tree in the front yard creaked and groaned; a window shutter flapped against the house; a fowl cock was crowing. He remembered being awakened by a fowl cock during mid afternoon naps in the old house in the Walk, when he was very young. This was before he started out to primary school. He recalled how much he looked forward to the arrival of his older brothers from school, and his father from his work place.

A grey mist surrounded him, it was almost as if he were up in a cloud, and trying to figure it out merely sent his senses reeling further in the fog. He sat up, trying to figure out where he was. He closed his eyes, compressing his lids against his sockets and opening them again to see if the effect was still there. A stinging sensation on his right hand diverted his attention and he looked to see what it was. His hand was braced against a mosquito net and on the other side several of the insects were perched, relentlessly draining his lifeblood.

Carl shook the net. The mosquitoes wavered for a moment, then settled down again on his forearm. He swatted them. Red blotches appeared on the fabric.

Just how did he get there? He'd arrived during the wake, talked to many people, and drank coffee with them. He remembered heading up the stairs to the room. It seemed so long ago. He recalled stripping down to his underwear and placing his pants and shirt on a chair before he dropped off to sleep. Someone must have pulled the net around the bed later.

He looked at his watch. The time was 6:30. He hadn't slept this soundly in a long time and he thought of Natasha and the kids –they'd still be asleep. In another half-an-hour Natasha would be rousing them to prepare for school. Since the separation, he missed that part of his life: the idle chatter around the breakfast table, dropping them off to school, discussing the day's events at the end of the day.

Sunlight was streaming through the open window. Slanted shadows from the wooden bars high overhead cast a scattered pattern on the floor and on the dresser across the room. Things were spotlighted by the sunlight on the dresser. A bottle of after-shave lotion, a hairbrush, a framed photograph of his father dressed in a pinstriped suit.

The opening in the net was on the right. When he parted it and stepped outside it was like going back in time and summoning a memory imbedded in his subconscious for what seemed like decades.

In a corner of the room was a clotheshorse with odds and ends of apparel draped over it –underwear and ties and crumpled shirts. Augusto's presence was everywhere and in everything, and Carl had never felt closer to his father. However, Augusto was gone, forever, and there would never be another opportunity for Carl to tell him that he was sorry he hadn't been around to ease all the pain and sorrow of the post-independence period of his life, and for any grief that Carl had caused him. Why was it, Carl thought, why had they focused so much on their differences when there was so much they had in common? Why could they not have bridged the gap that separated their two generations?

A wooden wardrobe stood next to the dresser where it had been since as far back as he could remember. Carl walked over to the wardrobe, passed his hands across the polished wood grain and opened the twin doors, and as he did, the confined odour came rushing out to greet him. His father's clothes were still there: the pinstripe suit that he'd worn in the photograph was stuffed into the right side; white shirts with stiff collars lining the other side. Nothing much had changed in the Old Man's outfits over the years. Tears welled up in Carl's eyes. He reached in and caressed the collar of the suit and ran his right hand across the shoulders.

Little things came back to Carl: a ride on the bar of his father's bicycle; sitting on his father's lap to take a family picture –he was the youngest when that was taken; Augusto caressing his hair and introducing him to a friend. Those times were fleeting. With a large brood of children and a younger one always on the way, dedicated moments of his father's time became a thing of the past whenever a younger one came along. He had always cherished those brief intervals with his father.

As he closed the doors Carl noticed his reflection in the mirror. He looked at his overnight stubble and passed his hands across his face. He could detect the trace of grey that had started to appear: specs of white on a red background.

He found his bag with his shaving set and cream and he headed for the washroom where there was a bucket of water near the sink. Brown sludge spurted from the tap when he opened it and he realized why the bucket had been placed there.

He wanted to see how much he could remember about his surroundings and after he'd shaved and dressed, he stepped out of the bedroom and found himself in the gallery. A double door led to the veranda and he slid open a series of bolts at the top and in the middle and stepped outside.

He recalled early morning rains that came and swept the sludge of the previous day and washed away the torpor of the night into the Canal. Only, there was no longer a Canal. He could see this from the veranda. The Canal was all filled up with debris and castoffs, a dumping ground: the shell of a car, a bicycle frame, bags of garbage, mounds of dirt, and it was where tall paragrass and wild eddo bush grew high. Earl said it had been renamed Freedom Boulevard shortly after independence. The intention was to make it a showpiece that reflected the young nation's aspirations. Far from being a Freedom Boulevard, the Canal now reeked and filled his nostrils with a variety of repulsive odours every time the breeze zipped across from the north-east. There was hope, however –he heard birds somewhere: the shrill cry of a kiskadee, the high pitched discordant whistle of a blue sacki, the cooing of a dove.

The mango tree was still there, branches drooping, its leaves suffering from blight –black spots evident everywhere. The same tree that he and Lincoln had climbed. Below the tree, it was where they had left the lizard after Lincoln had severed its tail. When Carl returned later that day he'd found the tailless lizard being carted off in a funerary procession of red ants. Funerals: Jordan Knights parading down the Walk, men dressed in stark white gowns and turbans, mourning the loss of one of their own.

A dog barked somewhere. Three houses down the Walk was Mister Mike's house, where he and Lincoln had pelted the two dogs in copulation, where, about a year later, they had met one of the dogs...

***

Lincoln always attracted trouble. Trouble just seemed to find him, like the way mosquitoes find their way with unerring accuracy to one's ear holes and nostrils at night. Trouble, like that day back in March, when they had come across Mister Mike's dog lying in the shade of the spice mango tree, nursing her litter.

The closest Carl had ever seen an intimate moment in an animal's life was when their cat had her litter the year before. There were eight little fur balls rummaging around the cardboard box under the bed in his parents' bedroom. His mother had told him not to touch the kittens before the nine days were up, that the cat wouldn't take kindly to the smell of humans on her litter. He had thought of it all that night, whether he should tell her that he'd already picked up two of them the same morning they were born. Later that day, he discovered that the cat had eaten two of her kittens. His mother was furious, but all through her interrogation of the household he'd remained silent, reliving the terror of that horrible moment when he had checked the box and found the remnants of the two kittens he had named Blackie and Brownie.

Carl crossed the rickety bridge to Mike's front yard. He left Lincoln behind and edged closer to take a look at the dog and pups. The dog was on her side, her paws outstretched to give maximum room for her pups as they jostled one another blindly to retain their delicate hold on her nipples. Carl watched as the dog's eyes moved closer to her nose; her ears standing erect. Her nostrils, black and wet, started to flare as she tilted her head and sniffed the air. The pups sucked away, four little black and white blobs, miniature images of their mother fidgeting against her underside.

From the corner of his left eye Carl saw Lincoln casually pick up a stone and saunter away, heading up the Walk, with no apparent interest in the dog or its pups. The dog followed his movements, her body pulsing rhythmically in the heat. As Lincoln cleared Mike's yard, he turned around and in one swift movement, tossed the brick at the dog. He was already running up the Walk when the missile landed and hit the dog.

She might have been no more than a common bitch, but with the instinct of a mother protecting her young, the black and white dog shrugged off her pups with a vigorous shake, as if she was just coming out of a bath. Noiselessly, except for a low rumble emanating from deep within her stomach, her lips drawn back in a snarl to reveal sharp canine ripping devices, she came after Carl. He was so close to her that he could see her lips curl back in a furious snarl and hear the snort that escaped her nostrils. He jumped up swiftly and took off for his house, the dog close behind him.

He'd always been a good runner –one of the best in the neighbourhood for his age group, but it was the longest three hundred yards he ever ran, much longer than all those races up and down the length of the Playground. Why did it take so long? Why was Lincoln perched on the paling post instead of trying to repel the dog? Why was Lincoln laughing and cheering –was it for Carl or the dog?

The dog seemed to be mere inches behind. Still, Carl thought he could make it before the dog caught him, but as he reached the gate he could see that the chain was wrapped around it. Lincoln had closed the gate! That left Carl with one chance to evade the dog now snapping at his heels. He scaled the gate and he'd just made it to the top when the dog lunged at him and snapped at his pants.

Carl sat on the fence and watched as the dog trotted back down the road, a low rumble still coming from her stomach, a fragment of his pants locked in her jaws. Lincoln was laughing.

Lincoln jumped off the fence and Carl followed him, keeping an eye on the dog going to rejoin her pups.

"It don't look too bad," Lincoln said.

Carl leaned over to look at the area where the dog had ripped his pants. A small section of his pants was missing and he felt a stinging sensation on his leg where the teeth had grazed him.

"Do you think I have to go to the hospital?" Carl said.

"Nah, I had worse," Lincoln said. "You one lucky boy."

***

Carl caressed his right leg. He hadn't told anyone about the dog attack that day. He'd simply applied iodine from the medicine cabinet and the scratch had eventually healed, but every now and then he could still feel the stinging sensation of that experience. Some injuries never go away, he thought, as he rubbed the area –they remain, evidence of past experiences and moments of indiscretion that haunt you for the rest of your days.

The sun was sneaking its way over the cane fields in the south. A tractor-trailer load of cane-cutters passed on the Walk: men with cutlasses, straw hats, sacks on their backs loaded with meals and sustenance to carry them through the arduous day's work. In the opposite direction, a load of cane was heading to the sugar estate. In the old days the estate moved the cane on mule-drawn punts on the Canal with a direct connection to the factory where the stalks were ground and the cane juice extracted.

The Canal. So many of his friends lived there. So many things revolved around it...

***

Carl had to be around nine – and he remembered it was during school break.

The family had returned late in the afternoon from Plantation Madeira where they'd spent the weekend at Grandmother Lilly's place. Carl could think of no better way to prolong the return to school than spending some time in the Playground.

He did not even change over to his home-clothes when they returned to the Walk, still giddy from the train ride, and he hurried over to the ground to take advantage of the limited time left before nightfall. The Playground was already packed: long queues assembled for the seesaw and the slide and the three swings all taken up. Carl opted for a swing and waited impatiently in line for his turn to come, noticing the long shadows on the grass and the gauldings already heading for the Backdam for the night.

When Carl's turn finally came he stuck to the swing, refusing to let it go. Below him the shadows had lengthened further, he could see his movement on the paling as he rode higher, the chains creaking and groaning from the momentum of the back and forth passage.

A sudden hush caught his attention. Silence, as if all the kids in the ground had suddenly been struck dumb. Why were they all gathered around Akbar who lived next door to Lincoln? Joseph, Thomas and James were also congregated around him. As the swing completed its arc from the high-end above the huge beam supporting the chains, words filtered upwards to Carl. Snatches of conversation: "Lincoln ... drowned...dead" were heard and registered with disbelief.

He came off the swing in a rush. A wave of nausea engulfed him –he hadn't eaten since lunch. His head swayed. His stomach was empty but he still wretched on the grass. Could it be true? How was it that Lincoln, such a good swimmer, described as being like a fast moving powerboat in water, how could he have drowned in the Canal?

Carl lingered on the fringe of the crowd around Akbar who was sobbing and supplying the details of what had happened within the last hour. Akbar was one of the kids in the Canal; he had been there swimming, had seen it all. More words worked their way into Carl's brain, a steady throbbing sound like someone banging in his head with a ball-peen hammer: *hanging on the chain between two punts...crushed... dragged down to the bottom...*

He didn't wait for the closing of the Playground. Somehow he had to ease the drumming in his brain. He staggered down the Walk, limped up the stairs to his house and crawled onto the sofa in the hall, only vaguely aware of his surroundings.

The slanting rays of the sinking sun had set the slats of the jalousie windows aglow but pools of darkness were all around: in front of the door to the portico; behind the coffee table in the gallery; below the cabinet in the dining room. The kitchen door was ajar and through it floated strains of the wind rustling through the Genip tree at the back; voices that seemed to come from afar, children laughing and playing, jeering and calling to him from the Playground.

Drowning; he knew what it was like. He had been almost there, once, and now all the details came rushing back. He kept seeing Lincoln's face: his cateyes staring intently through the unruly lock of hair.

Carl felt his head grow larger with every passing minute. The hair on his scalp and back of his neck bristled, his eyes felt as if they were about to pop in their sockets. What was that odour that clung to him? He detected it in his nostrils, the ever present, ever destructive smell of death. Had it followed him from the cemetery in Plantation Madeira where Grandmother had taken them to see the graves of her parents and siblings? All through that short visit, he'd inhaled it: a decaying, putrid, ever present odour that lingered in the very air that he breathed. Everything around him was assuming unfathomable proportions: he was in a room with the ceiling inclined to meet the floor at the far end and all the furniture piled up against one of the walls. Shadows detached themselves from dark corners, assumed shapes of moving objects and taunted him from the far-end of the room. Doors opened and closed and opened, and looking through one of them he had a vision...

The mid-afternoon heat had risen to the usual level of stifling proportions. Up and down both sides of the Canal, the vapour rose in pools that floated slowly off the road and seemed to be held there in a haze through which everything unfurled in distorted segments. The occasional burst of breeze that stirred down the Canal sent ripples through the reeds at the side of the parapet. Animals stood at the side of the road, panting and heaving. People lazed around in hammocks in bottom-houses and fanned themselves. And, the kids had taken refuge in the Canal.

Lincoln was there. He was plunging from the parapet. He was throwing somersaults that sent surges of water slapping against anyone who happened to be too slow to get out of the way. He was coming up under an unsuspecting victim and pulling the person's short-pants down, swimming off with it and throwing it on to the roadside where the kid would have to retrieve it, naked. Throughout this all, Lincoln was laughing.

From up the road came the resounding echo of a whip cracking in the air as a mule-train made its way westward.

The punts in the mule-train were linked with short lengths of chain hooked into metal clasps welded at the front and rear of each craft. Six mules up front kept the convoy moving, each mule bound to a punt by a length of chain, the chain pulled taut as the mules made their way down the road.

The convoy came to the Low Bridge and the mule team was halted. The chains were unhooked and as the punts coasted under the bridge and cleared it, the head man reconnected the chains. The momentum of the convoy was lost by this time. The air was rent with metal clanging against metal as the rear punts caught up and collided with the lead punt, and a chain reaction boomeranged from the rear to the front of the convoy.

Lincoln was clinging to the connecting chain between two punts in the middle of the convoy, hanging on for a ride, when he sensed the change and saw the distance narrow swiftly between the two punts.

Carl saw his friend's eyes, those cat-eyes that could dazzle and awe most people. He saw the shock on Lincoln's face; Lincoln knew what was about to happen.

Lincoln tried to let go of the chain as the two punts closed in. His mouth was shut tight, his eyes bulged, opened wide, then closed slowly as the pain registered. Lincoln's bones were crushed mercilessly; the water turned crimson with the blood that flowed.

Carl kept remembering the things he and Lincoln had done together: the first time they climbed the mango tree; the incident with the bats hanging from the roof; the day they stoned the dog. His entire body was racked with a fever that rose to his head, creating visions of Lincoln returning to take him into the watery grave that had so prematurely taken his life. Why was it that he had been spared from drowning, and why had Lincoln paid the ultimate price? He recalled the Pastor who preached during Sunday School sermons about evil acts committed by young boys and the perils of going to hell. Did the Pastor know what he and Lincoln had done to the two dogs stuck together? Could the Pastor know of the palmflies they had stripped the wings off and watched as they hopelessly tried to get off the ground? Was Carl being punished for this and all the other wicked things he had done with Lincoln?

Carl remembered his parents coming home. His mother rubbed him down with Limachol and mentholated spirits, his father trying to reassure him all the while that everything would be fine. The alcohol based balm cooled his head and calmed his nerves, the voice of his father, composed and soothing, gave him hope that he would live, that he would not join Lincoln, wherever he was being sent. Finally, he had lapsed into a fitful slumber.

***

The fowl cock crowed again. It was now brighter outside, shadows starting to form, birds flying in formation from the Backdam to feeding grounds from where they would return at the end of the day.

Carl made his way down the stairs. No one seemed to be up and around. In the front yard, under the tarpaulin, there was a man lying on his back on one of the benches, his hat over his head. Carl opened the gate and slipped out. If he recalled correctly, the Cross Road was to the right.

He passed people on the road. A car went by, a donkey drawn dray-cart, a cyclist. A woman was sweeping under her bottom house with a pointer-broom and stopped to look as he passed. He waved at her and she returned the greeting. Overhead, slow moving dark clouds cluttered up the morning sky and a cool breeze embraced him; rain was in the air.

Nothing had changed much in the Cross Road since he left. From what he'd seen so far, time had stood still in the entire country: very little change in the infrastructure, the airport still the same, no new roads, no improvement in water and drainage.

The tall coconut tree still stood in the middle of the Cross Road, its branches drooped and withered, the trunk scarred and pockmarked. Carl stood under the tree, on top of roots that now spread like tentacles reaching out to grab passers-by.

A number of lads were approaching from the other end of the Cross Road. Carl watched them, and counted. There were six in all. They were not dressed like labourers or cane-cutters going off to work, yet seemed to have a singular purpose in mind. He watched as they came closer.

The gang stopped in front of him and before he knew what was happening, they had cornered him.

"What yuh doing here dis early in the morning?" the boy directly in front of him said.

Carl shook his head. He wanted to say: What are *you* doing here? What business is it of yours? He hesitated; he'd detected something menacing about their attitude and stance and the last thing he wanted was a confrontation with a gang of ruffians on the day of his father's funeral.

Carl said: "I'm just out for a morning walk, that's all."

"You not from these parts, Putagee," the boy said. "I going ask you one more time. Why yuh here this early in the morning? You a thief-man or something?"

Carl had heard the disparaging term used for the Portuguese nationals when he was back in British Guiana. He'd had enough of it. "Is it any of your business what I'm doing here?"

"Well, we going make it our business, then," he said. He appeared to be the leader.

The leader reached into his pocket and the others closed in on Carl.

Here we go again, Carl thought. Something like this had happened sixteen years ago, to him, to James, and it hadn't turned out for the best. He backed away. Perhaps he could outrun them to the house.

"Leave him alone," someone said, from behind Carl.

Carl looked around. It was young Jimmy, his white shirt open in front and shirttails flying in the breeze.

Carl didn't want a repeat of the confrontation he'd had sixteen years ago. He said: "Watch out, Jimmy, they might be armed. Let's just go."

"He's with me," Jimmy said. "My uncle who come for the funeral."

The leader nodded and backed off. The group moved out farther.

"Didn't know dat Jimmy. We think he some stranger coming in to mekh trouble for the neighbourhood."

Carl stood next to Jimmy and watched the men retreat in the direction from which they had come.

"Uncle Carl," Jimmy said, "it's not safe to be walking around on you own."

"I wanted some fresh air," Carl said. "Are they friends of yours?"

Jimmy shrugged. "I know them. They're good guys. They keep a lookout in the Walk. Plenty thief-man around these days."

"I think they would have attacked me if you hadn't come along."

"They would have just roughed you up."

"What do they do, these guys? Do they go to school or work?"

Jimmy shook his head. "Not really –they drop out of school. No point in going on if no jobs around. They try to catch their hand doing odd jobs here and there. Most times they stay at home, though."

Carl was relieved. He braced against the coconut tree. "Thanks for your help. I wanted to see if this tree was still standing. Do you know the significance of this area? Do you know what happened here?"

Jimmy hesitated. "Yes," he said, after a while. "My father was killed somewhere here."

Carl nodded. "Right here," he said, "this is where it happened."

"You were there, I heard," Jimmy said.

Carl took a deep breath. "Yes, I was there the night it happened. I can tell you about it…

"We were coming home from the cinema, James and I. He'd taken me off to see a double bill at Paramount, something he did every now and then —something very impromptu. *Your brain needs a break from all that stuff they're cluttering it up with at school.* He always joked about that. *There's just so much you can fill your brain with,* he'd say, *and most of the stuff will be of no use to you in real life, anyhow.*

"We'd had a good time at the cinema —he bought everything, as usual, my ticket and snacks and drinks before and during shorts in-between the two movies.

"I was still at school; he was working at our father's store in Georgetown. You can imagine how great it felt for someone like me to have his older brother pay so much attention to him. Your father was like that: generous to a fault, and carefree. He never looked further than what today brought him. Did you know he dropped out of high school after the first year? Nothing at school seemed to hold his interest for long.

"I remember the double bill well —*Dr. No* and *From Russia With Love*; both James Bond movies. After the first movie, when shorts were showing, we went out to buy some more snacks from the roadside vendor. We were just about to return to the cinema when a bomb went off, placed under the cinema, in the crawl space.

"You can imagine what happened afterwards: panic. A rumour spread that more bombs would go off. Everyone was scared. We didn't want to take chances —we bolted towards the Cross Road and were heading home when we saw a gang coming in the opposite direction, just like it happened a few minutes ago.

"This was before racial attacks started in the city, so we had no reason to think that we would be at risk. They were mainly young Black kids from the housing scheme, a dozen or so of them, some of them your age, most of them around just twelve or thirteen. You can well imagine how surprised we were when they came across to our side of the road and surrounded us."

Carl sighed. "I thought for a moment that it was happening all over again, when that gang confronted me a few minutes ago."

"They never really hurt anyone, before," Jimmy said.

"First, they asked for our money. James gave them everything he had. I had no money on me. Just when we thought everything would be fine, one of them punched James in the face and before you knew it, they all descended on us like a pack of mad dogs.

"Your father was not the most powerful person in the family but he was in a few scrapes at school and could defend himself. I was just nineteen –the age where you think you can whip the whole world, until you come up against twelve kids who feel the same way. We started to fight back, run a few yards until they caught up with us, fight again and try to keep them off, but they were too much for us. They were raining blows on us, back and front. James got the brunt of it since he kept me behind him. He shouted to me to run and get some help. We were not far from home –you can see that. Just a matter of minutes away and I thought I could run there and get back in time with help. I ran. I left your father alone. I ran home. Your grandfather was there, along with Joseph and Thomas and we came back, with sticks. The mob had moved on –looking for more victims, I guess. James was lying in a pool of blood on the ground.

"We rushed him to the hospital. He had broken ribs, a punctured lung, his face was beaten almost to a pulp, and he was unconscious. He never made it out of the hospital. Something that I've thought about. I'm sure he was thinking of me when he sent me for help, but what if I hadn't left him? Would he still be alive today?"

"There was nothing you could do," Jimmy said. "If you remained with him you would be dead, too. They would have had two funerals instead of one."

"Sometimes, I wish that I had remained with him," Carl said.

CHAPTER 9 -People Past And Present

TUESDAY 25TH NOVEMBER 1980

The neighbourhood hadn't changed much. Carl noticed this as he and Jimmy walked back home. The buildings were familiar to him. They were the same structures he'd left back in 1964, now showing signs of wear and tear. Some of them were dilapidated, facades were weather beaten, paint peeling or stripped. Roofs had zinc sheets corroded or missing. Even the branches of the ubiquitous mango tree drooped and sagged.

They turned into the Walk from the Cross Road. On the left was the Pastor's church, across from that the Playground and behind it, Repentigny Burial Ground; houses on the north end of the Walk and the Cane Field on the south. They passed the house of the half-a-foot man –Carl couldn't remember his name, but they had a nickname for him: Langra. Did he still drive the dray cart? Next to him was Cromwell's house. Did he still wear dresses instead of shirt and pants? Wilfred's house was next –what had become of him? Mohamed's house was the third one down. His wife used to work in a Government Grant in the interior, clearing bush with a cutlass and cutting lumber with an axe. She was the woman who had lost a joint on one of her fingers and received substantial monetary compensation for the accident. Several joints later, the company became wise to her scheme and she was fired. Next to Mohamed was the Lee family. Mister Lee and his wife: they'd kept trying for a boy and ended up with six girls. Carl remembered the combination of Mister Lee: his Black and Chinese heritage, and his wife: East Indian and Portuguese, that the union produced the most attractive girls in the Walk. Were they all now married with children of their own?

The Dias house had been one of the most prominent in the Walk, rebuilt when Augusto's business boomed back in the fifties. Now, it reflected bad times, like every other house. The only exception was Winslow Carrington's, its three stories towering over all the others, sparkling and shining with a fresh coat of white paint. A long time ago the house was the worst in the neighbourhood: planks missing in the gallery up front, corroded zinc sheets on the roof, broken glass in the window panes, no back stairs and the one in front missing several steps. All that and the obvious tilt seemed to indicate that the house was on its last legs and would collapse with the first strong breeze that came along. That was then; the house had been rebuilt and was the best in the area.

Winslow lived with his grandmother who had a stall in Stabroek Market and made her living by selling straw baskets. How would they have managed to finance the type of structure on her meagre earnings and his job with the government?

Next to Winslow's house was Reds Robertson. Winslow and Reds never got along in the best of times and had a history of confrontations. Carl could remember one. He was around ten and had run off with Wilfred and Cyril to see a movie at the Paramount. No one at home kept track of Carl: one of the benefits of being one of five boys growing up in a large household...

***

The Paramount was showing a James Stewart Western double bill.

Carl and his two friends had arrived early and joined the queue going into the ticket booth which was a ten-foot tall, three feet wide enclosed overhang connected to the main building and referred to as the Tunnel. The purpose of the Tunnel was to maintain an orderly flow of people to the small letterbox slot in the wall through which tickets were sold. In practice, scalpers bought out all the tickets ahead of time and associates blocked the entrance to the Tunnel, resulting in a shoving match as people tried to obtain tickets.

One of the scalpers was Reds. He was mixed with Portuguese and Black. Reds' appearance reflected the mingled genes of his heritage: light skin; broad nose; thick lips; short, white kinky hair.

Reds' voice could be heard, shouting above the din: "Thirty-five, Sixty. Thirty-five Sixty. Get your ticket before the show start."

Carl and his friends had left the queue and were now standing on the bank of the Canal, debating whether to wait for the crowd to ease and get tickets from the booth or buy tickets from a scalper. If they waited, they risked missing the opening sequence of the movie. Carl watched as, one by one, the windows were closed from inside the cinema. In a few minutes advertising slides would start, followed by the first movie. Pockets of people were also waiting around for the rush to ease and others were buying snacks from a roadside vendor. The aroma of black pudding, boiled corn and channa, ripe tamarind, freshly baked cassava pone drifted across to Carl as an old woman dispensed her snacks from a tray perched on top of a wooden soft-drink crate. At the rear of the cinema, just behind where the screen was housed, a group of boys squatted on the ground throwing dice, money clutched like lottery tickets offering a chance to a fortune.

The crowd around the booth was intensifying its efforts to buy tickets, shoving and jockeying for leverage to get closer to the slot. This had resulted in a scrambling mass of bodies, arms intertwined, faces beaded with perspiration.

"There's no way I'm going back in there," Cyril said.

Wilfred was looking at the light side of the situation, as usual. "Man, it looks like that saloon fight right out of Spoilers with Wayne and Scott."

There seemed to be only one solution to Carl. "Well, we might as well buy from Reds."

"You crazy, man, how do we know he selling good tickets?" Cyril said.

"Well, do you want to go back in line and join the rush?" Carl responded.

Carl had seen the scene unfold so many times that it was not difficult for him to imagine what would happen. If they ever made it inside the tunnel, he had visions of them being trapped there, caught among the massive bulk of bodies jammed tight into the small edifice, not being able to go forward or retreat. They would be lucky if they still managed to obtain tickets.

Carl's dejection deepened: they would miss the 5pm showing. The next show was at eight thirty –he'd never attended a late show. He'd be pushing his luck since he would be surely missed at home. The thought of returning home without seeing the movie was driving him to desperation.

"I don't know about you two, but I'm going to take my chances with Reds," Carl said.

Reds had taken up a position by the steps leading to the door where the ticket collector sat. A small group was crowded around the scalper –people with the same desperate look like Carl.

Carl joined the group and handed over a quarter and a dime to Reds. Wilfred and Cyril did the same. They collected their tickets and made their way up the stairs, Carl in front. Carl handed his ticket to the door man and was just about to part the black curtain and step into the cinema, when the man grabbed his hand.

The man was built like several barrels stacked up one on another: a large round head, substantial body, thick, sinewy legs. He shook his head and gave the red ticket back to Carl.

"No good," the man said. "Dis for yesterday show."

Wilfred and Cyril looked at their ticket. The same colour.

"You need a blue ticket," the collector said.

Carl retreated down the stairs to the bank of the Canal, followed by Cyril and Wilfred.

"You see, is exactly what I said would happen," Cyril said.

"Guess there's nothing much we can do, now," Wilfred said. "I don't have any more money."

Carl was faced with the same problem. He was sure that it was the same with Cyril.

"This is not right," Cyril said. "We should get our money back from Reds."

Carl shrugged. He was not prepared to confront Reds. Cyril reminded him of the story of the rat that came up with the solution of placing a bell on the cat to warn them when they were faced with imminent danger, only he wanted some other rat to do the job.

"Look, Reds right over there. You go talk to him," Carl said.

Cyril looked away. The idea did not seem to appeal to him.

From behind Carl, someone shouted, "Hey, you, shrimp," and grabbed him by his shirt collar.

The man spun him around and pinned him against the lantern post. Carl raised his hands to protect himself –he thought he was in for a beating. From the corner of his eye he saw his two friends slink away.

The man stood in front of Carl. "Yuh remember me, shrimp?" His voice was gruff but calm, his grip tight on Carl's shirt.

Carl squinted at the man. Of course he knew who it was. Winslow –the tallest, largest, most feared boy in the neighbourhood. He appeared to be several sizes too large for the black T-shirt that clung to his torso, his brown khaki pants seemed at least three inches too short for his length, and his facial features had all expanded. The limp in his walk, one short leg dragging after the other, like a wounded dog pulling its back leg behind it, was what Carl remembered most. Carl looked down at the right leg, wondering, if somehow Winslow might have recovered fully from the polio attack that had crippled him as a child.

"Do yuh remember me, shrimp?" Winslow repeated.

Carl nodded. Winslow was noted for his disappearances from the neighbourhood. He was caught shoplifting, held for several days in youth detention in the city and finally released on his grandmother's recognizance. He was picked up again for stealing from a vendor in the Market. This was before the fight at school, an incident where he knocked a schoolmate down on the ground and trampled him, breaking several ribs; it had earned him a four-year stint in Onderneeming, the boy's school in Essequibo County.

Carl knew about Onderneeming: about the remoteness of the location. To get there meant crossing the Demerara River by ferry, taking a long train ride, another ferry across the wide expanse of the Essequibo River, then traveling by bus for many miles into the interior. It was an inaccessible place where relatives found it difficult to visit, a place that Carl never wanted to see.

Winslow was back.

As Winslow released his hold, Carl said: "Yes. You're Winslow, but, I haven't seen you around for the longest while. What happened to you?"

Winslow smoothed out Carl's shirt and patted him on his shoulders. "I see you talking to Reds. Watch out, he likes boys, especially fair-skin ones like you."

Carl sighed and shook his head. He'd heard of Reds' reputation and knew what Winslow meant. Reds was like Cromwell, who preferred male companions over women, only, Reds was the masculine side of the equation.

"You got a small piece for me today?" Winslow said.

Carl had willingly shared his pocket money with Winslow many times. He'd even passed on school supplies, along with helping Winslow with his homework.

Carl shook his head.

"What you doing here? You going to see the movie?"

"No. We couldn't get tickets because of the rush outside…" Carl started to explain.

"Give me the money," Winslow opened his hand, "I get it for you."

Carl shook his head. "I can't," he said. "Don't have any more money. Reds sell us bad tickets."

Winslow shook his head, his wide nostrils flared, his eyes widened. He looked more menacing than ever as he folded his hands into fists. Carl recalled the many confrontations he'd seen with Winslow and Reds in the Walk, most of them over the smallest transgression –it was clear that there was never any love lost between the two of them.

"Mother fukker," Winslow said, "up to he old tricks again."

Carl watched as Winslow crossed the thirty feet that separated him from Reds.

"That's Winslow." Cyril had a way of stating the obvious.

"Where did Stumpy come from? He looks meaner than ever," Wilfred said.

Carl smiled. His two friends had found it prudent to be close to him again. Wilfred was referring to Winslow as the crippled character played by Walter Brennan in one of Carl's favourite westerns, *Rio Bravo*.

"Where's Stumpy been all these years?" Wilfred said. "The last time I seen him was when he had that fight in the schoolyard. You remember –when he trampled that kid?"

Carl shrugged.

"Probably been in jail," Cyril said. "Guys like him end up there, eventually. There's no hope for people like them."

Winslow approached Reds, engaged him, and pointed in direction of the Canal. Reds leaned to his left, looked at Carl and his two friends, sneered and shook his head.

Carl had a clear view from where he stood high up on the bank. Winslow had his face just a matter of inches from Reds who was backing away until he could go no further than the wall of the cinema.

"Give me three tickets, now, or you not leaving this place," Winslow said.

"Fukk you," Reds said. He pushed Winslow away.

"Look like if we going to get our own Spoilers with Wayne and Scott today," Wilfred said. "We don't have to go inside to see the movie, after all."

Many more people from the crowd outside the cinema must have had the same expectation –shouts of *Fight, Fight*, rang in the air and people started to flock around the two men. The card and domino players, the men in the tunnel, all came over to witness the upcoming clash.

Winslow grabbed Reds' left hand and in another minute they were both pushing and shoving, Reds resisting, Winslow trying to wrest the tickets out of the man's hand. On it went for another few minutes and then, Winslow grabbed his cheek, held his hand up and stared at it.

Carl saw blood on Winslow's hand.

"Look like Stumpy got slashed," Wilfred said.

Winslow's reaction was swift, even as blood dripped from the cut on his face. He kicked Reds in his stomach and was all over him as the man dropped on the ground, the razor blade falling from his hand.

Winslow held his face again, amazement spreading all over his features. "Mother –fukker, I going kill you here today," Winslow said.

Reds was already up on his feet and running down the road, Winslow chasing after him.

Carl watched the two men as they headed towards the market place.

"Guess we will have to see the movie another day," Wilfred said.

***

Jimmy opened the front gate and they entered the yard.

The man who was sleeping under the tent was up –he had a black garbage bag in one hand and was collecting plates and cups. Glasses had been stacked on one table, empty beer bottles collected on another, and enamel cups placed on a third. The man turned and waved to Jimmy as they headed into the house.

Jimmy laughed. "He's supposed to be a night watch man."

Sounds were coming from the kitchen in the rear of the ground floor but no other sign of life was evident. Jimmy led Carl up the stairs to the washroom.

"Water is in the bathroom," Jimmy said. "The pressure is not up as yet, so you got to use the bucket. There is soap and a towel there too."

The water was cold. Carl had been bathing with water of the same temperature for the first nineteen years of his life, but he couldn't recall it being so cold. Yet, the people in the household, all of Repentigny, even the whole country, bathed under similar conditions. He had grown soft in the North American phase of his life, he concluded. Using the basin in the bucket, he splashed water on his feet first, then worked his way up to his chest. By the time he was ready to wash his hair, his body had grown accustomed to the temperature and he felt invigorated by the water.

He was tightening the belt around his pants waist and sensed a presence behind him and when he turned around he found that two children had entered the bedroom. They were standing, almost in shadow, just inside the doorway. One was a little girl, no more than six. Her brother stood next to her; he was about two years older. They both wore school uniforms: the girl a blue skirt and a white top, the boy a khaki short pants and a short-sleeved white shirt, and everything was neatly ironed with seams clearly standing out.

How long had they been standing there, Carl wondered.

"Hello," he said. He pulled on his shoes and tied the laces. No response. They stood, still, observing every move he made.

"Did you come to get me?" Carl said.

Earl appeared behind them. He smiled as he placed his hands on the children's shoulders. "They're just like their mother –they don't say much."

"Who are they?" Carl said.

"They're my kids."

"Their mother?"

Earl shook his head and laughed. "She ran off with another man since three years ago. I have no idea where she is now. She might be back in the North West District where she came from."

Carl thought of Alexei and Irina, both were around the same age. How were they making out without him. Did they miss him as much as he missed them? How was Natasha making out without his help?

"Sorry to hear that," Carl said. "They must miss her a lot."

Earl shrugged. "Not a big deal."

"What happened?"

"The church brought her here to train her as a teacher. I met her –at Teacher's Training College. Before you know it, she was pregnant. We got married, but you know how *Buck* people stay –they can't remain in one place for long. Is very easy to fool them. She met up with some man in the city one day and before you know it, he make all kinds of promises to her and she run off with him. Not even a look back or a word of goodbye to me or the children." Earl said this nonchalantly, as if he'd resigned himself a long time ago to accept the situation.

The two kids had distinctly Amerindian native features and seemed to have inherited very little of Earl's gene pool. Both of them were short and squat; they had similar diamond shaped faces with high cheekbones and large black eyes.

Despite their background and the fact that he'd made disparaging remarks about their mother, Earl seemed to be close to the children. He pulled the two kids into his arms and said: "They're both mine. I try my best with what I have and wouldn't give them up for anything in the world."

"What's your name?" Carl asked the girl.

The girl stuck her thumb into her mouth and drew even closer to her father.

"Her name is Ruth. The boy is Anthony," Earl laughed again, snickered, and whispered to Carl, as if he were sharing a private joke. "We call them Buck Girl and Buck Boy."

If the children were aware of the derogatory reference to them they did not show any sign. Carl was amused about how very little had changed since his time: a nickname for everyone, especially if the person had an unusual name. Wilfred, his old friend, had such a penchant for labelling people. He would have been proud of the names given the two kids. He might even have come up with the names himself, but he would have culled them from a movie he'd seen. The only movie Carl could recall seeing about South American natives was *Green Mansions*, and in it, Audrey Hepburn played the native girl!

Earl led the way down the stairs into the kitchen, his two children beside him.

People were in the kitchen already seated around the dining table. Carl took an empty seat next to Uncle Jules. The kitchen was abuzz with activity: five women cooking around a kerosene-oil stove, people coming and going from the front and back yards with coffee cups and saucers, children running in and out, as if everyone was celebrating a national holiday, instead of the passing of someone. Just the way a wake was held, Carl recalled: a coming together of the entire community.

Uncle Jules was eating. His plate was filled with sliced fried potato and he was scooping up mounds of it with pieces of *roti*. "Did you sleep well, Cal?" Uncle Jules said.

Carl nodded. "Yes, Uncle Jules. One of the best rests I've had in a long time. Except for that fowl cock crowing early in the morning, seemed to be right next to my ears."

Everyone in the kitchen laughed.

A woman placed a plate in front of Carl; it had the same contents as Uncle Jules.

"This is Sumintra," Uncle Jules said. " Earl's mother."

Carl nodded at the woman. Given Earl's age of around twenty-nine, Carl figured that the woman had to be in her early or mid fifties. She was about five feet eight, short dark brown hair that showed no trace of grey, smooth features that seemed to be moulded out of clay. Her face was freckled. She had also taken good care of herself –no lines on her face, had a small waist and breasts that stood out prominently.

"I understand from Uncle Jules that you've been a great help to my father," Carl said. "You and Earl. I want to thank you both for all you've done."

"It was nothing," Sumintra said. "The least we could do. I'm only sorry that Earl didn't take better care of you last night when you arrived." She glanced at Earl and he squirmed in his seat.

Carl recalled that Earl and his mother were engaged in what appeared to be a heated conversation during the night. Was he their focus of disagreement?

"No problem," Carl said.

"I told Earl that you must have been tired after your long trip," Sumintra persisted. "He should have taken you straight upstairs to rest up. Instead, he left you in the middle of the crowd with everybody hanging on and bothering you."

"Really, it was no bother," Carl said. "I was much too wound up to go to sleep right away. Besides, it was good to meet the people who came for the wake."

"Told you so," Earl muttered.

Sumintra walked back to the stove. "Here is Patsy," she said, as a Black woman turned around from the counter and smiled at Carl. "She's Jimmy's mother. Do you remember her? She also helped a lot."

Carl nodded at the woman. "Thank you, too, Patsy," he said.

Of course he remembered Patsy. He'd had occasional meetings with her when he was still in British Guiana. A few times James had taken him home to his apartment and she'd been doing the same thing she was doing now: cooking at a stove. Augusto had been critical of the relationship from the start. Matters became worse when James started to live common-law with Patsy. Augusto had kept his dealings with his son on a strictly business basis from then, since James still managed the store in the city. The situation got worse when the Old Man heard that James was planning to marry Patsy later that year, the same year James was killed.

"You remember Shirley and her two sisters Marilyn and Theresa?" Sumintra introduced the remaining three women – they were mixing flour and rolling the mix into flat dough for making *roti*. "They from next door."

The tradition still lived on, Carl was happy to see: neighbours pitching in at a time of tragedy, something he remembered happening often when he was in British Guiana. Neighbours keeping watch over children, helping out during times of floods, cooking for weddings or funerals –Guyanese hadn't lost the touch of humanity for which they were known.

A close resemblance between the three Lee sisters was evident. They turned around, almost in unison and waved to Carl. But, it was Shirley who stood out most. She still had the shoulder length black curls spiralling around her head and the deep, recessed dimples on both cheeks. When she opened her mouth there was a flash of even, white teeth that looked as if they'd been chiselled and crafted with precision.

"Shirley!" Carl said. "I can't believe it. She was just this high," he held his right hand about three feet off the ground, "and look at her now. Your two sisters were just babes when I left."

"That's me, alright," Shirley laughed, and her two sisters giggled.

"You had three older sisters, as I recall. Irene, Pammy, Amy…what's happened to them?"

Shirley squinted, her hands held akimbo, as if she was reprimanding him about something. She laughed. "I'm surprised you remember all their names so well. Which one of them you had your eyes on?" she said.

Marilyn and Theresa giggled. The people around the table sniggered. Carl could feel himself getting red in the face. He was sure that it was obvious. At one time or the other, he'd been smitten with each of the three older sisters. First it was Irene until he found out that she was older than him. After that, it was Pammy, until Amy came along. He'd left British Guiana. Now, here was Shirley, with a presence that was even more overwhelming than her older sisters.

"Anyway," Shirley said. "Too late –you lost your chance. They all married and living in GT. They've got their own family now."

Everyone seemed to find the humour in this; their laughter rang around the table, again.

Shirley winked and said, "I'm still available." She tilted her head back and laughed and her white-laced blue dress and long curls swung back and forth like pendulums when she turned to the counter to work on the roti.

"Yes," Sumintra said, "Somebody better grab her up before they lose their chance."

"How is it that three, extremely good looking girls like you aren't married yet?" Carl said. "What's wrong with the guys around here?"

"The right man just hasn't come along," Shirley said, without turning around.

"How about Earl, he's available," Carl said.

Earl shook his head vigorously. "Not me. My time come and gone...don't want to go through that again."

"Earl just lives for his two children," his mother said. She sighed and there was a tinge of regret in her voice. "I wish he'd move on and find a good woman to mother them, though. Maybe have some more children, too."

"Good looking girls all over GT," Uncle Jules said. "There bound to be one for every man who looking for a wife." He was finished with his breakfast. He went over to the sink to wash up. "Some men even end up with two, but one was always good enough for me."

"What I always say," Sumintra said. "One woman, one man."

"Did you decide how you wanted your father buried?" Uncle Jules said when he came back to the table, a much more sober note in his voice. "The funeral director is waiting for clothes to dress him in and I didn't know what kind of ceremony you wanted for him so I didn't make any arrangements."

Carl thought for a moment. "I saw his pinstripe suit in the wardrobe upstairs," he said. "Seems to be the one in most of his pictures –might as well let him go in that. I met a priest on the flight –he was kind enough to offer to do the ceremony. If Earl can take us into GT, we can see Father Martin at the archdiocese in Brickdam and drop off the clothes after that. I also have to confirm my return flight to Toronto."

"Whenever you're ready, is okay for me," Earl said. "We can hit the archdiocese first, on the way to Lamaha Street where the funeral home is. The airline office is in-between."

Carl, Earl and Uncle Jules were on the way to the funeral parlour. They'd already made two stops.

The first stop had been to the Archdiocese where Carl had hoped to see Father Martin but the priest was in the middle of a meeting when they arrived. Carl wrote a brief note and asked the clerk to pass it on to Father Martin. The woman came back and said that the priest had agreed to do the ceremony. Carl wrote down details of the time and place and where his father would be buried and left them with the clerk.

The second stop was to the airline booking office. Earl handled the arrangements through a friend of a friend. He managed to secure a confirmation for Carl's return flight on the coming Sunday. Having friends in high places helped to speed up the process.

"Most of the buildings look so run down," Carl said.

"You ain't seen nothing yet," Earl said. "I going to give you a ride through the city so you can see how things look today."

Earl had turned into High Street. They passed the Legislature: the building was a pale imitation of the once proud Victorian structure built back in the last century. Carl looked at it. He recalled the day of the disturbances in 1962. Today, very few people seemed to be around the building, compared to back then when thousands protested outside. Even the building seemed to be mourning the loss of democracy.

Earl must have read his thoughts. "There is no session going on," he said. "We haven't had one for some time. The opposition is boycotting the assembly, due to the elections being rigged over and over again. They don't see any point in attending. They claim it's just a rubber stamp. As for the public, they don't seem to really care, anyway."

"Boy, Cal," Uncle Jules said. "Is a good, good thing that you and all your brothers left this country. There's no future here anymore."

Stabroek Market loomed large against the morning sky. The zinc-topped structure that occupied a whole city block and backed on to the Demerara River, was enclosed by iron grating, a large clock with Roman numerals sitting on the tower in front. The hands on the clock were showing 2pm. Carl looked at his watch: it was eight in the morning.

"The clock is broken," Earl said. "Been like that for years. They don't have money to fix it."

"Broke, like everything else in this country," Uncle Jules said.

Sidewalks outside the market were jammed and there was a spill over crowd on the road. Pedestrians hopped between cars, drivers honked, cyclists negotiated between pedestrians, and the cacophony emerging from inside and around the market dominated the airwaves. The car park, where hire-cars were stationed added to the bedlam as taxi drivers pulled in and out without much thought for the niceties of the road.

A long line of people moved swiftly along the outer fringe of the sidewalk, many of them were women with children trailing behind them. Earl slowed the De Soto to a crawl as traffic stalled in front of him. One of the children, a girl dressed in a tattered and faded dress, broke off from the crowd and ran towards the car. She pushed her right hand through the car window and kept pace. She was mere inches from Carl and he could see hollow cheeks, dark spots under her eyes, and knots in her hair.

"Please, Mister," she said, her mouth opening to reveal gaps in her front teeth.

Carl reached into his pants pocket and pulled out a Canadian dollar and handed it to her.

"You going have the whole gang swarming you," Earl said. "And, you'd better look out how your hand is hanging outside the window –you might lose your watch. They move fast around here and disappear in the crowd before you can even blink."

Sure enough, as if the others had received some telepathic message of the bounty handed down to one of their own, they changed direction and made a beeline for the car. The traffic moved on and Earl sped up, leaving them behind.

"This is a lot worse than I remember it," Carl said.

A block away, the crowd was still thick on the sidewalks. The market had extended north, far beyond the original structure. Roadside vendors dominated the scene here and they were perched on short stools or sat on empty sugar bags as they shouted the price of their wares and vied for customers. Behind the vendors was a chain-link fence that restricted access to an area that contained burnt out buildings. Sixteen years after the looting and arson, some business men still hadn't rebuilt what they had lost in the arson and looting.

"Here is where your father's store was," Uncle Jules pointed to the fence.

"Yes, I remember," Carl said.

In his younger days he'd spent many Saturdays at the store. He knew that he was never of much help at such a tender age, but what had appealed to him most of all was the closeness he felt to his father. Next door used to be a Chinese Cook Shop where his father would take him for lunch: fried rice, noodles, wanton soup, prepared by a cook dressed in his white singlet due to the oppressive heat that built up in his windowless establishment. After that, they travelled a route that took them around Brown Betty Ice Cream and he was treated to a cone. What mattered most, was that he'd never had to share his father during those times.

"What happened to the land these stores were on?" Carl said.

"People couldn't afford to rebuild," Uncle Jules said. "They couldn't even afford the taxes after a while. The city owns some of the land."

So, this is what most likely happened to the land his father's store was on. A piece of land that was in his father's name for decades, worth hundreds of thousands of dollars at the peak when business was expanding in the city, had been either sold dirt cheap by him or taken over by the city.

People were waiting outside a supermarket. A long queue stretched around the block.

"What's going on here?" Carl said.

"People lining up for flour and rice, bread, cooking oil, anything that's in short supply right now," Earl said.

"They paying black market prices, you know," Uncle Jules said. "The cost of living keep going up and up and the money people working for staying the same. I don't know how people managing these days."

Carl waved to the roadside vendors. "People still trying to make a living, though."

"Nothing much else to do," Earl said. "A lot of the stuff you see here comes in barrels from relatives in Canada or America."

"Everybody trading these days," Uncle Jules said.

"Not many jobs around," Earl said. "All the major companies were nationalized, so you either work for the government or you don't work at all. To work for the government, you have to get a party card and pay your membership dues. They get you every way."

"All the young children have to join the national service now, you know," Uncle Jules said.

"Yes," Earl said. "After high school, you either go to University or join the army. No other choice."

"You think Guyanese mothers and fathers want to send their girl children to serve in the army?" Uncle Jules said. He was indignant. "We hear stories about young girls getting raped while doing national service in the interior. Families rather keep their girl children at home or send them over seas."

They passed Royal Bank of Canada building. People were lined up, waiting to be let in by an armed guard. The uptown core where Fogarty's and Booker Bros. Departments stores were located was crowded with people going about their business.

Earl went up Camp Road and they came to the funeral home. An attendant came out and took the suit. He said that the undertaker would see them in a few minutes.

The undertaker was Manning. He greeted them in the office when they entered.

Manning was mixed: Black and Chinese, but it was the Black in him that commanded attention. He had black, kinky hair, thick lips, and a broad nose. Just about the only thing Asian about him was his eyes. He was a small, wiry, lean man who rarely smiled. It seemed as if he always wore his sombre profession on his face.

"What arrangements do you want to make for the funeral?" Manning said.

"Well," Carl said, "I think we should have a showing at the house before we go to the cemetery. Don't you think so, Uncle Jules?"

Uncle Jules nodded. "If you can get there by around two-thirty or three, that would give us time for a showing. He was well known in the neighbourhood. People will want to take a last look at him."

"That can be arranged," Manning said. "Did you plan on having a service at home or the burial ground, or both?"

"I think one at the cemetery will be enough," Carl said. "At any rate, the priest can't make it earlier than that."

Manning nodded.

"Is there anything else we need to discuss?" Carl said.

Manning shook his head. "Your uncle already picked out the coffin and said you'd arrange payment later." He looked at his watch. He said, a smile barely cracking his stern visage: "Would you like to see him while you're here, to have a quiet moment with him. Things might get very noisy at the funeral, you know."

The thought of seeing his father without sharing the moment with strangers crowded around the coffin, appealed to Carl.

"Come this way," Manning said. He led them through a door, down a corridor to a room at the rear of the establishment.

A blast of cold air greeted Carl as the undertaker opened the door. The room was well lit with coffins perched on biers lined up on the far side. Carl counted ten coffins of various dimensions and colours and the lid of the one at the very end was lying in an upright position behind the coffin.

Manning pointed to the last casket. "Take as long as you want."

Carl led the way and took a position on the left of the coffin. Uncle Jules and Earl stood across from him. Carl hadn't seen his father in sixteen years. Looking down now, on his father's body, it seemed to him that he was seeing a stranger. Augusto's features had changed radically. His cheeks were puffed up and inflated by jowls, his forehead much farther back on his head, his nose contorted at the base. Must be the angle, Carl though, or is this what death does to you?

So, this is what it comes down to at the end of your life! A man is brought up with values instilled in him by his family, he educates himself, builds a career or business, raises his own family, makes his name in a community, but in the final analyses, it all comes to nothing. You come into the world with nothing and leave the same way.

Carl looked back: Thirty paces had separated him from his father and he'd crossed them in a few seconds. The gap that separated him from his father had finally been bridged. Was it only because one of them was now immobile, unmovable, and passive? Why had it taken so long to heal the fracture? Tears welled up in his eyes. He shook his head slowly and sobbed. He reached for his handkerchief and swabbed his eyes.

Uncle Jules was looking at his brother and nodding. "You finally going to meet your maker," he muttered.

Earl was standing still, looking, and staring. Was that a tear trickling down his cheek? He must have grown very close to Augusto over the last few months, Carl thought.

In the De Soto going back to Repentigny, Uncle Jules said: "Your father would have wanted you to have this. I didn't see any reason for him to take it where he's going." Augusto's watch, handed down to him by his father, Salvador. "This should go to the oldest. Since Joseph is not here, you can decide if you want to keep it or pass it on to him."

Carl could think of the many times he'd seen his father pull out the watch from his fob and check the time. The Old Man did it at the store all through the day; at supper when they were around the table; at night in his study. He'd wind the watch gently, look at it, say *Time is money*, and he'd be moving on to something else. He'd made his final move now, and time didn't really matter anymore.

CHAPTER 10 - Family Values

Memorandum.

From: Special Assistant

To: The President

Washington, March 8, 1962

SUBJECT: Memoranda on British Guiana to State and CIA

The point of these two memoranda is that both State and CIA are under the impression that a firm decision has been taken to get rid of the Reform government.

The desired effect is to make sure that nothing is done until you have had a chance to talk with the Colonial Office.

The attached memos will give you an impression of current British attitudes.

British Guiana has 600,000 inhabitants. The Chairman would no doubt be gratified to know that the American and British governments are spending more man-hours per capita on British Guiana than on any other current problem!

"I offer this toast," Augusto Dias said, holding up his glass, "to John on his tenth birthday,"

They were having a family reunion at the house in the Walk –the first time they had all managed to get together since the riots back in February.

"To Little John," Joseph said, from his position next to Augusto.

Joseph had come to Georgetown by ferry from his job downriver at the Demerara Bauxite Company. His wife Frances had accompanied him. The trip was tiring and exhausting and they were due to return the next day. Carl was amazed at his oldest brother's appearance. Joseph's hair had gone totally grey and he looked as if he'd lost twenty pounds off his one hundred and eighty pound, five feet, ten frame. *It's the stress of the job and living where we do*, had been his explanation. Unlike the senior management of the foreign owned bauxite company who lived in a gated community in the town of Mackenzie, Joseph and his wife had to find housing across the river, in the town of Wismar. This meant crossing the Demerara River by launch every day to work and to get back home. The crossing was not the source of his stress, since the journey itself took no more than ten to fifteen minutes each way, but it was living in an insecure environment, not knowing what would happen next, that was taking a toll on him.

"I don't know how much longer I can take it," Joseph had said. "The company has put all new development on hold, now that there's talk about independence. They feel if Reform takes power, they will nationalize all foreign companies. Why invest more money if this happens? I can imagine that this is the same thing with all the other foreign owned companies in the country. So, any promotion for me continues to be on hold."

Joseph had been hired as an Assistant Manager not long after obtaining his certificate from the Government Technical Institute in Georgetown. His reputation for hard work had earned him the respect of the company's senior management and he had hoped one day to join their ranks and move to the senior staff compound in Mackenzie. In the current situation, it didn't look as if this would happen.

Carl looked in his glass. The wine came from Augusto's private stock. Since the riots earlier that year and the subsequent uncertain political situation, most in the business community affected had found it impossible to refinance their activities. No one had been able to collect insurance so far –policies simply did not provide coverage against insurrection and public disturbances. His father was no exception:

his store hadn't been rebuilt. He'd also been running a lucrative import business in wine but, now, this had dried up due to the lack of foreign exchange. Augusto had resorted to making his own wine for the local market place.

"I've been saving this fine Madeira for just an occasion like this," Augusto said.

Augusto held up his hand to the sunlight streaming through the jalousie window and watched the red liquid swirl around the glass. Carl could imagine what was going through his father's mind –on so many occasions he'd referred to the softness, the depth of flavour and the overpowering burnt taste of the Vinho da Roda wine of the round voyage, about the effect that the sun and heat had on the quality of the wine brought on the long passage from Madeira to the tropics. Apart from his ancestry going back to the generations who came from the Funchal region in Madeira, his father was most proud of the fine wines produced there. He talked about the tonic value of the wine he called *Milk of the Old* that would enable him to live beyond a hundred. He had a substantial inventory of the wine, waiting for the economy to pick up before he would release it to the market.

"A toast to Madeira," Augusto said. "An island noted for greatness: once the greatest sugar producer in the world, once one of the greatest banana exporters. Now, known for the finest wines in the world."

"To Madeira," came the response from those seated around the table.

"And, a toast to those who are no longer with us," Augusto said. He raised his glass to a series of pictures mounted on the walls around the room. Directly behind him was a picture of his father Salvador, next a picture of his grandfather Alvaro, and next to Alvaro, a painting of his great grandfather Carlos. On the opposite wall, pictures of Uncle Jules and Augusto's family were mounted, along with a wedding picture of Augusto and Carl's mother, Mary.

Silence reigned around the table, whether in deference to the toast, or merely because they were engrossed in their own thoughts, but slowly, everyone raised their glass and sipped wine.

John had the smallest amount of wine in his glass, due to his age. Carl was not surprised to see John lower his glass at his father's words –every year for the last number of years he'd been noticing John's behaviour at family gatherings, and he could hardly blame the youngest member of the family for his attitude. How could John drink to a toast when the reason for celebrating his birthday also marked the anniversary of their mother's death ten years ago?

Being the youngest of the family meant John held a special place in everyone's affection, but, to Augusto, his youngest son seemed to be a constant reminder of his wife's death. The Old Man had the habit of saying how lucky John was to have survived his mother's passing. Carl tried to make up for Augusto's attitude by paying special attention to John. Recently, however, John was gaining a reputation for being the rebel of the family –skipping school and staying out late with his friends. Carl had to track him down many times and lead him back to school where he seemed stalled in standard three in primary school.

"I'm planning to run for the legislature next election," Augusto said.

Carl didn't think anyone would be surprised at the news. Augusto had been hinting about this ever since the riots back in February. With the store no longer in operation and time on his hands, he'd been playing an increasingly active part in the Conservative Party –lead by one of the most successful business men in British Guiana and the British West Indies.

"A good move, father," Thomas said. "You're bound to get elected this time."

Thomas had just turned twenty in June. He was the son that Augusto was most proud of. After obtaining his Advance Level certificate, he had joined the youth arm of the Conservatives, hoping eventually to play a role in the party. Thomas was not only starting to adopt the mannerisms of their father

–he talked about buying a three piece pin stripe suit and a chain watch, he was also heard often discussing politics with Augusto and hoped to follow in his footsteps.

"We have to do everything we can to get this government out of office," Thomas continued, "it's the only way stability can come back to the colony. There should be no independence if Reform is still in office." He was echoing their father's stand, right down to the last word.

Augusto beamed and nodded.

"I think the Kennedy administration will put enough pressure on the British government to make sure of this," Augusto said. "After last month's fiasco in the Bay Of Pigs, the Americans are determined to do things right, this time. There is no way that they will accept a Communist leaning government in an independent British Guiana. The American public will never stand for it."

Was he speaking officially on behalf of the Conservatives, or merely spouting his own opinion based on conversations with other party members?

"I read in the newspapers that the Conservative leader is going to Washington," Joseph said. "Is he going for talks with the Kennedy administration?"

"I suppose so." Augusto was noncommittal about the purpose of the trip.

But, he didn't have to say it –Carl already knew the truth...

***

Since the riots back in February, there had been non-stop traffic between Georgetown and Washington with leaders of both opposition parties shuttling there to have meetings with the Kennedy administration. The centre of power was shifting from London, with Washington calling the shots when it came to freedom for British colonies. Ironically, from once calling on the British to liberate former colonies according to United Nations resolutions, the American government was now applying pressure for them to postpone independence for British Guiana.

The Chairman of Reform had said this in a speech he gave at Liberty House in October after his return from London where he'd gone with the two opposition leaders to engage in independence talks.

Carl recalled most of the speech. He was seated at the back with Wilfred and Cyril, in a crowd of several hundred, men and women, East Indians and Blacks, some minorities and a few of mixed heritage, like Carl. The Chairman had always claimed that his party was the only one that truly represented all the people of British Guiana, and Carl had seen evidence of it in the assembly room that afternoon.

"Brothers and sisters," the Chairman had begun, "we have to prepare for a long battle ahead of us. As you know by now, after the riots in February, the British Government said it felt compelled to postpone independence talks and we spent the last few months trying to get them to restart, almost as if the British rewarding the opposition parties for the role they played in the riots."

"Thanks to the Republicans and the Conservatives," Wilfred whispered on Carl's left. "Their supporters have been openly gloating about it since then."

"I suppose Augusto is happy, too," Cyril whispered.

Carl ignored the remark about his father, but, how could he deny it? Both his friends were aware of his father's stand on politics in British Guiana.

The Chairman said: "Well, we finally got the talks back on track. I've just returned from negotiations with the British Government, along with the leader of the two opposition parties. However, it's ended in a stalemate, again."

The news had been broadcast widely over the media but it still caused a buzz in the hall.

The Chairman sounded hoarse. He'd been debating the issues at the conference and trying to drum up support from every quarter of the British opposition and labour movement. Prior to returning to British Guiana, he'd gone to many Commonwealth countries, including India, where he'd met Pandit Nehru and solicited the Indian leader's backing against the British government's stand.

"The opposition is calling for fresh elections before independence," the Chairman said. "We've already had an election recently. Why should there be another election before independence? The people elected us. We have a majority. We should be the party taking the country to freedom. What more could they want?"

"We're going to win again, anyway," Cyril whispered to Carl.

"On top of that," the Chairman continued, "Duncan Sandys, the Colonial Secretary, is hinting that the British Government will arbitrate a solution if we can't come to one among ourselves. This is disappointing news."

Cyril shook his head. "There's no other way but for us to fight for independence," he whispered.

"Friends, we've come a long way on the road to freedom. They're doing everything in their power to deny us independence. The Americans are determined to keep us out of power, and the British don't make a move without consulting them. We know the Americans are intervening in our internal affairs and the British are doing nothing to stop them. The Americans continue to funnel funds to the unions in the country –remember what happened before the riots when the unions went on strike against us? Nothing changed since then. They're going slow and threatening a countrywide strike, again. We know, freedom never came easily and we will continue to fight for it with all our might."

Wilfred pulled out his pocket comb and passed it through his hair. He replaced it in his shirt pocket and said: "Hey, maybe we should get John Wayne and Richard Widmark on our side –Davy Crocket and Jim Bowie. They did a good job fighting for Texas independence at the Alamo."

"They died there, too," Carl said.

***

Augusto pulled out his watch from his fob and opened it. As if the face of his watch had offered him some hope and reassurance, he said, "I seriously still believe that there is a great future in this country. We can truly make it into the jewel of the Caribbean when democracy is restored in the colony."

British Guiana once had the most advanced political framework and had been way ahead of the rest of the British Caribbean on the road to nationhood. There had always been free elections in the colony. Reform had picked up the most votes in every election and this was unlikely to change.

"I don't know, father," Joseph shook his head. "There is already a small exodus of Portuguese and others from the business and upper class leaving the colony for abroad. Most of them are going to Canada and the US where they're being received with open arms."

"They're chicken," Thomas said. "They don't have the guts to stay around and fight for what they want."

"Call it what you want, Thomas," Joseph said, "I can't really see peace coming to the colony after independence is granted by Britain. The Reform party, backed by East Indians will always run the government under the present system –they have the bulk of the population behind them. If they don't, the Republicans, backed by Blacks will –after all, they're the next major group. Where does that leave all the minorities? We will be caught right in the middle."

"There are always alternatives," Augusto said.

Joseph shook his head. "Father, face it. Reform can never lose and the Republicans will never allow them to rule in peace. There will be violence in the streets if this happens. There might even be a civil war. Look what happened back in February –if all the riots and the looting and burning weren't signs of things to come, I don't know what else I can tell you."

"The Conservative will be able to form a government soon, you watch and see," Thomas said. "Common sense will always win over race."

Joseph laughed. "You're dreaming," he said, his voice raising an octave. It wasn't often that Joseph lost his composure but when he did, his voice grew shrill and he was unable to contain himself. "The Conservatives will never form a government here in this country," he shouted.

Carl couldn't help smiling. He'd been determined not to participate openly in the debate going on, for fear of showing where his sentiment lay, but this latest suggestion from Thomas was about all he could take. "That's about the most ridiculous thing I've heard in a long time," he said to Thomas.

Everyone turned around and looked at him; he was sitting at the bottom end of the table, far from the heat of the conversation.

About the only ones around the table not participating in the conversation were John and James. John, at his age, had no idea what was going on and James had never gotten involved in any political discussions within the family. James had taken some time off from managing the winery to attend the family council –he was working longer hours now, since the family fortunes hinged on the winery as the main source of income, but he always said that it didn't really matter who was in power –they were all out to fill their pockets and get rich. He'd never voted for any party and said he never intended to.

"Regardless," Augusto broke the silence, "the Conservatives can and will be a strong partner to the Republicans and they can and will form a government if the electoral system changes for the better."

"Mark my words, the Portuguese minority will always be used just to achieve an end," Joseph said. "When they're no longer needed, they will be discarded and discriminated against like any other small faction in the country."

Augusto looked to his right, to the pictures hanging on the wall.

Here it comes, Carl thought.

"My ancestors came to this country over a hundred years ago," Augusto said. "They worked and slaved to make a living, to get us where we are today. This is my country, as much as any other man alive, and I'm not abandoning it to a Communist take over. They're going to have to take me out of here in a pine box."

What Carl's father really meant was that he considered the retention of the status quo to be the only way out. Carl's interpretation of his father's words came from listening to his business and social philosophy over many years. When his father talked about rights, he meant rights for the upper class who owned property; when he referred to democracy he meant rule of the many by the few. He'd always said that people in the colony were not capable of ruling themselves and this had often reminded Carl of his approach to his own brood. The same way the Colonial system worked: it was paternalistic, often treating people as children, rewarding those who complied and punishing those who were rebels. Under such a system there was no recognition that colonies might want to be self sufficient down the road, that there should be a long-term plan for ensuring that they had all the right skills needed to go on their own. Years after self-government came to the colony, the Governor and Executive still had the right to overrule decisions made by the elected Reform government and they still controlled foreign and financial matters. The upper class in the colony, made up mainly of business and property owners still held the greater portion of the wealth. Things would never change unless there was a radical transformation of the entire system.

The Chairman had said it often in his speeches at Liberty House when he quoted from the Manifesto of Karl Marx: *The proletariat have nothing to lose but their chains.* Carl believed that Marx's approach to a socialist economy might be the solution for everything that ailed the colony.

"I agree with you, father," Thomas said.

"I'm not sticking around to find out," Joseph shook his head. "Frances and I are going abroad, the first chance we get. I don't see any future in this country, not for a long time to come."

"I'm sorry to hear that," Augusto said. He smiled. "You have to do what's best for you and your wife. Thomas and I will stick it out here." He looked at James. "We know we can always rely on James to run the business." He ignored John. He looked at Carl. He seemed to hesitate, as if he wasn't sure what to say.

"I'm hoping that Carl will join us, also," Augusto said.

Carl did not respond.

CHAPTER 11 –Last Rites

TUESDAY 25TH NOVEMBER 1980

Carl sat in the Berbice Chair on the veranda upstairs. He was alone, watching the flow of people entering the front yard for the viewing of his father's open casket. A steady, growing clamour was floating upwards from the ground as people gathered under the tent. Tiredness, bordering on exhaustion was threatening to overwhelm him. He'd kept an almost non-stop pace since he arrived and now, he was savouring the brief interlude, alone with his thoughts.

He'd taken a last view of his father's body before retreating upstairs. He'd stood there watching people join a queue, then, seen them beat a hasty retreat afterwards, as if they'd performed the unpleasant part of the rite, and now they could move on with the rest of it. He'd watched as Uncle Jules placed a bottle of Madeira in the coffin, tucked it under Augusto's right hand and muttered a few words.

Carl passed his hands along the arms of the *Berbice Chair*, an *Easy Chair*, something more like a cot without a mattress; the sturdy wood frame, made of polished mahogany and lined with canvas, had stood up well over the years. He had pulled out the two leg rests; his feet were resting on the extensions, a position he'd often seen his father take. Augusto seemed to find his escape here often, along with time in the study that was filled with books and documents connected with his business. Only, now, his father was no more.

Overhead, the sky was growing dark and rain clouds threatened. There would be a deluge soon. He remembered times like this, when he was a boy.

One of them had been a year of mixed blessings...

They had just suffered through one of the driest spells anyone could remember. The parched earth cried out for rain and the tall resilient para grass turned brown and finally died. Trees seemed to be on the brink of collapse as branches drooped and leaves wilted.

To the people in the Walk, it might have seemed as if they had been fetching water from the well forever. Even the level in the Canal dropped to an all time low, black mud showing on the bottom in some areas with fishes sputtering vainly in an attempt to reach deeper water; the hassar, houri and curass and the occasional piranha all trapped in the sludge.

September came and went and still there was no sign of rain. Mother Nature seemed content to tease the residents of the Walk with small gestures of what she could do, as if reminding them of her power. An occasional dark cloud passing swiftly towards the Demerara River; a cool breeze filtering through the house and sending blinds rippling against the window panes; a heavy downpour that stopped as quickly as it started, just enough rain pouring from the spouts to leave a twisted trail on the earth as if someone had accidentally kicked over a bucket of water. This was all they had experienced for more than three weeks into the season.

Just when it reached the level of desperation, things changed. The nights turned cooler. Crickets chirped endlessly –they seemed to be shouting *Quick-Quick, Quick-Quick* to passers-by as they hurried home to beat the coming downpour. Legions of crapoud croaked interminably –a bellowing, pulsating cacophony that reverberated throughout the night. Dark clouds hovered overhead or sailed restlessly across the bright, silvery moon. Swarms of candle-flies fluttered through the darkness in the Backdam.

It started off with lightning. Not broken strings of jagged forks that arc across the dark sky and leave a moment or two of luminescence in their wake, but bright flashes that lit up the entire sky from the Demerara River to the Backdam, from the Atlantic to the cane fields of the Veldt. Blinding light that left everything suspended for brief moments, like when someone walks into a dark room, flicks the light switch on and off, leaving the scene indelibly etched on the mind. Thunder followed and a slight pitter-patter on the leaves, a drumming on the zinc sheets of the roof, a roar of the wind crashing branches together.

The rainy season had finally started.

The rain fell as it never had before. Torrential rain, sheets of water cascading down, as how the towering Kaieteur Falls sends never-ending volumes rumbling over its wide gorge. Spouts overflowed into yards, water ran off to the gutters, spiralled down the small sluice running underneath the Walk, merged with the Canal and rushed to the Demerara River, only to be blocked by a closed koker due to the tides and the swollen river. So, the run-off remained in the canal. From the other direction came the waste dumped by the sugar estates; a putrid, black liquid seeking escape to the river for eventual blending with the Atlantic. Only, there was no release.

The rain fell for three days and nights. On the fourth day, Christians went to church and prayed that they would see the end of it. Muslims trekked to the Masjid and begged Allah to be merciful. Hindus went to the Temple and appealed to their deities for help. Finally, it stopped on the fourth night. Even so, the river remained swollen with high tide and the koker was kept closed to prevent the Canal from rising even more from the backwash, something that was sure to happen if the sluice was opened.

Meanwhile, the water level had risen to the point where it overflowed the banks of the Canal and swept through to bottom-houses. The odour from the stagnant body of water filled the air and drifted to the surrounding areas on the breeze blowing in from the Atlantic. Fishes floated on the water, upturned bellies white and bloated. Fences were undermined and fell; logs that lined the walkways floated away half submerged, looking like alligators.

Carl revelled in the change, as if God had answered his prayer. A flood meant it was impossible to distinguish the gutters from the actual Walk. One step in the wrong direction would mean being submerged in water. A flood meant that classes would be cancelled. He liked the postponement of school; it made him feel as if it was an extension of the long August break they had not too long come through, and a chance to play in the water, sail logs down the Walk, catch tadpoles at the sluice, prance in the water with his friends.

When the flood finally receded, the gutters became foaming, swirling tributaries of water. He remembered: he was standing with Lincoln, peeing into the water, vying to see who could project his stream the farthest. Lincoln had asked him if he was going to be circumcised one day like their Muslim friend Akbar. *They do it with a razor blade you know*, Lincoln had said. Carl had squirmed, hastily tucked away his *willie*, and resolved that no one would use a razor blade on his penis, not ever.

***

Earl was waving to him from the front yard. Carl could see him through the slats of the jalousie section of the veranda. Father Martin had arrived and it was time to start the trip to the Repentigny burial ground.

Hundreds of people were gathered in the yard and outside on the road –Carl saw this when he came downstairs. His father was widely known, but the turnout was much larger than he expected. Did his father have an impact on the lives of all these people at one time or the other? The undertaker placed the lid over the coffin and Carl caught a final glimpse of his father's body just before it was sealed. In those few seconds, the picture of a sedate, composed Augusto imprinted itself on his brain and he thought that this last image would be the one remaining with him for the rest of his life.

So many faces; people he knew: Earl, Jimmy, Patsy, Sumintra, Uncle Jules, and people he thought he recognized: Wilfred, Shirley and her two sisters, and so many others whose faces all blended or became a blur as the funeral procession started the walk to the burial ground. He was sure that later, he might meet people who'd tell him that they were at his father's funeral and he'd thank them, but he'd be at a loss, unable to recall their presence.

The dark clouds opened up in the middle of Father Martin's last rites and the rain poured down.

Standing under a tent along with the other mourners huddled against the downpour, Carl couldn't help but think that the reason he'd travelled close to three thousand miles, was ending. His father would soon be laid to rest in hallowed ground. Then, what? He'd be making his way back to Toronto, returning to a job for which he'd grown tired even though he still had good prospects and a bright future, to a relationship that he was unsure of, to a life that had grown so pointless that he'd been questioning the meaning of his very existence over the last year. If he could turn back the clock, what would he change? To what extent, anyway, did he have control over events as they'd unfurled over the three and a half decades of his life? Ultimately, how much control did anyone really have over his life?

Here was his father being placed next to his father and his father before him. People whose origins started in a far off place around the world, men who had found themselves in a corner of the globe that would hardly have featured in their future plans before economic conditions drove them out. All the others buried there, headstones marking their final resting place: a British soldier who died of malaria back in 1920, far from his home; Blacks brought over as slaves from Africa; East Indians and Chinese bonded as indentured workers, and his brother James –the start of a new generation, now lying side by side with previous ones. His mother Mary was also buried there –her headstone now sunken and atilt with the twenty-eight years since her passing. Her third child: a girl, Bernadette, with a small headstone marking her name and 1940 as the year of her birth and death. Carl would most likely be buried in Toronto, Thomas in America, Joseph in England.

Jimmy was among the mourners. He was standing next to his mother, Patsy. Carl could see them looking in the direction of James' headstone. What were they thinking? Did they harbour bitterness against Augusto for not accepting them into the family because of colour, or had all been forgotten and forgiven now that he was dead? Earl was standing next to his mother. He was looking down at the coffin. She was crying and Earl had his arm around her, trying his best to console her. Death affects people in strange ways, Carl realized. Although they'd only lived a short time with Augusto, they'd grown close enough to him to be moved by his passing. Uncle Jules was stoic, his face impassive, like a man coming down to the end of his years and accepting his age and ultimate fate.

Someone else was there too, standing next to Uncle Jules, someone whose face Carl had not seen in over sixteen years. But, weren't faces like scraps of information imbedded in the subconscious, stored away and not forgotten, recalled in an instant when a connection was made? It was John.

John was looking at their mother's grave. What was he thinking? Was he reflecting over the many times Augusto had told him about his birth: *One life moving on, a new one starting*? Carl was just seven when their mother passed on, tired and exhausted from so many years of child bearing. Carl had done the calculation: eight children over sixteen years of marriage, averaging one every two years. Quite a feat for a small framed, delicate woman. *A baby factory* is how someone had once referred to her. Four who had passed on: a child died shortly after birth, two of them were stillborn, one –James, died in the riots. Four still alive but scattered to the four winds; her, not surviving to hold her youngest in her arms or see him grow to the man he was today.

Carl looked at his younger brother. He'd changed over the years. John was always considered the runt of the litter when they were growing up, someone who always needed to be sheltered and protected, but he was far from that now. When Carl left in 1964, John would have been twelve and still stretching. John had grown to all of what looked like six feet now. He towered over Uncle Jules and was supporting their uncle with his right arm. John's youthful features had changed from what Carl remembered. His brother's face now bore strains of a life lived on the edge; gaunt and riddled with pockmarks, and there was a scar on the left side of his forehead. John finally looked up in Carl's direction and they made eye contact. John smiled and Carl nodded.

Father Martin was blessing the burial plot. Rain continued, now reduced to fragments of drops that Carl could hear on the tarpaulin overhead.

All these graves and tombs, mausoleums and head markers: people who passed on with nothing left of their life but a token of their existence. How were they remembered –for the good they'd done in their life, or for evil deeds? Who remembered them –relatives and friends? Or had they been forgotten, maybe their memory relegated to pictures taken, letters written, events that had occurred long ago?

Someone was missing. Grandma Lilly died in 1963, three years before the colony gained independence and assumed the name of Guyana, one year before Carl left the country. Carl remembered going to her cremation, her ashes interred on the plantation. He was just eighteen.

Yet another disconnection: a going of separate ways, in death, as in life. Grandfather Salvador and Lilowtie had met in Georgetown when she ran away from home and a strict family, back in 1910, when she was fifteen. She was pregnant with Augusto when Salvador married her and gave a name to his first son. From then on she was known as Lilly. By the time the second son, Julius, came along, the difference in religion and background had created a wide chasm that they couldn't bridge: she was Hindu and he was Catholic.

Salvador had amassed land in Bonaventure, started a coconut plantation and opened a store in Georgetown where he also ran an import-export business. When they parted ways, she retained the coconut estate while he went to Georgetown to focus on the business. The split also resulted in Augusto going to the city with his father while Jules remained with Grandma Lilly in the country. Relations had remained cordial but never warm enough for Salvador and Lilly to be reconciled.

Carl had always felt close to his grandmother. There was a time…he was a boy, old enough to remember, young enough for it to leave an indelible impression. He hadn't started primary school…

***

Grandmother Lilly had come down to Georgetown from her plantation. She was in the kitchen, three of them – Grandmother, his father and his mother. They were having a family discussion, one of those where only the adults were allowed, so the kids had all been consigned to the gallery in the front of the house.

The trip from her estate on the East Coast took several hours by train and an additional half-an-hour by hire-car from the station on Lamaha Street. For a woman who was already in her seventies it would not have been an easy trip to make, plagued as she was by the ravages of her diabetic condition and in the last year she'd curtailed her travelling. It must have been something very urgent to bring her down to the city this time.

A visit meant little tokens for each of her grandchildren. When she arrived and opened the cloth bag she toted, the one with the polished wood handles and faded printed flowers, four pairs of eyes peered into the bag with high expectation, like kids eagerly awaiting the opening of gifts on Christmas morning. A regular visit meant an overnight stay and late into the night she would regale them with tales of the countryside where she grew up. She would sit in the old wooden rocking chair that creaked and groaned from the burden every time she moved around in it, then she would reach over to the side table for the small can of tobacco, a box of matches and cigarette paper that she'd placed there.

Sitting beside her, a privileged place reserved for the younger ones, Carl always watched closely. He knew the routine well from the many times he had seen it.

Grandmother placed several pinches of the tobacco to form a ridge in the middle of the paper, flicked her tongue out and licked the edge of the paper several times, then sealed it around the tobacco. As the cigarette dangled from her lips, she painstakingly extracted a match from the small box and when she struck it a tantalizing burst of sulphur floated across to Carl's nostrils. Grandmother filled her lungs with smoke and then flicked the ashes into an empty matchbox. She held them in suspense as she slowly picked off a loose strand of tobacco from her lips.

After that, she'd regale Carl and his brothers with tales of spirits that roamed the countryside in the old days. Tales of the *Bacoo*, the African spirit kept in a bottle by the *Obeahman* who could summon it to carry out his evil doing; of the *Ol'Higue*, the bloodsucking old woman roaming from village to village looking for prey, especially little boys and girls to feast on; and the *Moongazer*, the spirit that came out on a full-moon looking for travellers foolish enough to be out on the road at night. The *Flying Dutchmen* –spirits of Dutch overseers and plantation owners whose restless souls still roamed around the grounds of their old haunts at night, riding their white steeds on patrol, the horses snorting and panting to the steady beat of slaves chanting in the background.

According to Grandmother, her mother had witnessed many of these phenomena and she herself had seen many things when she was a little girl. These stories always left Carl feeling exposed and vulnerable. At times he felt as if he was caught outside in the middle of a thunderstorm with lightning bolts striking trees all around him.

Grandmother stopped and took another drag from her cigarette. On the wall, just over her head a lizard paused, its light grey skin almost blending with the white wall, its four legs outstretched. Carl saw the lizard slowly turn its head and look in his direction. The lizard's two bulging eyes followed the movement of the insects as they buzzed around the dim light from the kerosene lamp that cast a halo over Grandmother's head. The lizard's long tongue suddenly flicked out and snatched a paper moth from the group circling around the lamp. Carl moved closer to Joseph.

This was not one of Grandmother's regular visits. She'd suddenly appeared out of the blue at the front gate and there were no gifts for distribution. She was all business and she got straight to the point. Carl doubted whether there would be tales told later that night.

It was early. Long before his father set out on his weekend outing into the city, something that he'd been doing of late.

"I don't know what to do, who to turn to," Carl's mother said.

Through the doorway to the kitchen Carl saw his mother. She sat at the table, wiping tears from her eyes.

Carl grew increasingly alarmed as the words drifted across the hall to the gallery. He was the one closest to the kitchen and he could hear the conversation.

"You're a shame, a downright disgrace to the whole family," Grandmother said, "jus' what yuh t'ink you're doing? You must mend your ways boy, or I will kick yur ass out of this house so fast you won't know wha' happen to you."

Grandma Lilly was dressed in a yellow short sleeve blouse. The skin of her arms, shrivelled from age and dry as the bark of the mango tree in the front yard, stood out against the sagging flesh that had replaced her biceps. By now she was really angry. She opened her eyes wide and tilted her head up to the ceiling when she spoke to him, as if she was appealing to some heavenly body for help.

Carl looked at his older brothers –Joseph, Thomas and James. They were playing card games and if they knew what was going on, they showed no sign of it. With every passing minute, Carl grew more concerned and resentful of Grandmother's tirade. She was a very strong and forceful person, but to throw her son out of his own house! Surely this would have been too much, even for someone as fearless as her.

"A man of your age, with so many kids. 'Ave you lost all your self-respect," Grandmother said. "How can you be gallivanting all around the town, when you have a wife and children at home?"

Throughout the one-sided conversation Carl's father remained silent, as he sat there with the Sunday Graphic. He had that look on his face –Carl knew it well, the same one Carl had when his mother had caught him stealing sugar out of the sugar bowl. Carl knew his father was not reading. He'd read all three newspapers-the Graphic as well as the Sunday Chronicle and Sunday Argosy earlier that morning, as was part of his routine: to sit in the Berbice chair and read the papers from the front page to the back. Now, he was merely going through the motion again, like a rerun of an old familiar movie. Carl felt connected with his father and hated his Grandmother for what she was subjecting him to. What would happen to his father if she kicked him out of the house! Most of all, like a child left to wander the streets on a dark night, he was concerned about what would become of him.

"Have you no shame?" Grandmother repeated. "Fooling around with a younger woman when you have a wife and young children at home depending on you! If Salvador was alive today he'd kick your ass right outta here."

Grandmother's arrival was no coincidence; it had been timely and she'd caught Carl's father before he set out of the house. It had something to do with the early Sunday morning trips his father had been taking into the city. Sometimes he took Carl with him: three times –Carl remembered them well, not only because of the treatment he received when he was there, but because it was something that he, and only he among his brothers had been privileged to share with his father. He remembered the route well: along Main Street, past the public library and the guarded, enclosed compound of Government house where the Governor ran the colony, to the range house in Kingston where Aunty lived, not too far from the seawall where the sea crashed against the concrete barrier, close to the lighthouse painted in white and red.

On the second trip Carl realized that Aunty was looking just as big as his mother when she was having the last baby, the one they said was stillborn and taken away by God to a much better place, even before the baby was able to open her eyes and see the world. That was not too long ago. Both his Aunty and his mother with big tummies, and at the same time, too.

Aunty was his own special Aunt, never to be shared with the others in the family, and she was always kind to him; gave him ice cream and soft drinks and black cake on those visits. She had lovely eyes, his Aunty, she reminded him of the cat that had eaten its kitten, only, Aunty had many red spots on her face, the only person he'd seen with so many spots. On the last visit, she was not as big. They had a religious function with a priest and many other visitors, and a little baby lying there in the crib as she showed him off to everyone. Mostly, his father was there with her. The two of them alone, with Carl loving the treats she gave him.

It was only natural for Carl's father to be afraid of his grandmother, even though he was a powerful man in his own right. Grandmother inspired respect. Not just because she was huge: she was massively built, from hard work in the coconut plantation when she was young. The years of tobacco smoking had enriched her voice with a deep baritone. Sometimes it came across as a rasping, grating sound, like coarse sandpaper drawn across wood. When she spoke everyone sat up and listened, and that was what his father seemed to be doing, now that he'd abandoned the pretence of reading the newspapers.

Grandmother shook her head. "I want dis nonsense to stop, today," she said. "I don't want to have to come back down to go through this again with you. If I have to, the whole world will know about it."

Carl's father bowed his head.

"Do you understand what I'm saying, boy?"

Carl's father nodded. Then, he withdrew to the portico adjacent to the gallery.

Grandmother left later that day. Carl never went on visits to Aunty again.

***

The atmosphere was now loaded with moisture and Carl's clothes stuck to him as if he'd just been caught in a sudden downpour.

Carl heard Father Martin's voice: *I am the Resurrection and the Life.* The priest sprinkled holy water on the coffin. *Grant thy mercy, O Lord, we beseech Thee, to Thy servant departed, that he may not receive in punishment the requital of his deeds who in desire did keep Thy will, and as the true faith here united him to the company of the faithful, so may Thy mercy unite him above to the choirs of angels. Through Jesus Christ our Lord. Amen...*

Carl had resolved in the walk to the burial ground, that he would not surrender to an emotional reaction at his father's funeral. He had fed himself the logic that, after all, it was over sixteen years since he had last seen the Old Man. They had drifted worlds apart even in the years leading up to his departure.

Carl watched the gravediggers lower his father's polished mahogany casket into the hole. He wanted to reach out, touch his father, tell him that he understood that his turn would come one day.

Father Martin gave the final petition: *May his soul and the souls of all the faithful departed through the mercy rest in peace.*

Carl watched as the gravediggers started on the mound of earth at the side of the hole. As dirt filled the void where the casket lay, the finality of it all struck a cord. This was the last act, a confirmation that his father was no more and it started as an involuntary gesture, a hesitant sob, his entire body reacting to the numbing sensation in his brain. He broke down in convulsions that racked his body and started the tears trickling down his cheeks.

Carl shook his head. Death was supposed to mean absolution of all sins and past transgressions, and his father had committed his share in his lifetime. Who hadn't? Right there, at his gravesite, was a son, John who'd always been made to feel guilty over their mother's passing. Close to him was Jimmy who had never known the love and affection of his grandfather. Somewhere out there in the city, was a child born to Augusto just about the same time as John, maybe a child who was still around, having never known or felt the closeness of his father or siblings.

Carl thought: if there was life after death, his father was sure to find it with those who had gone before him – whose courage and bravery to seek fortune in a far away place he'd always been proud of. Carl and Uncle Jules had now carried out Augusto's last wish and buried him with his ancestors.

CHAPTER 12 – The Wake

TUESDAY 25TH NOVEMBER 1980

It was all over.

Father Martin had come around, extended his sympathy to Carl and quickly left for another function. The undertaker left in his hearse, leaving a gravedigger to complete the job. People started to make their way out of the cemetery. Carl watched them carefully pick their way across the ground that had turned into a soggy morass. The procession was slow. Some were carrying umbrellas opened up against the drizzle that had started again, others had a variety of items held over their head: a printed copy of the service, a Bible, a handkerchief.

That was it, Carl thought. The underlying attitude at the end of every funeral he'd attended: it was over and time to move on to something else. A cemetery was the last place people wanted to linger and socialize on a wet day. Carl remained standing in the same position, watching the gravedigger shovel the last of the dirt. The man was taking his time. He would scoop and throw it on the mound, pause, scoop and throw, puffs of smoke rising from the cigarette dangling between his lips. How many graves had he done for the day? What number was Carl's father? Was this something that a gravedigger kept track of?

The cigarette was down to a stub by the time the last of the dirt was thrown in the grave but the man still would not let go of it –he held the butt between his thumb and index finger and dragged out the last few stimulating puffs before he threw it on the ground. He was a thin man, his back stooped, his clothes hanging by threads on his emaciated body, his face grizzled and grey, and he looked for all the world like someone who approached his profession as if time was on his side. Why would he have to hurry? His clients were the least to complain about the way he approached his job. He took his time, tamped the mound with his shovel, stood back and looked at his handiwork, twisting his head right and left as if he were checking the mound for its symmetry.

This is what a man's life finally comes down to in the end, Carl thought: Ownership of a six feet deep plot of land that would eventually be marked by a headstone commemorating his coming and going. In the final analysis, life was for the living. The dead already had their place in the sun when they were entities and once you've moved on, a plot was waiting for you someplace, somewhere.

In a few weeks, after the site had settled, a dome would be cast and the headstone installed. In accordance with Augusto's wishes, Uncle Jules had selected a marble headstone to be carved with the words: *Augusto Dias 30 August 1910 –24th November 1980. Died as he lived. No more, No less.* Would it be something that he might see one day, Carl wondered. He doubted it. He couldn't see a reason that might draw him back to Guyana in the future, unless it was for Uncle Jules' funeral, and even for that, he was sceptical whether he might return, considering the grand inquisition he'd been subjected to at the airport for this trip.

Uncle Jules and John were still standing on the opposite side of the grave –Uncle Jules dressed in a worn tweed suit, John in a navy blue jersey and jeans. They were watching, with the same fascination that seemed to imply there was some deeper meaning to the entire process of filling a hole with the dirt that had been excavated from it just hours previously. Or, was Uncle Jules reflecting that with the passing of his older brother, he was now the last of his generation?

And, John, what was he thinking? Was he now looking back with regret, about all the years of separation and alienation and the time he never spent with their father? Blood always runs thicker than water. Despite the disagreements Carl had with his father, there was now no denying the fact that there was a bond between him and Augusto, and surely it had to be the same for John.

The gravedigger placed his shovel over his shoulder and slowly made his way out of the grounds. Carl walked the few yards that separated him from his brother and uncle.

A certain amount of reserve was displayed in John's demeanour. Carl sensed it as he got closer to his brother. John had an upright bearing, stern features, and a look in his eyes that suggested he would much prefer to be someplace else. Had the sixteen years of separation between them created an unbridgeable chasm? John was only twelve when Carl left the country. The intervening years would have seen him develop into a man, moulded by forces he'd been subjected to and events that had transpired in his life. What had life been like for him?

Carl did not hesitate. He reached out, grabbed John and embraced him.

"I'm so happy to see you," Carl said.

At first, it was like taking hold of something rigid and unyielding, like holding on to a mannequin. As they swayed back and forth, Carl felt a firm body: well-developed biceps, a bulging chest and wide shoulders. Carl eventually felt the tension drain out of his brother's body as his shoulders slumped and his entire being seemed to relax.

"I know," John said. "'Been a long time."

"Much too long," Carl said. "We have so much to catch up with."

"I just know he would come," Uncle Jules said. "John always find his way back home sooner or later."

They laughed, the three of them, even though Carl thought that his uncle had just described his younger brother as if he were a family pet that was in the habit of wandering off and finding his way back home when he'd had enough of the outside world.

Carl and John walked back to the house in the Walk, sheltering under Uncle Jules' umbrella. The day was being swiftly transformed from late afternoon into evening, a light breeze percolating through palm fronds and mango leaves.

By the time they arrived, the yard was packed. People were crowded under the tent sheltering from the drizzle, some hovering under the mango tree, using its broad leaves for some measure of protection. The tables were set up. Games were already on the way: several groups were engaged in playing cards and domino tickets were being slammed down with the intensity and seriousness with which most players took the game. Bottles of rum and foam cups were stacked in front of players. Later in the evening steaming cups of coffee or tea and biscuits would be brought out to sober up the mourners and they would start over, another long night, and Carl yearned for some peace or quiet, to get away from it all.

They made their way through the crowd towards the front door, people greeting them as they passed and Carl acknowledging or nodding. Still so many people –would it ever end? He knew he shouldn't be surprised at the way things were done, but it was draining his energy and left little time for contemplation. He wanted to be alone with his brother and he'd wanted to find out about his father's last days.

They entered the house: still more people coming and going in all directions. He saw Earl and his mother talking to a group of people. Shirley was there, talking to Patsy.

Carl steered Uncle Jules and John up the stairs where there was a calmer atmosphere. The three of them stood on the veranda.

"I have to sort out the Old Man's things," Carl said. "I have no idea what he's got stored away in his office. Do you know if there's a will, Uncle Jules?"

Uncle Jules shook his head. "Do you know how many times I talked to your father about making a will? I don't know whether or not he made one."

Somewhere back in time, had his father reached a stage where he just simply didn't care in whose possession the property ended? Had he come to the conclusion that it was too much of a bother to make a will?

Carl turned to John. "If there's no will, what do you think we should do with the property and all his stuff in the study?"

John's response was instantaneous. "As far as the property goes, I don't want a share, never did –I told the Old Man this the last time I saw him." He snorted. "As for his stuff, whatever it is, I want no part. It means nothing to me. You and the others can have it or throw it out in the garbage, for all I care."

Carl was startled at the passion in his brother's voice. Death didn't seem to have eased John's pain or soften his attitude towards their father. He could understand his brother's feelings. After the shabby treatment he'd received and years of detachment from their father's affairs, why should he start taking an interest now?

Carl had no idea on the magnitude of the job ahead, but it was something that had to be done in the next few days, and he was on his own. Both Joseph and Thomas had made it clear that they would not exercise any claim to the property. Since Carl had no intention of returning to Guyana anytime in the future, either to live or visit, the property and other assets presented a problem to be sorted out.

"I'm heading back to the countryside," Uncle Jules said. He pulled off his tie and stuffed it into his jacket pocket. "Things will be a mess if I don't. I hope you will come up to see us before you leave, Cal. You too, John."

John shook his head. "I'm leaving early tomorrow morning, Uncle Jules. I have to catch a bauxite ship heading to the U.S."

Less than twenty-four hours in sixteen years –that was the sum total of the time he'd be sharing with his younger brother. Would it take another sixteen years for their paths to cross again?

"Well, keep in touch. Write me from whatever port you end up in," Uncle Jules said.

"I'm catching a flight out on Sunday, Uncle Jules," Carl said. "I will visit you before I leave."

Uncle Jules seemed pleased. "Okay, I will be expecting you. Of course you know we're no longer in the old estate. I will leave directions with Earl and he can bring you up."

Earl came up with a tray. He placed it on a table on the veranda. A bottle of rum, three glasses, a tumbler of ice lay on the tray. "This wake will go on until late tonight, I'm sure you know that, by now." Earl said. "You might as well take things easy."

"Can you take me to the hire-car stand?" Uncle Jules asked Earl.

"Sure, are you ready?"

"I will have one drink before I go," Uncle Jules said. He poured rum into a glass, raised it to his mouth and drank it in one smooth motion. He shook his head vigorously as the rum made its way down his throat into his stomach. In another minute, he and Earl had retreated down the stairs to the ground floor.

Carl stood on the veranda with John and watched the De Soto pull out of the driveway, through the gate, heading down the Walk towards the taxi stand in Georgetown. From there, Uncle Jules would catch a hire-car to his house in the country.

From the ground floor, sounds of the people under the tent rode on pockets of breeze up to the veranda. It was a steady caress, men arguing over the strategy that someone had adopted in playing out a hand of cards, someone calling out for more ice, a man's voice imploring for a chance to be in the game.

Carl placed ice in two glasses, poured a drink for himself and one for John. He watched as his brother emptied his glass with one swift movement.

John pulled out a pack of cigarettes and a lighter from his jeans and placed them on the table. He extracted a cigarette from the pack and lit it.

Carl said, as he sat down: "Sixteen years –it's a long time. Where have you been?"

John sighed and a look of resignation crossed his face. He shrugged and took a seat. "Here and there," he said.

"Were you always at sea, or did you settle down somewhere?"

"Never stayed in one port for more than a few weeks at a time. Whenever there was a ship going someplace, I was on it."

"How about marriage?"

A far away look seemed to overtake John's face, as he looked into his glass, at the two shrunken cubes of ice, then, outside to the front yard and back to Carl.

"Came close to it once," John said. "I met a woman, in Port Of Spain, a mixed up cook-up rice for a woman with a bit of everything in her, Chinese, Portuguese, Black, Indian, even some native, way, way back. We really hit it off great. She wanted marriage and children, though." He shook his head. "Is this the kind of world for anyone to bring up children?" The question was rhetorical, it seemed. He continued: "Even if I could get my head around that, I realized, that after a while I would be on my way again, and it wouldn't be fair to her. She'd see me perhaps once a year, if that much."

A wandering man –his brother seemed to be always on the go. Had things grown so hopeless between him and their father that John wanted to be as far away as possible?

John took a long drag on his cigarette, contorted his lips and released fumes in the air. He had a habit of rifling through his short hair and his left hand was constantly caressing a scar on his forehead. He must have seen Carl looking at the scar.

"You're curious," John said, as if he felt that he had to explain. How many times over the years had he been asked to tell the story? "Got it in a bar in Port Of Spain a long time ago. Somewhere I shouldn't have been in the first place. Someone hit me with a bottle. He ended up with a broken nose and a fractured skull."

"He singled you out, just like that?"

A trace of a smile flashed across John's face. "He claimed I was trying to pick up his girl. Truth is, I was, only I didn't know she was his girl at the time. We ended up in a one big fight."

"Did that happen a lot to you?"

Lines creased John's thin face and his light brown eyes lit up. "What? Picking up someone else's girl, or the fighting?"

"The fighting."

"A few times in the early years, when I was much younger and rash. I guess I had something to prove, to myself, to everybody else. I don't know. Not anymore. I try to keep out of trouble, even though, with my size, there's always someone out there trying to test how far he can push me. I realized, though, it's not worth it. Anyway, I'm getting too old for that kind of stuff."

Carl smiled. His younger brother no longer needed supervision. He recalled a period when John was notorious for skipping school and hanging out on street corners or around the cinemas. He'd even taken to gambling one time. Carl had to hunt him down on many occasions and escort him back to school.

"Did you ever finish school, after I left?" Carl said.

John shook his head. "Dropped out back in sixty-eight, just before I was going to write the Primary School Leaving Certificate. Saw no real need to get a certificate, much less going on to high school. What would I do with it? Didn't even want to work for the Old Man. I took a job in a sawmill cutting lumber, worked as a stevedore on the docks, hung around for a while, doing mostly nothing. The Old Man was mad as hell over the whole matter. I didn't really care back then."

How much had he himself contributed to John's lack of direction and aimless roaming? Up to the time he had left British Guiana, he was the only one who took an interest in John. The age gap between John and Joseph and Thomas was so wide that they barely knew John existed at times, so busy were they with their own careers. His father was too obsessed with the political situation to pay any attention.

Carl said. "Was that the same year that you signed on and went to sea?"

John nodded. "I heard later that the Old Man was even madder over that. He must have been sorry that he ever signed the papers for my passport application. He had no idea where I was or what I'd done."

"How did he eventually find out?"

John laughed, the most relaxed moment Carl had seen his brother experience since they met at the funeral.

"I signed on through a shipping agency on Water Street. I just turned up there one day. They were looking for able-bodied sea men and my size impressed them enough to give me a try. I heard later from Uncle Jules that the same agency used to handle the Old Man's customs paperwork for his wine imports. They probably thought they were doing the Old Man a favour. I can imagine that someone there mentioned it to him one day. *How's your son doing on that ship he signed on to?* How it must have floored him! Hearing from a stranger that his son was out of the country."

"So, you just decided to do another one of your disappearing acts?"

John turned away. He sucked long and hard on the cigarette and exhaled, the fumes spiralling upwards from his tilted head. He passed his hand through his hair several times, always ending up on the scar. "I figured no one would care, or miss me. Everyone was too taken up with his own problems. Besides, they didn't owe me anything, and I didn't have to give them an explanation."

On another occasion, John was no more than eight or nine. He'd hopped on a punt going to the cane fields in the Backdam and was missing for a whole day. Everyone in the family was frantic, searching all over, not knowing whether he'd been kidnapped, drowned in the Canal, or in an accident and was lying hurt someplace. Late that afternoon he came back, just wandered in, like a stray dog coming home after a day's foraging, as if what he'd done was the most natural thing in the world.

"Like the time you ran away and caught the train to the plantation in the country," Carl said. "You actually told Uncle Jules that the Old Man knew you were going up there to spend time. Uncle Jules knew better, of course. He brought you back the next day and the Old Man was mad as hell. He gave you a good walloping with his belt."

"I remember that," John said. He threw his head back and laughed. "I did give him some hair raising moments over the years, didn't I?"

"We all did, at one time or the other," Carl said. "It's not easy for a single father to raise four boys –I know something about children now and can appreciate that. To give him credit, he took most of it calmly. *Boys will be boys*, he often said about our pranks and transgressions."

John nodded. "Can't deny that," he said, after a while, almost as if he were reluctant to admit there had been some redeeming qualities in their father. He said: "You're married, I guess?"

Carl shook his head. "I've lived with Natasha for many years, until early this year when we thought we'd like some time away from each other. We've got some problems –mostly of my making, I have to say. We have two kids –a boy and a girl, Alexei and Irina."

John shrugged. "Not sure if to offer you sympathy or congratulations," he said.

"I'm hoping it will work itself out when I get back. I'm starting to feel there's hope, since I've been away from them."

John looked at his cigarette. The tip glowed in the dark. "You're right, though," he said. "Can be a bastard of a thing to raise kids in this world. All four of us proved that, in many ways."

"Who was the worse of us all is questionable. Although, at times, I think that I took the prize for that. I doubt that the Old Man could ever get over what I did."

John was still looking at the tip of his cigarette, as if it held answers to questions that were plaguing him.

"Did he ever talk about it with the rest of the family?" Carl said.

John shook his head. "Not a word, as far as I know, but we didn't talk very much about anything, anyway."

Sometimes, silence says enough, Carl thought.

"Do you think you will still come back, now that the Old Man's gone?" Carl said.

John shook his head. "I doubt it. There's nothing here for me, never was when I think about it. I remember Joseph saying that there's no future in this country – the reason why he left, isn't it? Just when you think the worst is over, you hear stories about how bad things have become. It's like diving into the ocean and hoping to hit bottom, you never can. Not that I've got big plans for the future right now. The only reason to return would be for Uncle Jules –I don't know how long he will last. He was always kind, about the only one who took an interest in me, apart from you. I'd like to be here for him, when the end comes, depending on where I am and what I'm doing."

"How about the Old Man, did you see him when you came back?" Carl said.

"I saw him twice. The last time was just last year."

"That was a lot more times than I saw him over the same period."

John poured another drink into his glass. He looked through the jalousie slats. "You didn't miss much," he said.

"Did he say anything about me?"

"No, nothing at all."

"How did the last visit go?"

"He was the same. In the end, I was even sorry that I came to see him."

"What happened?"

"You know how he was, always talking about his father and his father before that and what they went through to get to this country. He'd go on and on, about his business, the riots and the looting, and how Reform betrayed the country. He was still living in the past. You have to move on, sometime."

Sumintra brought a kerosene lamp and a bowl of chicken wings and retreated back downstairs. Moths circled around the lamp and mosquitoes buzzed around Carl's ears. Outside, candle-flies darted back and forth, their iridescent glow punctuating the dark night.

So, their father still clung to the belief that it was Reform who betrayed the country; a bittersweet irony. Under the change in voting system to Proportional Representation imposed by the British Government under pressure from the Kennedy administration, the Republicans and the Conservatives managed to form a coalition, even though Reform had garnered more votes than either of the two opposition parties. Their coalition took the country to independence in 1966. Once in power, the Republicans had the clout and the mechanism to rig the first post-independence election so that it ended up with a majority, something that was impossible, given the fact that their Black supporters did not comprise the major segment of the population. From there on, election after election was engineered to keep the Republicans in power. The Conservatives had lost their gambit to obtain influence in the running of the country and its supporters were left stranded, like fish washed up on the banks of the Canal after a flood had receded. Augusto's political future and financial stake started to wane with the downfall of the Conservatives. He had risked everything in a gamble that didn't pay off.

"I'm sorry that you were not able to make up with him on your last visit," Carl said.

John raised his glass to his lips and paused. He said: "I knew it would eventually lead to the same old story. There's so much anyone can take, you know. Everything he told me always came right back to the day I was born, the day our mother died. Why did he have to keep on reminding me about it? Wasn't it enough that I knew she died the same day? Did he have to make me feel that I was the reason for her death, that it was I who killed her?"

"You did resemble her most of all, from what I remember," Carl said.

A film of moisture clouded over John's eyes. He sighed and looked through the jalousie again. The noise from below had not abated. Someone was shouting for Jimmy to come and bring another bottle of rum. A dog was barking somewhere down the Walk. A blackout was in effect and the flickering glow of lamps and candles seeped into the black void up and down the Walk.

"Everybody keeps telling me that. What do I know? She died when I was born."

"You came along at a time when there were problems in the colony. On top of that, the Old Man was still struggling with his business."

"I didn't ask to come into this world, you know. He was the one who couldn't keep his hands off her. Why didn't he use some kind of fucking contraceptive if he didn't want more children?"

Carl sighed. Contraceptives were not widely used by the older generation back then, and even so, how do you tell dedicated old-school Catholics to use them? When he thought more of it, John's close resemblance to their mother must have been very painful for Augusto over the years.

"Why did he have to start up with it again?" John said, when he turned back to face Carl. "Hadn't I heard enough of it when I was here? I came to see him, not to go through the same old story over and over again."

"I think it's something we'll all be wondering about from here on –the motivation and reasoning for the things he did. For what we all did, for that matter. I'm sure, like me, that you look back at some of the things you did when you were young, and ask yourself, what in the world could I have been thinking of? They were so senseless and downright stupid, with so much potential for harm. The fact that none of us was here in his final days, we'll probably be carrying around the guilt of that for some time to come. I'd like to think that it was the memory of good times that the Old Man carried to his grave. This is how I would like to remember him. Sure, he must have had regrets; it couldn't have been easy, having four sons and none of them around him in his final years."

John shook his head. "There's just so much you can take, though. I swore at him and left without even saying goodbye."

Was that a tinge of regret that Carl detected in his brother's voice? An irony: the son who had the greatest conflict with their father, was the last of the brothers to see him alive.

The bottle of rum was almost depleted and there were stubs of a pack of cigarettes in an ashtray. Carl was still nursing his first drink and had eaten some of the wings, but he'd watched John pour drink after drink without eating, and yet, it seemed to be having very little effect on him. His brother was a seasoned drinker with a cigarette always between his lips.

"I'm glad you kept in touch with Uncle Jules over the years," Carl said. "I'm sorry the two of us didn't do the same."

"I wouldn't call it keeping in touch. I sent him the occasional letter, saw him whenever I came back here, which is not more than three times over the years."

"How about Joseph and Thomas, did you ever get in touch with them?"

John shook his head. "Never knew where they were, or where I would end up most of the time."

The way it would probably continue, Carl reflected, with a great deal of sadness. John seemed destined to roam the world for the rest of his days, going from port to port, looking for something that would explain why things turned out the way they did. In the end, what would happen to him? Would he finally shack up in a room in some run-down port? Would he die and be buried at sea, his body consigned to the depths? Would they even know what happened to him?

The front gate opened, car lights penetrated the darkness. Earl was back. The gates were swung shut and the car headed to the garage.

"I did try, you know," John said, after he'd poured another drink and lit a cigarette.

"I'm sure you did," Carl said.

"After you left, there were still demonstrations and picketing going on. The Old Man was always up front there with other Conservative and Republican supporters. I joined him and Thomas, waving banners against the Reform government. I thought the Old Man would be pleased. I wanted so badly to gain his approval. Well, it never happened. One morning I woke up, I asked myself, what am I doing with all this demonstration crap that was going on? I fucking didn't even know why they were picketing and what they were hoping to achieve at that stage. I just gave up." He snorted. "I doubt if he ever noticed I was fucking missing."

"So it ended," Carl said. "I left in nineteen sixty-four, Thomas the same year, Joseph in sixty-five, you in sixty-eight. From that time on, the Old Man had none of his children around. Tell me, how did you manage to get here so fast for the funeral?"

John seemed surprised at the question. "I didn't," he stammered. "I just happened to be on a ship going to pick up a load of bauxite from McKenzie. I dropped in at Uncle Jules' place and heard the news."

The oil in the kerosene lamp had diminished and the flame was just a flicker waving in a cool breeze that swept across the veranda. Carl had watched people exiting, saying long goodbyes, making their way home in the dark, some of them staggering and reeling from the night's imbibing. The crowd below was down to a few hangers-on waiting until the very end, perhaps to be kicked off the premises. He heard footsteps on the stairs. Earl appeared.

"There's food waiting for you downstairs," Earl said.

Carl was happy for the break. An awkward silence had ensued after he heard that it was mere coincidence that had brought John to the country. He was sceptical that his brother would have taken the time and energy to attend the funeral even if he had heard the news and been given the opportunity.

Far from easing his conscience, his long conversation with John had only succeeded in making Carl feel even guiltier that he hadn't been back to see his father, and how lonely Augusto must have been in his last few years. Listening to John talk about his wanderlust, Carl had found himself thinking about what a lonely life his brother must lead, and with that, he thought of Natasha and Alexei and Irina and how much he missed them.

Carl followed Earl downstairs to the kitchen. John trailed behind them.

The kitchen was filled with scents of freshly cooked food: the pungent odour of a curry simmering in a pot, the aroma of dough and oil and fresh *roti*, the starch of boiled rice recently strained.

"The two of you should have had your meal long before now," Sumintra chided them as they sat down at the table. "Empty sugar bags can't stand up, you know."

Carl smiled –he hadn't heard that saying in a long time. The aroma of the food made him realize how hungry he was. This would be his first solid meal since breakfast.

Carl took a seat at the table. John sat across from him.

As he started on the plate of food Sumintra placed before him, Carl was thankful for the tranquillity that had descended on the house. Gone were the unrelenting dissonance of the card and domino players and the constant noise of the rum drinkers who had grown increasingly belligerent as the evening progressed. The occupants of the house seemed to have taken it all in stride but he would gladly have locked the gates and kept everyone out. He hoped for some peace and calm over the next few days to finalise arrangements for the property.

"I want to thank you, again, for everything you've done since my arrival," Carl said to Sumintra. "I don't know what I would have done without you and Earl."

"You don't have to thank us," she said, without turning around from the sink where she was washing dishes.

"Still, it couldn't have been easy on all of you over the last few days, coping with my father's illness."

"The least we can do."

"I'd like to ask you about my father's last days, if you don't mind," Carl said. "I'm sure John would be interested too."

Sumintra turned around to face him. "What would you like to know," She said, wiping her hands on her apron.

"How long had he been sick, before he passed away?"

She tilted her head up to the ceiling, turned and looked out through the window. Carl didn't think it was such a difficult question. When she turned to face him again her face was flushed –was it from the cooking she'd just done? Uncle Jules had said that he'd brought her and Earl over to care for Augusto. Was the weight of the burden of caring for his father over the last few weeks now taking its toll?

"Jules asked us three months ago to come over and take care of your father. Prior to that, he was sick for many months," she said.

So, she was brought over mainly as a housekeeper?

Carl hesitated. He wanted to ask her: Why you? But, he thought it wasn't the right time, considering all she and her son had done, and the fact that his father had just been laid to rest.

"What was wrong with him back then?" Carl said.

"The doctor said he was suffering from dehydration and lack of nourishment. The real problem, he said, was that your father seemed to have lost the will to live."

"I can see that," John said. He'd already wolfed down several *rotis* and was working on another, scooping the curry up with pieces of *roti* and stuffing his mouth. It seemed as if he couldn't get enough of this type of food –something that was probably rare when he was at sea.

John continued: "He was holed up here all by himself in this big house. He'd lost a lot of weight –You should have seen how thin he was. The house was a mess, papers all over the place, dishes piled up in the sink. I swear: I even saw rats running around. I suspect that he was drinking too. I could smell it on his breath."

"He didn't look that bad... today," Carl said. "He must have been doing much better. I'm puzzled how it happened so suddenly."

"He was doing well," Sumintra said. "I cooked good food for him and he was eating again. I used to take his meals up to his room. I took good care of him."

"I'm sure you did," Carl said. "What happened? How did he die?"

"The doctor said: hypertension, colitis, and complications from cirrhosis of the liver. He was in pain when I took up his dinner that night –he was lying in bed, all curled up and moaning. He didn't want to go to the hospital –he said that he would never get out of there alive. We finally got him to agree later that night. He was in so much pain that he couldn't bear it any longer."

"Didn't people know that he was drinking?"

"In the last few months he used to lock himself up in his room and his study all day and night. No one was ever allowed to go into his study. I think he had liquor stored up there. Sometimes I did suspect he'd been drinking, but what could I do. You know how strong willed your father was, nobody could tell him anything he didn't want to hear."

"Who took him to the hospital?" Carl said.

"We all did, me, Patsy, Jimmy, in Earl's car."

"Who was there with him when he passed away?"

Sumintra's eyes misted over. The spots on her face were conspicuous, like a child showing signs of the aftermath of a small pox attack. She was the first East Indian he'd seen with freckles and they stood out prominently on her fair complexion. Singh –was it due to genes inherited from past generations of East Indians? How far we've all come, he thought –her ancestors all the way from the Punjab? His from Portugal, Patsy from somewhere in Africa. Continents on opposite ends of the globe, and yet, they'd taken routes or been led to British Guiana a long time ago.

Sumintra turned away to look through the window again.

Earl took up the story. "We sent word to your uncle who came down with hire-car early that morning."

"What was his condition like? Was he conscious, did he know who was there?"

"He was going in and out of consciousness most of the morning, moaning and groaning about the pain. At times I thought he knew who we were, but I wasn't sure. They did give him some painkillers, but that didn't seem to help much. He was too far gone, I guess."

"Did he talk to any of you? Did he say anything at all?"

"A lot of mumbling," Earl said. "A lot of words all jumbled up. He was talking about his father and grandfather, about Madeira and wine. He said something about *mistakes made, can't go back and undo what's done.*"

A dying man seeing his life flash before his eyes?

"But," Earl cleared his throat and hesitated. He looked Carl in the eyes. He seemed to be putting a great deal of thought into what he was going to say. He looked at his mother –she'd turned around to listen to him. Something, an understanding of sorts, seemed to have been exchanged between the two of them. "I know he did say at one time: *where are my children? I want to see my sons.*"

Carl had stopped eating a while back –his plate was still half-filled with food. He pushed the plate away and looked at John who lowered his head. Carl felt the hair on his arms and the back of his neck bristle, a giddy sensation suddenly overtaking him. *I want to see my sons.* His father's last words, and neither he, nor any of his brothers had been there to hear them or hold his father and offer him what little comfort they could.

"I'm sorry we were not there," Carl said. "I really appreciate what everyone did for him, in those last few days and hours of his life."

"We were happy to do it," Earl said.

Where do we go from here? They had been kind and generous, they had brought sustenance to his father when it was most needed. Should he offer them payment for all they'd done, or would he be insulting them if he brought up the subject? Before he left for Canada, he would have to broach the topic about occupancy of the house. Had rent been discussed with Uncle Jules? These were all questions that he needed to ask before he came to a decision on the future of the house, and he needed to ask them delicately. Today was not the right time.

CHAPTER 13 – The Strike

From: Secretary of State.

To: Embassy in United Kingdom

Washington, June 21, 1963, 7:03p.m.

Eyes only for Ambassador from the Secretary.

President wants you to know high importance he and I attach to reaching understanding with UK on British Guiana. This is principal subject President intends raise with the Prime Minister at Birch Grove and is main reason for my talks in London.

Our fundamental position is that the UK must not leave behind in the Western Hemisphere a country with a communist government in control. Independence for British Guiana with government led by RE-FORM is unacceptable to US. Our objective in London is to get HMG to take effective action to remove the Chairman's government prior to independence. As you know there has been long series of high-level exchanges this subject. Last fall the PM agreed to this objective but he has now reverted to view UK should wash its hands of British Guiana by granting early independence, leaving the mess on our doorstep.

I hope you will let it be known to the Foreign Secretary and the PM that President and I intend to focus on this subject while in England. I think it most important that we involve the Foreign Secretary. This is not jus a Colonial problem but one with the highest foreign policy implications. I would welcome your thoughts on how best to convince our British friends of deadly seriousness of our concern and our determination that

> *British Guiana shall not become independent with a Communist government.*

The house was alive: an active, energetic, pulsating entity that set its own pace and demanded attention.

Carl was in bed. Something had fallen on the rooftop, landed with a bang, followed by another and yet another: mangoes reaching maturity, swollen with juice, unable to maintain their tenuous hold on the stem, finally free-falling like parachutists jumping from an airplane. He had a headache, and this morning in particular, the sounds were like cannon balls being fired next to his ears. The slightest movement of his body sent waves of percussion thumping through his head, penetrating deep into his brain.

It was early, Friday. He had a hangover. This drinking during the week has got to stop, he thought.

He could hear the breeze moaning through the rafters, and the constant ping-ping of water dropping from the downspout. Moaning, groaning sounds caused by the wind sneaked through the eaves; floorboards creaked and shutters rattled. He heard voices from the house next door infiltrating through the windows and bouncing off the walls. One of the Lee girls was shouting to her sister to get going or they'd all be late –Just where in hell were they heading so early in the morning? He thought they were crazy. He heard a kisskadee calling: *kiss, kiss, kisskadee* and it seemed to be coming from the bathroom. A lorry passed on the road outside and the walls of his bedroom reverberated with the rumble. From the rooftop came the deafening trill of a fowl cock crowing.

There seemed to be no end to it all.

For Christ sake, he thought, the house had been completely rebuilt, expanded to twice its size and they'd only started reoccupying it last year. How can it be making all these sounds?

Finally, he was drifting back to sleep when he was awakened again. Something was caressing his cheeks –he thought it was a butterfly. He opened his eyes and looked around; nothing except the flickering ray of a sunbeam sneaking through one of the jalousie windows, creating a pattern of movement: dangling, gliding, swaying on his face. He turned around to face his bookshelf on the opposite end of the bedroom.

He rubbed his forehead. He knew he'd been out drinking with Wilfred and Cyril. He remembered coming in around one o'clock in the morning, sneaking in through the back door, thankful that no one was up. What happened before the drinking session? The evening was a blur, the afternoon missing from his consciousness, the morning a total washout. Working backwards was something that always gave him results when he was faced with a situation like this. He would start with last night, the cause of his hangover and headache...

***

The El Dorado Rum Shop and Beer Parlour in St. Jamestown was quiet when Carl arrived there around eight that evening, along with Cyril and Wilfred.

He remembered: He was the one who suggested they go for a drink. Frustration had been building up all week. He'd been wondering about his life after high school –he wasn't sure what he wanted to do. His options? Work for his father – no way! Join the civil service –boring! Go to Teachers Training College –not very appealing. On the way home that evening, as they passed the parlour, impulsively, he'd offered to buy his friends a beer. They'd readily accepted.

The place was almost empty: a bar man serving two customers sitting on stools, a solitary waitress standing around the jukebox.

Carl and his two friends took a table at the far end of the room and the waitress approached. She looked bored. She was East Indian – long black hair hanging free around her head, straight nose, small ears, and full lips. She had a round tray in one hand and she placed it on the table and leaned over.

"Hi, my name is Jasmine. I'm your waitress for the night. You boys want something to drink?" she said.

Jasmine wore a low-cut blue dress and had bosoms that heaved and rolled with her every gesture and movement. Carl was sure that if she leaned over a few more inches they would pop out of her bra.

Carl looked at Wilfred and Cyril and raised his eyebrows.

"Beer," Cyril said.

"Same for me," Wilfred said.

Wilfred had his eyes fixed on Jasmine's bosom.

"Me too," Carl said. "Something foreign, though."

Jasmine smiled. Her initial boredom had evaporated with the order for foreign beer. Perhaps she thought it had increased her prospects of a substantial tip from clientele who could afford it.

Jasmine picked up her tray and walked away. A few steps from the table, she looked back without turning around, her torso rotating a full sixty degrees from her slim waist. She had large eyes and she opened them wide, as she said: "You boys want a private room upstairs?"

Carl shook his head. El Dorado was a full-service bar, known for accommodating patrons who wanted additional fare after a night of drinking. He'd been there a couple of times over the last year. Tonight, he was not interested.

Jasmine walked away, slowly, her hips swaying, her rear gyrating, as if to the rhythm of the song coming from the jukebox *Sweets for my sweet, sugar for my honey*.

"Man, that is one big-batty woman." Wilfred said. "Did you see how she leaned over the table. Her boobs almost popped out."

"You wish," Carl said.

"How come you always looking at women backside?" Cyril asked him.

Wilfred sighed, long and hard. "I'd sure like to pluck Jasmine's flower. That's a woman to die for!" he said.

Wilfred turned to Carl and said: "Why didn't you take the private room upstairs?"

"To do what?"

"Remember East Of Eden, when James Dean visited his prostitute mother and he wanted to remain there? Well, I could live with Jasmine. She'd be my very own flower!"

"You're all mouth-talk," Carl said.

"He won't even know what to do with her," Cyril laughed.

"Would you?" Wilfred retorted.

Customers entered. A group of four men and two couples along with two single men. The group of four headed for the two billiard tables, the two couples occupied separate tables, and the single men went to the bar. Jasmine left the jukebox and approached one of the two tables to take orders.

More people came into the bar. The noise level in the room started to increase. A man was moving across the room, pausing at tables. Carl remembered him; it was Maxwell who lived at the far end of the Walk and had done handy man work for Carl's father. He was someone who came and went with the weather: fetch water from the well in the dry season, clear the drains in the wet season.

"Hey, what's up little boss?" Maxwell said, to Carl.

"Hey, Maxwell, what're you doing here?" Carl said.

Maxwell's response was to take off his bag from around his shoulder and open it.

The bag was filled with loose, unfiltered cigarettes. With the strike on, there was an acute shortage of cigarettes and few smokers could afford to buy an entire pack at the exorbitant prices that were being demanded. Vendors were now breaking down almost everything that was sold in packages into smaller, affordable portions.

"Want to buy cigarettes'?" Maxwell said.

"How much are they?" Carl said.

"You can buy one for thirty cents or two for fifty."

"Wow, volume discounts," Wilfred said.

"Don't smoke," Carl said, and Wilfred and Cyril shook their heads.

Maxwell closed his bag. He raised his eyebrows and said: "'How about flour, sugar, rice, I can get them all for you, any amount you want. Or anythin' else you want."

"At black market prices, I suppose," Cyril said, with a sneer.

"But 'ow you mean, man, what else?" Maxwell said. "A man gat to make a living these days, you know. I buy 'igh so I 'ave to sell 'igh."

Carl shook his head. Maxwell sighed and said: "You all can reach me right 'ere if you change yur mind."

"It's people like him causing this problem we having with price increases," Cyril said, after the man had moved on.

"He's just trying to make a living," Carl said. "Everyone is, these days."

"What next?" Wilfred said. "Are they going to charge by the puff for cigarettes?"

"Won't surprise me," Cyril said.

By nine o'clock the bar was packed, a late night crowd swelling it to jam-tight proportions. The liquor was flowing, men were sitting at the bar drinking, groups of three sat at tables playing dominoes, with people standing over them. The two billiard tables had been occupied non-stop. The atmosphere was acrid with smoke and noise filled the air: chairs scraped on the floor, glasses clinked, and the jukebox played continuous music.

Jasmine had come and gone several times and replenished their beer. Every time she walked away, Wilfred sighed and swooned at her retreating form.

At one of the billiard tables, a man was bent over, about to place his shot. He shook his head and straightened up, and as he did so, his face was spotlighted under the overhead light. The scar on the man's face was prominent even in the smoke-filled atmosphere.

Wilfred spotted the man at the same time. "Look, it's Scarface," he whispered. "He's been seen down at the Legislature almost every day this week."

Winslow had changed his position and was now bending over the table to take his shot.

"You mean he was picketing with the Republicans and Conservatives?" Carl said.

"Republicans, most likely," Cyril said. "Which other party could it be?"

Cyril's inference was clear. He was saying that the Republican was the party of Blacks, Winslow was Black, what other party could he belong to? Ever since the original Reform split into two, there was a gravitational pull of East Indians towards Reform and Blacks to the Republicans. Many Blacks, however, had remained with Reform and the Chairman often boasted about the universality of his party. Almost as if to substantiate his claim, the Chairman had placed a few Blacks in his cabinet.

Cyril's racist comments did not fit in with party philosophy. Cyril, along with some party members, held to the view that Reform should only have an East Indian membership. Wilfred, on the other hand, was open to all the other nationalities in the country and did not see a promising future for an independent country unless there was representation by all races in government.

"I don't know," Carl said. "He could belong to the Conservatives."

"No, he's definitely Republican," Wilfred said.

"How do you know that?" Carl said.

Wilfred laughed. "I have my sources," he said.

Wilfred was making his way upwards in the hierarchy of the Reform Youth Movement, and had already attained the position of Secretary. With the work his father had done in the early days of the formation of Reform party, Wilfred's rise was expected to be meteoric. The only real hindrance to his move upwards was the fact that Wilfred sometimes had a frivolous approach to politics and Carl sometimes considered him an uncommitted socialist. Nevertheless, he was always up to date with party goings-on.

"Police carried out a surprise raid at all three party headquarters early this week," Wilfred said. "They were looking for arms and ammunition. They were probably hoping to find some at our headquarters, but they didn't..."

Cyril interrupted him: "As if we'd be so stupid to keep arms and ammunition at party headquarters."

Carl looked at Cyril. Was he, therefore, implying that Reform *did* have arms and ammunition and was storing them some other place?

"They didn't find any arms at the Conservative or Republican office either," Wilfred continued, "but, they were surprised at something else that turned up at the Republican head office: documents about a secret organization responsible for creating insurrection and assassinating government ministers. The Chairman received an advance copy of the report."

"How does Winslow fit into that?" Carl said.

"He's believed to be one of the members of the group, along with a bunch of criminals. There is also American involvement in the plot."

Carl looked across the room to where Winslow was still playing billiards. Carl was sorry to hear that his neighbour was involved in a dirty tricks campaign. Still, everything seemed to be driven by race these days, and why not? Winslow, who had something of a deprived childhood with little chance for advancement, probably felt a lot more comfortable being part of the Republican party, rather than the East Indian dominated Reform.

"Tell him about Perough," Cyril said to Wilfred.

"Perough has to leave the country. He was sent here to organize the trade union movement and disrupt the government."

"Probably working for the CIA," Cyril said.

"Or, the American labour movement," Wilfred said.

Or, both, Carl thought.

"I know about Perough," Carl said.

"Aha, he approached you too?" Cyril opened his eyes wide.

"Yes, he did, at school, not too long ago."

"What did he want?"

"Same thing he probably asked you and Wilfred to do –tell him who's in the youth arm and what we're up to."

"Did you give him the information?"

Carl felt his stomach heave and his head sway. The fact that Cyril felt there was even a need to ask, made Carl wonder how he really felt about their friendship. For the first time, he had an impulse to reach over and punch Cyril, but he realized after a while, that it was the alcohol that was driving his precipitous thoughts and he managed to retain control of his emotions, but not before he said: "How could you even ask me a stupid question like that? Do you, for one minute think I would even consider giving him information?"

Cyril started to stutter. He did this when he became excited. He said: "How come you never told us about this before now?"

"How come *you* never told me before now?" Carl said.

"Kennedy is travelling to meet Prime Minister MacMillan in London later this month," Wilfred said. He seemed to be attempting to diffuse the situation. "The Chairman is sure they're going to postpone independence talks, using the strike and disturbances as the reason. They're going to argue that they can't discuss the subject if there is no stability in the colony."

"Playing right into the opposition's hands," Carl said.

"There was another explosion last night, this one at the Ministry of Home Affairs," Cyril said. "All part of the campaign to destabilize the government."

Opposition supporters had begun squatting at government offices at the start of the strike, trying to block workers from functioning. When that had proven ineffective, they had resorted to placing dynamite and other incendiary devices in the buildings. It was the start of a terror campaign designed to delay independence talks and ultimately lead to the suspension of the constitution, again.

Carl shook his head. "I can't understand why they want to do this," he said. "They can't gain anything much from it. All they're doing is hurting innocent people and damaging public property."

"They attacked the Chairman and other cabinet members outside the Legislature last week," Cyril said.

"The Assistant Commissioner and the Chairman's body guard had to fire shots in the air to disperse the mob," Wilfred said.

"Must have been another attempt to assassinate the Chairman," Cyril said.

Nothing had been reported about that in the media. But, that was Cyril, always seeing a conspiracy in everything.

"Was Augusto down there, too?" Cyril asked.

"Yes, he was," Wilfred replied.

"So, he was involved in the attempt, then?"

"There's no way my father would have been involved in that," Carl said.

"How do you know that?" Cyril said. "If he was down there picketing, he had to take part in it"

"There you go, jumping to conclusions," Carl said. His voice was reaching a high pitch, again, something that he couldn't help, and the alcohol was driving most of it. "I know my father has strong convictions about Reform, something he and I don't agree on, but there is no way that he would be involved in an assassination."

Carl had to stop and think, however: was he leaping to his father's defence purely out of blood ties? How well do you really know anyone? His father had stooped very low to report the Communist affiliation of both Cyril and Wilfred's fathers back in 1953, and he still had undisguised contempt for Reform and everything it stood for. Was it, therefore, unreasonable to believe that he could be involved in a conspiracy to assassinate the Chairman?

"I'm not jumping to conclusions. The facts are there for everyone to see," Cyril said.

"Then, you're even more stupid than I thought," Carl said.

"Who do you think you're calling stupid?" Cyril stood up, his stand now menacing.

"At least the Assistant Commissioner took some action," Wilfred said.

"Only happens once in a blue moon," Cyril said. He sat down. "The whole police force is anti-Reform and always turns a blind eye to action taken against the party and the government. We need to start arming our own supporters to defend themselves."

A rumour was circulating within party ranks that Reform might bring in Cuban troops to repel the strong-arm tactics being used by the opposition. Carl didn't think there was any merit in the rumour since foreign affairs in the colony were still controlled by the British Government and they would never allow such a move to take place, unless the party was using clandestine methods to smuggle the Cubans into the country. Cyril seemed to be working himself into a fit over the entire situation.

Of his two friends, Carl considered Cyril to be the most radical. His views did not provide for any compromise with the opposition if it meant reducing Reform's power.

Maxwell had circulated around the entire bar and was making his exit. Jasmine was delivering a tray of beer to a table. Winslow was sucking on his beer and looking at another player about to execute his shot at the table.

"Opposition supporters have started attacking East Indians in the city," Wilfred said.

"What's Augusto and the Conservative doing about it?" Cyril said.

"I don't think that the Conservatives are involved in this as much as the Republicans," Carl said.

"It's turning into a racial confrontation," Wilfred said. "The violence is spreading to East Indian dominated areas where they're retaliating against the few Blacks who happen to live there."

"Had to happen, and we're all going to be caught in the middle," Carl said. "Before you know it, the violence will spread all over the country."

"Might all end up in civil war," Cyril said.

Tension was growing between the two major races in the colony, urban Blacks versus rural East Indians, with minorities caught in the middle. Despite his loyalty to Reform and what it stood for, Carl was anxious about how it would all end, especially for the Portuguese, like him and his family.

Carl was feeling the effects of the alcohol that he'd consumed over the course of the night. He stood up, his head reeling. Time to leave –he would take a taxi home.

***

Beer followed by rum: A lethal mixture under the best circumstances, even worse on an empty stomach, as bad as pouring oil on a fire. That's what had done him in, Carl concluded.

A lorry passed on the road outside. Another rumble. Carl's stomach was feeling it. A wave of nausea overwhelmed him and he was glad that he was still in bed. He tried to recall how many beers he'd had last night. He counted: one when he went into the El Dorado, another by eight-thirty; one more after he came back from the washroom. Total: three. He ordered another round when Wilfred started to dance with Jasmine. He'd bought a bottle of rum afterwards and they had started on that, finishing it before the night was over.

The visit to El Dorado had been a badly needed respite for Carl after a long day. He remembered: They'd gone to Liberty House, party headquarters after school as volunteers, helping to package foodstuff for people who were suffering from the effects of shortages caused by the strike. This was how it should always be, he thought: a government that governs for all, not just its supporters, like with Reform helping people in the city even though they had very little support there.

They'd remained at Liberty House until after seven, when they'd left for home.

Something else had happened earlier that morning, an event that disturbed Carl and left him with a feeling of helplessness...

He had passed through St. Jamestown, riding his bicycle on the way to school. Shops were all closed, proprietors selling through a small opening in the shutters. Long lines of people were waiting to purchase whatever was available. Just a week ago, food riots broke out at the Market Place. Almost all basic staples: rice, flour, cooking oil were short and shopkeepers had taken to rationing supplies, and in most situations, only selling to their regular customers.

He passed St. Jamestown Bakery. A long queue had formed outside the entrance to buy bread. A guard was admitting customers, one at a time. The cake shop, owned by a Portuguese woman was completely shuttered, so was the pharmacy next to it. The rum shop was open even though it was mid morning and a man staggered out and headed down the street. Some people still had money to buy rum. Some people didn't know where their priorities lay.

The strike was taking a toll on the city. The situation was reaching crisis proportions and would only get worse before it got better. The opposition continued to block importation of food supplies that would ease the shortage and the government was trying to bring in supplies from Cuba to alleviate the crisis.

Bands of Republican youths were roaming the city attacking East Indians. They didn't care if people had a political affiliation or not: If you were East Indian you were presumed to be a member of Reform. Carl had run into such a gang on the way to school that morning. He was on his bicycle, heading up Camp Street, just passing Regent when he saw them heading south. There were about a hundred Black youths, the oldest not more than thirteen, and they were spread out across the road, blocking traffic from moving in both directions. There were no police officers in sight.

Carl saw several East Indian boys in school uniforms accosted, punched and relieved of their bicycles and schoolbooks. He knew –if he had the misfortune to be an East Indian in the wrong place at the wrong time, he too would surely be in harm's way.

***

Another mango fell on the roof, another explosion in Carl's head.

He heard a rap on his bedroom door. What now?

The knob turned, the door opened and his father entered.

"Carl, I heard you coming in very late last night," his father said. "Where were you?"

Carl always believed that half-truths were better than a total lie. He was with Cyril and Wilfred, he had been to school earlier that day, and at one time or the other, he did plan to study with them after school.

"Had a study session with Cyril and Wilfred," Carl said.

"As late as that?"

I'm eighteen, I can stay out how late I want to, Carl thought.

Carl nodded. "Final year," he said. "Advance levels coming up."

With the successful completion of his Advanced Levels he would finish high school and get on with the next phase of his studies. He still hadn't decided what the next phase would be, though.

"You've been out late many nights this week," his father said. "You're still a young man, you know. Too many late nights are not good for you. You're burning the candle at both ends."

That's what all old men tell their young sons. They forget that they did the same thing when they were that age. This happens when old men become hypocrites.

"I have everything under control."

"I still think you should limit the number of late nights."

Carl didn't have the energy for an argument. He sighed and nodded.

"Carl, I want you to come with me down to the Legislature," his father said.

An imperial command. Augusto had never made a request like that before.

Another cannon fired close to Carl's ears. He shook his head, slowly, painfully. It was going to be one of those sessions, and he had no stomach for it this morning.

"We're picketing again, today. We need all the support we can get," Augusto said.

His father had been down to the Legislature almost every day since the general strike started back in April 18th. The strike and picketing were the latest attempts by the two opposition parties to cripple the Reform government.

Carl remembered Cyril's remarks about the unruly mob.

"Was there an attempt to assassinate the Chairman?" Carl asked his father.

Augusto pulled back his shoulders and snapped his head upwards. "Não seja ridículo. Don't be ridiculous," he said. "Where in the world did you get that preposterous idea from?"

"Just a rumour I heard. Was there a mob down there?"

Augusto shrugged. "They can call it anything they want. We are not a mob. We have the right to protest against an unjust law. This is what democracy is all about. Do you think they can do things like that in Cuba or Russia?"

How do you know? You've never been to Cuba or Russia!

Carl was silent. It was one of his father's favourite tactics. He often fell back on attacking countries with socialist or Communist governments whenever he was confronted with criticism about methods employed by the Republican and Conservative parties. His father made no distinction between Communism and Socialism. To him the end always justified the means. Even the socialist leaning Labour Party of the U.K came in for severe censure by him when they undertook measures that were meant to raise the living conditions of the working class there. If it had anything to do with trade unions or was not to the benefit of unfettered free enterprise, his father was totally against it.

"The Chairman's bodyguards are just too trigger-happy," Augusto continued. "They think they're in the wild-west playing cowboys and Indians. They suddenly started firing at us without any provocation."

"Did they fire at you or in the air?"

"Doesn't matter, someone could have been seriously hurt. They have no right to do that. There is still law and order in this colony."

But you and the other supporters of your party have the right to stop the Legislature from carrying on its legitimate business and passing meaningful legislation that will benefit all the workers of the colony!

After last year's incident, when that mob moved in on the Chairman's car and started rocking it back and forth, Carl could see where the Chairman's bodyguards were not taking any more chances.

"How can you blame them?" Carl said.

Augusto raised his voice and the sound of it bounced off the walls and ricocheted back and forth in Carl's head. "De que lado você está, afinal? Whose side are you on, anyhow? Don't you comprehend what's happening to this colony, that it's all heading downhill under Reform?"

And you think that the Conservatives, with big business behind them, will take care of the common man? Or that the Republicans are not in it just for the power grab?

"I'm not taking sides," Carl said. He couldn't help it. He'd also raised his voice in response. "All I'm saying is that the leader of the government deserves some respect, no matter which party leader it is, doesn't he? Wouldn't you want the same treatment for the leader of the Conservatives if he was head of the government?"

"The Conservatives and their leader would never act like that. If the Chairman wants respect he must act like a leader, not like a Communist stooge under the control of Moscow or Havana."

As opposed to being a stooge for London or Washington, I suppose?

Carl shook his head. He knew he couldn't win this argument and he was sorry he ever started it.

"Well, are you coming or not?" Augusto said.

"Can't." His voice was much calmer, in an attempt to be conciliatory. "I have mid-term exams coming up soon."

"This is very important."

"I'm getting together with Cyril and Wilfred for a study session."

"The future of the colony at stake."

"My future is at stake, Dad."

"We have to take action now," Augusto urged him, "while both the Conservatives and Republicans are united. We have to defeat this legislation before it gets off the ground."

It was all a reaction to new legislation that the Reform government had introduced back in March, meant to revamp the process of certifying unions by enabling a free vote by workers. Reform felt that there was too much centralization of power in the Consolidated Trade Unions, an organization that claimed to represent all unions in the colony –both rural agricultural and urban factory. Reform, with its rural based support, knew that if there were a free vote, the Reform backed Union of Agricultural Workers would be accepted as the primary bargaining unit, and this would break CTU's stranglehold over the unions, also enabling the new union to negotiate better benefits for agricultural workers and cement Reform's reputation as a champion of the working class. The opposition supported CTU knew that this would eviscerate its power –they were not going to let that happen.

Carl shook his head. "Can't do it, Dad," he repeated.

Augusto walked around the foot of the bed and stopped near Carl's bookshelf. He passed his hand through the spine of the books on the top shelf. What was he doing –checking for dust or Communist literature? Carl was happy that he only kept schoolbooks at home. Whatever reading he did on socialism was done at his friends' house or at party headquarters.

Augusto pulled out his watch, held it up to his right ear, and then, looked at it. He seemed to have something else on his mind.

"I hear that Cyril and Wilfred are now active in the Reform Youth Movement," Augusto said, as he turned to face Carl.

Carl froze. How did the Old Man hear that about Wilfred and Cyril? Joseph was the only person in the family to whom Carl had mentioned it. Was Augusto also fishing to obtain information on Carl's activities?

"I don't know about that," Carl lied.

"You do know, of course, that Reform is using its youth membership arm to indoctrinate young people and convert them to Communism?" Augusto said.

The two opposition parties are also indoctrinating their young people. What else could you expect from the big business supported Conservative party and the so-called socialist Republican party which was opposing Reform for the sake of opposing, even if the badly needed transformation of the colony was delayed?

Carl didn't respond.

Augusto continued: "The only way to make true progress in this colony is to get rid of Reform and its youth movement. To do that, we have to oppose every piece of legislation that they bring to the house."

The two opposition minority parties had indeed vigorously opposed the labour law when it was introduced in the Legislature. Demonstrations were held, with both party leaders and their supporters picketing and denouncing the government in front of the Legislature. On April 5th, rioting and looting broke out again in the city, in a mini Black Friday reminiscent of Friday 16th February last year. Here we go again, Carl had thought.

Carl would not get involved in the opposition's plans. The Republicans and the Conservatives could all go to hell, as far as he was concerned.

"Sorry, dad," Carl said. "Not something that I want to get into at this time. I want to focus on my final year."

His father's disappointment was clear –Carl could see it: raised eyebrows, bottom lip pursed, a frown overtaking his features. He was fast getting red in the face.

"Eu sei disso! I know that!" Augusto said. "I'd like you to spare a couple of hours. It's very important. You could learn a very valuable lesson from all of this."

So, that was what his father was hoping to accomplish! He was trying to pre-empt Carl from getting involved with the youth movement.

Carl's father was not one to give up easily. "The entire labour movement is being threatened with extinction if this legislation is passed. Our party will not rest if this government doesn't back down."

That was the way his father often referred to Reform: it was *this government*, not *our government* or *the government*. Reform had been democratically elected, but his father would never consider that in his anti-government activity. As far as he was concerned, anything that Reform did was illegal and immoral.

"I hear you, Dad, but I still don't have the time."

"Thomas is coming. Why can't you come, at least this once?"

Because I don't want to, because Thomas is your lapdog who will do anything you ask him to do, because you, along with all the other members of the opposition, have done nothing but obstruct the elected government that is trying to bring meaningful change to a colonial system geared to keep working class people in chains for the rest of their lives.

"Just can't do it," Carl said.

His father shook his head, looked at his watch, circled back at the foot of the bed. He seemed poised to make his exit. He deliberated for a few seconds then, turned to face Carl.

"I hope you're not thinking of joining Reform youth arm, like those friends of yours," Augusto said. "Would be a very big mistake on your part. I won't stand for it, not while you're under my roof."

Carl sighed and closed his eyes. This was nothing new: His father was known for issuing ultimatums. It was one of the reasons why he could never tell the Old Man that he was already a member of the RYM.

Augusto headed for the door. In a few seconds he was gone and Carl heard footsteps echoing down the hallway.

Carl lay in bed, thinking of his father's parting words. If his father ever found out about the connection with the RYM, there would be a confrontation resulting in his father kicking him out the house. Since he had no intention of leaving the RYM, Carl would have to make other arrangements in future.

Another mango crashed onto the rooftop. Carl's head started throbbing again. The house was still alive.

CHAPTER 14 -A Life In Pictures and Words

WEDNESDAY 26ᵀᴴ NOVEMBER 1980

The room was dark, the only light coming from slivers of sunlight penetrating the slats of the Demerara windows.

Carl pushed open a window and it moved outwards on its upper hinges. The morning sunlight filled the room with dazzling brilliance. He opened a second, then a third window and turned around to take a look at the room.

Two walls of his father's study were lined with shelves and they were crammed with books and papers. A phonograph player with records stood on one of the shelves. A large desk stood in the middle of the room. He couldn't see the top of the desk –it was covered with stacks of papers, each stack aspiring to be the tallest of the lot and the top leaning precariously to the right or left. Five metal filing cabinets stood against one of the walls. Trays were on top of the cabinets and these sagged with piles of paper. Cardboard cases were stacked against the fourth wall. A Smith-Corona typewriter stood on the right side of the desk, a sheet of paper still wound in the carriage.

Where to start?

He'd been up early and seen John as he left to catch his boat. After his younger brother left, a feeling of complete desolation had overtaken Carl, knowing there was no conceivable way of getting in touch with John when he was at sea. It meant that the possibility of meeting his younger brother again sometime in the future was as remote as their recent one after sixteen years.

The room smelled musty. It was four times the size of the portico in the old house and that had been packed to the ceiling with his father's collection of documents, old newspapers and paraphernalia. When the money had started to flow, his father had redesigned and rebuilt the entire house to be the showpiece of the neighbourhood. The oak panel walls in the study were lined with teak bookshelves. The increased space had sufficed to expand Augusto's interests and his love of collecting memorabilia.

The idea behind the larger house was to eventually have all Augusto's sons and their family live with him. Carl had always felt that his father's motive was to rule over the household like a Lord of the manor and have his children follow his orders and carry out his wishes. In the end, the house seemed to have been turned into a mausoleum for Augusto's collection of papers and documents.

Where to start?

Pictures hanging on the wall showed Augusto and the leader of the Conservative party and members who were legislators. Carl remembered parties thrown for his father's business associates and the hierarchy of the Conservatives when his father was planning to run for the Legislature. His father had been making all the right connections and moving in the right circles, and for a while it looked as if the Old Man would rise in the upper echelon of the party. Carl even suspected that he'd been aiming for leadership at one time.

Where to start?

He walked over to the cardboard cases stacked uniformly against the wall. He was curious about them. He counted thirty-six cases piled in six columns.

The labels facing outwards on the cases: *Vinho da Roda Superior Madeira Wine.*

Exported for Augusto Dias. Agent for British Guiana and West Indies

These were his father's premium Madeira that he always boasted about, the wine that he expected to raise in value and make him a small fortune. After the disturbances back in 1962, when he'd lost everything in the store and the success of his business prospects rested solely on the wine business, he had stored cases of Madeira at home, fearful of a repetition of the looting and arson that took place back then.

Carl lifted off the nearest case from the top row and opened it. The case had cardboard cells filled with bottles. He pulled out one of the bottles. The bottle was empty; he could still detect the stale but lingering aroma of the Madeira, along with an instant recollection of Christmas and special occasions where wine was an integral part of the celebration.

He opened the top case in each of the six columns and found that every case contained empty bottles. He was puzzled and intrigued. What did it mean? In a fit of anxiety, he started opening all the crates in the lower tiers, rummaging through them one by one. In less than an hour he'd checked them all and the entire stash was now scattered over the floor. He'd found empty bottles in every case. All three hundred and sixty bottles were empty.

The vintage Madeira that Augusto had often boasted about was now gone.

Carl sat down on the chair behind the desk, his head resting on his hands. He was afraid of the implications of what he was seeing.

Sumintra had said she suspected Augusto was stashing alcohol in either the study or his bedroom. Carl had found no liquor in his father's bedroom. It was in the study that Augusto had kept the last of his imports. The market had dried up due to the poor economy, caused mainly by the uncertainty in the political situation. He'd rather drink it all than sell it at reduced prices, and in the end, it was this that had led to his failing health, and ultimately to his death.

Carl found it distressing: The Old Man had become a solitary drinker, drowning his sorrows at the bottom of a bottle. How many of the thirty-six cases of wine had he himself drunk? There always seemed to be a predilection for alcohol consumption in the tropics and Carl remembered his teenage years, the rum shop where he drank with his friends and their late-night drinking binges. His grandfather drank, his father drank, all his older brothers drank at one time or the other; it seemed to be something that became ingrained after a while. He remembered Thomas staggering home on several occasions after all-night parties and James having to be brought home by friends. Before he was married, Joseph was the biggest drinker of them all, Augusto threatening to take away his key and lock him out of the house if he didn't stop his wanton ways. Was a part of this inherited, or was it simply due to the culture, something that was inescapable, as sure as the rainy season followed the dry? It seemed to be made a lot easier by the low cost of a bottle of rum available in every rum shop in every street corner in a country where rum was an important export. If he hadn't left, would he have eventually ended up an alcoholic as his father?

Augusto came from strong immigrant stock. He was someone who knew what he wanted out of life and had made a fortune by the time he was thirty-five. What was it that had brought his downfall? Family lent stability and respectability to a man as he aged, something for him to live for and boast about. What could Augusto say to anyone? That all his children had abandoned him and left him on his own?

Now that he was separated from Natasha and their two kids and had no one to share his life, it struck Carl that his own life was unfolding similar to his father's later years. Was he doomed to go down the same road? He couldn't help wondering: would it have made a difference if the Old Man still had his sons around? Would it have made a difference if Carl himself had been there?

Carl stacked the empty crates as best as he could; he would ask Earl to arrange for their disposal. He moved over to the filing cabinets.

The cabinets were all locked. This had to be where the Old Man kept his most important documents. Sumintra had provided a ring with keys: a different key for each cabinet, and then still more keys on the ring.

The first cabinet had a label with the words *Accounts Payable Invoices*. Carl opened it and pulled out a folder. It contained invoices and payment reminders from The Great Madeira Wine Company for twenty-four cases of fine Madeira wine shipped to Augusto Dias And Sons. There was no indication that the invoices had been paid. All the other folders contained invoices from various suppliers.

The second cabinet contained more folders. Carl pulled out one: it had a numeric sequence of invoices from Augusto Dias And Sons to customers. The third cabinet contained Accounts Receivable invoices and correspondence between Augusto and different businesses.

Augusto had always been an organized man, someone who believed in a place for everything and everything in its place. Where did he keep the will, if he had made one?

The top drawer of the fourth cabinet contained two scrapbooks and the remaining three drawers were crammed with loose newspaper clippings. Carl pulled out the two scrapbooks. The first was filled; the second was empty. Was it that Augusto had never found the time to paste clippings into the second book or had he just given up? Carl opened up the first –the clippings had turned brittle and yellow, as if the book hadn't seen the light of day in a long time. Newspapers lay in stacks, some on the desk, more on the floor, clippings to be culled from them.

Augusto had written the date and some notation in red ink on the clippings. Carl rifled through the pages, pausing to look at a few that caught his attention. The headings on the clippings stood out, stark and damning. They brought back memories…

16th February 1962: *Governor And U.S Council General Lament Turn Of Events And The Introduction Of racism Into The Political Scene.*

Carl thought: British troops could have prevented the disturbances and the subsequent burning and looting if the Governor had acted sooner. Why would the U.S Council General lament something that was deliberately aided and abetted by the Americans through the C.I.A and the Guiana Labour Unions? It was the old divide and conquer approach. Hypocrites to the very end!

23rd October 1962: *Start of Independence Talks in London.*

Another exercise in futility for Reform!

25th March 1963: *Government Introduces New Labour Relations Bill.*

The Bill that was meant to uplift the standard of living for the sugar workers but ended up being vehemently opposed by the two opposition parties and becoming a cause for outside intervention.

24th May 1964: *Disturbances at Wismar.*

Disturbances: a vast understatement. When the details came out later about what had transpired at Wismar, it left most of the country in shock. A Judicial Enquiry later would reveal facts about what people had suspected, but these were never reported in the media.

Wismar was located across the river from McKenzie, the Bauxite town sixty miles down the Demerara River. Wismar was where his oldest brother Joseph lived with his wife Frances and daughter Bernadette. McKenzie was where Joseph worked. They were home at Wismar when the so-called Disturbance occurred, something that would not be easily forgotten by Joseph.

Long before the enquiry was held and the information came out about what had transpired, Carl had known what had taken place...

***

It was the late afternoon newsflash on radio that alerted Carl and everyone else at home to the events at Wismar: There has been a radio report of a : *"... disturbance at Wismar and hundreds of people are being evacuated by ferry to Georgetown. Evacuees are being housed temporarily at the vacant Textile Factory in the Veldt. Arrangements are being made for their relocation to more suitable accommodation. In the meanwhile, relatives are urged to make contact and facili-*

tate their move to more permanent quarters. The situation at Wismar is now under control..."

Carl had wondered: if the situation was under control, why were people being evacuated? Since there was no overland route, the journey to Georgetown would take close to four hours by river. If refugees were already arriving, whatever had transpired would have happened during the previous night. If Joseph was affected, it meant that he and his family would have had to spend a tumultuous night somewhere, before being rescued and brought to the city.

Augusto drove his car, Carl and Thomas accompanying him. They followed a stream of visitors through the front entrance and along a corridor to the factory in the rear. A door opened out to a landing that overlooked the shop floor. Carl paused on the landing and took in the scene below him.

There once must have been a steady hum rising from below: the buzz of forklifts moving bales of raw material, workers tending machines engaged in the manufacturing process, and crates of shirts and dresses being moved off the floor. This had all been gutted when the economy nose-dived following the 1962 riots and arson. In place of a busy shop floor, in an area as big as a cricket ground, was what appeared to be a mass of humanity, some of them on cots, many of them lying on sheets spread out on the ground. An attempt had been made to organize the refugees into rows, with aisles separating them, but it appeared that the building had filled up faster than expected and now, even the aisles were occupied.

It was impossible to determine exactly how many people were bedded down on the factory floor, but Carl estimated that it had to be at least a couple of thousand. McKenzie and Wismar were all essentially Black dominated areas with populations of tens of thousands. He hadn't even known that there were that many non-Blacks living in the region, and now, there had been a mass evacuation of those people, in what essentially had turned out to be an ethnic cleansing operation. A similar action was sure to follow in areas where there were East Indian majorities.

It was madness. Where would it all stop? Carl thought of the old saying: an eye for an eye. The only problem with that policy –everyone ended up blind!

Carl followed Thomas and Augusto down the stairs. They went through the first aisle looking for Joseph and his family. Carl saw a man sitting, staring into space, a woman next to him crying, a child sleeping in-between them. A man and a woman in the next stall were drinking something hot from a mug and eating salt-biscuits. A woman, sitting alone on the ground, was asking every passer-by: *Do you see my husband Ramlall anywhere?* A man had his head wrapped in a blood-soaked bandage. Many people were wrapped in sheets; Carl suspected that they had no clothes of their own. As he passed through the aisles, Carl realized that every cot, every position on the floor was occupied by people, who were perhaps asking themselves the age-old question: *Why did it have to happen to me?* Perhaps they were all reliving a night of horror that would remain with them for the rest of their lives.

Carl found himself trailing behind Augusto and Thomas. His father and brother seemed obsessed –they had to find Joseph. Carl was also interested in finding his oldest brother and his family, but he also couldn't overcome the magnitude of the disaster he was seeing, and it disturbed him. He wanted to stop and offer help to people, to tell them that they were not alone, that the Reform party and the government would see them back on their feet. How does one console people who have managed to escape a violent event with nothing but the clothes they're wearing, and in some instances, with loved ones who were missing?

They went through every aisle and Carl looked at every face, heard every moan and groan, smelled the ever present odour of fear. How was it that there was no limit at times to man's inhumanity to man?

Finally, they came to the last aisle. Up to that point there had been no sign of Joseph and his family. A growing sensation was taking hold, deep down, in Carl's stomach, that something terrible had happened to Joseph and his family. Could it be that they hadn't made it at all?

In the middle of the last aisle they came upon Joseph sitting on a cot, alone, and Carl and Thomas rushed over to meet their brother. Joseph had the same blank stare that Carl had seen often that day. It was the look of someone who had survived a battle where the enemy had attacked with overwhelming numbers, and he was now trying to figure out how he'd made it out alive when everyone else had perished.

"Where's Frances?" Carl asked.

"Where's Bernadette?" Thomas said.

Joseph did not respond. He looked at the two brothers as if he had no idea what they were talking about.

Augusto held Joseph by his shoulders and shook him gently. "Joseph, we've come to take you home. Where're Frances and Bernadette?"

"Frances? Bernadette?"

"Yes, your wife and daughter. Where are they?"

Carl looked around. He didn't see the familiar faces of his sister-in-law and his niece anywhere.

"Where are they?" Augusto repeated.

Joseph squinted, rubbed his eyes with his knuckles and opened them wide. He shook his head several times, as if he were trying to wake up from a nightmare. Reality must have come back to him suddenly; he pushed Augusto away and buried his head in his hands. "Frances and Bernadette," he whispered. "They're gone, gone."

Later that night, at home in the Walk, Joseph told his story...

"We heard rumours earlier this week. A member of the

Republican party, a member of the Legislature, was in town. He was telling the residents that they had to be vigilant, that there were Reform activists going from town to town, trying to stir up trouble, and that the people in the town had to take action to prevent this.

"We thought they were just wild rumours –how could East Indian Reform activists be trying to stir up trouble in a majority Black town? He was provoking the Republican supporters to take action against the minorities. We thought, though, that we had nothing to worry about. After all, there was a coalition between the Conservatives and the Republicans. Most of the Conservative supporters were Portuguese. Being Portuguese, we didn't think they would bother us.

"We were just finished with supper when our neighbour rushed over to tell us that there were gangs moving through the town, picking on anyone who was not Black. We still didn't think we'd be at risk. We thought they were only picking on East Indians. We decided to head for the ferry stelling to play it safe. We'd catch the first ferry to Georgetown.

"We lived about half a mile from the stelling. We were not too far from the boat when a mob appeared. They surrounded us. I pleaded with them, told them that we had been living there for many years, that we were Conservative supporters. They didn't care. They were mainly young people out of control. It was all a game for them. I tried to hold on to Frances and Bernadette but they snatched them from me and knocked me to the ground when I fought back. They took them off to a nearby building. I heard their screams. I didn't know what was being done to them, but I could imagine why a woman and a young girl would scream like that. She was just nine –Bernadette was just nine! I can still hear her and her mother screaming! I tried breaking loose several times; I was punched, hit on the head, stomped, and there was nothing I could do about it. They dumped the three of us in the river.

"I tried holding on to them in the water, but a swift current pulled us apart. I swam around, I don't know for how long, looking for them in the dark. I lost track of time. I never saw them again…never. I saw a light. It was a boat with British soldiers combing the river, looking for survivors. They rescued me. I didn't want to leave without Frances and Bernadette, but the soldiers told me that they couldn't guarantee my safety if I remained.

"What do you say when you see your wife and daughter killed right before your very eyes?"

Carl came across more clippings.

31st January 1964: *Reform Holds Country Wide Freedom Rally To Protest Imposition of Duncan Sandy's Formula For Proportional Representation.*

Carl had attended that rally.

4th March 1964: *Bomb Thrown Into Bus At Tain, Berbice.*

East Indians were retaliating against violent acts committed on East Indians in predominantly Black areas and Blacks were taking it out on East Indians for similar acts committed in East Indian dominated areas. The country was on the verge of civil war. Some politicians were even daring to call for partition of the three counties.

15th April 1964: *Bomb thrown at a Reform Member of Legislature.*

Politicians were being attacked.

23rd May 1964: *Over Sixty People Beaten and robbed In Georgetown.*

Wilfred and Cyril had narrowly escaped a beating several times.

26th May 1966: The last clipping in the scrapbook.

British Guiana Gains Independence Under coalition between Republicans and Conservatives Adopting The Name of Guyana.

A note was scribbled in red in-between paragraphs of the article:

1966: tumultuous year. Independence comes amidst a climate of fear and lack of hope for the future welfare of the country.

The last clipping: perhaps, for Augusto, it marked the end of an era, something he wanted to put behind him.

Carl moved on.

The fifth cabinet contained documents, many of which he'd seen over the years.

Two travel documents, both crisp and faded were stored in plastic envelopes. One was issued in 1843 in Funchal, Madeira, to great-great grandfather, Carlos Dias, described as twenty years, sixty-two inches, small eyes, and swarthy complexion. Another issued to great-great grandmother Maria Fernandes, seven years, accompanying her parents Jose and Theresa Fernandes. An invoice for forty-nine pipes of Madeira wine shipped by the Madeira Wine Company on the S.S. Nonpareil 13 de Setembro, 1873. A printed invitation to the wedding of his father Augusto Dias and his mother Mary De Santos in 1935 was in an envelope.

Family pictures, all sepia, separated by sheets of thin paper, each with markings on the back showing the identity of everyone in the picture. Carl flicked through: Pictures taken of groups based on filial connections, groups based on matrimonial connections, groups based on heritage. He'd seen them all before. A family tree showing the descent from the very first Dias, Carlos, down to the current generation, with accompanying notes on those who had preceded him back in Madeira, going as far back as the fourteenth century. Short biographical notes were documented on the descendants of Carlos, showing their accomplishments and business connections in the colony. Augusto had done his research well: it showed pride in people who had arrived with little or nothing and worked to accumulate great wealth in a system designed to foster improvement through initiative. The small Portuguese population had eventually succeeded in dominating the commercial landscape of the colony through cartels engaged in fixing prices. No wonder Augusto had a firmly entrenched view that there was no room for socialism anywhere.

Carl saw items relating to Augusto's business and entrepreneurial spirit. One was his business registration with the city and a dollar note labelled *First Dollar Earned*. Another item: a copy of his first income tax return filed with the Department Of Inland Revenue.

Carl came across a commendation granted to Augusto Dias in 1962 by the Chamber of Commerce. His father had been awarded it for making the highest contribution to underprivileged children that year. The award also praised him for a lifetime devoted to enriching the lives of those who were needy and destitute. Nineteen sixty-two was the year of the riots, the year when Augusto lost his business and a small fortune. It was the year when the city was reeling under the wanton destruction of property and business, when unemployment rose sharply and the economy had nosedived. Yet, Augusto had made a contribution, at a time when it was most needed, but when he could least afford to: a side of his father that Carl had never known. His father had often bragged of his roots, boasted of his business accomplishments to many people, but he'd never made public his charitable work. It was like moving a rock and finding that it hid the entrance to a cave where a treasure cove of riches had been stored right under your nose for many years. Carl thought: how well do you really know someone, even though you've lived under the same roof for so many years?

Carl went to the desk. Two drawers on the right side were both locked. One of the keys on the ring opened the two locks. The top drawer contained books. His father had a habit of walking around with small appointment books in which he jotted down notes about important events and meetings.

Carl opened the second drawer and came across notebooks, a large number of them in several stacks held together by rubber bands. They looked like journals –they had dates on the covers. He didn't know that his father kept journals.

All the mementos: the scrapbook, the journals and appointment books written and then locked away, the newspapers and clippings lying around –did Augusto ever go back and revisit them in later years? A man takes his time to chronicle his life and after he passes on, does it really matter to those who come after him? Is anyone ever really interested in a life lived? Your children, Carl realized, have their own memories to create for themselves, photographs and memorabilia that they hope their own children will one day cherish and look back on.

Carl opened up a stack and looked at the first journal. The year: 1953 written on the label.

A rap on the door interrupted him. He looked at his watch. The time was almost noon. He'd been at it for close to five hours. By the time he had torn him self away from the journal and opened the door, he found no one outside, just a tray on the floor with a sandwich and a glass. He picked up the tray and took it to the desk.

He ate while he continued to go through the journal. The sandwich was made from left-over chicken. The glass had cane juice.

An entry in the 1953 journal sparked his curiosity and he paused to read it:

Monday, 21 July. *My last visit to Kingston today to visit her. It is something that I do with a great deal of sadness, but it has to be done. There are too many people who will be hurt if I continue this relationship, including Maria and my children. Better that two people are hurt than my entire family. She was very upset that I wouldn't continue to see her after today and I left with a promise to continue to support her and the boy. I intend to keep my promise.*

Carl had always thought he might have imagined grandmother's visit when she'd chastised his father for his philandering ways. He'd mentioned it several times to Joseph, James and Thomas to see if they could recall it; they had all denied any knowledge. Were they really ignorant of the episode or simply trying to cover up for their father?

He returned to the journals, looking for the events that would have been recorded in 1964 and he found one.

19 AUGUST 1964:

Carl leaving today on his scholarship. Heated discussion with him. Told him that it was a bad idea. Still think so. Nothing more to add.

Carl remembered...

***

Carl had been thinking of it for over a week, of the way he should break the news to his father.

He found himself rationalizing. After all it was his life and he had the right to do what he wanted. His future was at stake and he had to make the decisions that would have an impact on him. This also meant he would have to live with the consequences, regardless, but he was prepared for this. In any event, the Old Man had made it clear that he would be kicked out of the house if Carl did not comply with his way of thinking.

Carl had thought of writing a note for the Old Man and leaving it in his study, for him to find after Carl left. He thought of confiding in one of his brothers and getting him to tell Augusto about it. Who could he tell? Joseph was still up in McKenzie, Thomas was too close to the Old Man and couldn't be trusted to convey the right message. John was much too young to be entrusted with the job. At the end of all his rationalization, if he wanted to be true to his convictions, he needed to tell the Old Man in person. He was not ashamed of what he was about to do. On the contrary, he thought it was necessary, another step in his development.

So, he waited for evening, when Augusto came home.

As usual, after supper, the Old Man went to his study. Carl found him there. His father was going through some papers.

"Can it wait?" Augusto said, with all the hostility of someone who's had a hard day. "I'm in the middle of something right now."

"It can't" Carl said. "I have to speak to you, right now."

Augusto looked up from the file he had spread out on the desk. Carl could tell that the Old Man was tense. The contortion in his features: raised eyebrows, an unmistakable grimace, the glare, all reflecting what he was thinking: *why is it so important at this moment?*

This is not going to be easy, Carl thought.

"Since I now have my A levels, I want to tell you about what I'm doing for the next step in my career," Carl said. "I've been offered a scholarship to study abroad."

"Oh," his father leaned back in his chair. He seemed pleased, his features relaxed for the first time. "Sounds good. Where?"

That part of the news was something Carl wanted to keep for last.

"I'm also switching to Economics and Political Science."

"I thought you wanted to do journalism."

"I've changed my mind."

"Sounds sudden to me, but if it's what you want to do, then, it's fine. What are you going to do when you come back?"

"I'm not sure. Maybe, get into government, or politics."

Augusto smiled. Maybe he thought that Carl's plans included returning and taking up a role in the Conservative party.

"How soon is this all going to happen?"

Carl hesitated. It needs to come out, he thought.

"Very soon. I'm leaving tomorrow morning."

At first, his father didn't respond, but Carl watched him go through an entire range of emotions, the type that people experience when they receive news for which they were unprepared. At first there was a surprised look, then puzzlement, swiftly changing to indignation that he was only hearing of the news now. Later, it would be anger.

"How come you didn't tell me anything before now?"

Carl thought of a number of reasons he could give: *Because you were too busy; Because you would not have understood; Because the two of us don't see eye to eye on so many issues.* But, he said, "It happened quickly, just over the last few days and I didn't have much time to decide."

"Well, if that's the way it is, that's the way it is. Who's giving this scholarship and where is it to?"

He couldn't avoid the question anymore.

"The scholarship is being offered by the government."

"Oh. Where are they sending you?"

"…to the University of Havana."

Silence reigned. The Old Man's face turned a darker shade of scarlet. After a few seconds, he rose from his chair. Carl wouldn't have been surprised if his father rushed over to him and grabbed him by his neck and shook him. Augusto turned away and went to the jalousie window, staring outside at the dark night, seeing what, Carl couldn't figure.

When he turned around to face Carl, Augusto said, in a calm voice: "You mean Reform is giving you this scholarship? Why don't you say so?"

Carl could tell that his father was struggling to control his emotions.

"Yes, it is so."

Augusto shook his head. "This is a big, big mistake you're making, something you will regret forever."

"I don't think so," Carl said.

"I do! You're a young man, yet. I know you're filled with ideas about equal opportunity for everyone and you think there should be no poverty in the world. In Cuba they will use all your ideas and they will fill your head with nonsense and nothing else but Marx and Engels and Communist propaganda and before you know it, they will bring you back here to indoctrinate other young people and implement their Communist manifesto."

His father: always looking on a dark side that he thought dominated the Reform party, never accepting that the party had a brand of socialism that the country badly needed to redress decades of injustice. The Chairman himself had said this to President Kennedy at his last meeting, when he'd declared that he was a Socialist -Not a Communist.

Augusto said, "Tell me exactly what you hope to achieve by doing this?"

Augusto sounded as if he wanted to have a debate. Carl was not prepared to have one, since he had no intention of changing his mind.

Carl shook his head. "There's a lot that needs changing when the colony gets independence. Reform will need all the help it can get when that happens."

"You're a lot more naïve than I thought, if you think that Reform will not take the country down the path of Communism. That is, if the British Government grants independence under them. It's clear to everyone: Kennedy will never allow that to happen, not after what happened in Cuba, not with all that oil next door in Venezuela that the Americans depend on. Kennedy's going to put all the pressure he can on the British Government."

"All the more reason why Reform will need all the help it can get."

"I suppose that your friends Wilfred and Cyril are also getting scholarships?"

Carl nodded.

"I'm not surprised. They were both a bad influence on you, from the very start."

This was something that made Carl unhappy and he wanted to defend his friends and retort in an angry manner: *Are you saying I'm incapable of making my own decisions?*

"I don't think that's fair," Carl said. "I made the decision. They had nothing to do with it."

"Our party heard about these scholarships, about students being sent to Russia and Cuba to fill them up with Communist propaganda. I didn't think for one moment that a son of mine would be involved. I just can't believe it."

"Cuba actually has a very advanced education system, perhaps the best in the West Indies."

"Education is not all they're going to teach there. Before they're through, you and your friends will be revolutionaries, ready to return here to take up arms and fight. Can't you see that's what the plan is?"

"It's just an educational scholarship, nothing more than that."

"How do I explain this to relatives and my friends?"

Carl was silent. Here it comes: *he's going to put me on a guilt trip.*

"Do you realize what this will do to my standing in the party, when they hear that one of my sons is going to Cuba on a scholarship? How do I explain this?"

"Nothing to do with me, Dad."

"I was hoping to run for the Legislature next election. I'm hardly likely to get the nomination, now."

Carl knew: After the appeal to higher motives would come the bribe.

"Look, why don't you think about the UK? I've told you this before, I will pay for all your tuition. It will be a much more acceptable degree when you come back. If you don't come back and you remain there, or go to Canada, or the US, it will be something worth a lot more than the University of Havana."

You're almost broke, Old Man, barely hanging on to this house. How are you going to manage paying my tuition fees?

Carl shook his head. "Everything is finalized. I'm going to Cuba."

The rich shade of pink had returned to Augusto's face. He rose from his chair and slapped the desk with both hands. "Caramba! God damn!" he said. "What do I have to do to convince you that this is not good for you? It will only end up hurting you in the end?"

"I've made up my mind."

Augusto threw up his arms. "Know this, then, if you take this scholarship, I will no longer have a son."

Carl said: "If that's the way you want it..." He left the study, went to his room and picked up his suitcase.

***

Another entry in Augusto's Journal for 1964, 21st August. Carl was already out of the country.

Deciphered with a great deal of difficulty.

There was a bomb blast at the U.S Embassy earlier today.

This appears to be an escalation of the violence that has taken hold of the country recently, only this has struck closer to home, once again.

How much can one family take? James paid the ultimate price last year. Joseph and his family suffered at Wismar, Carl is in Cuba, doing who knows what, and now Thomas has felt the full force of the violence. The country is bleeding, and it's all because of the increasing tension between Reform and Republicans. Where will it end? Civil War? Already there are radicals in the two major parties calling for the three counties to be separated. If only people will come to their senses and grasp the opportunity for stability that the Conservatives represents! If only our party could appeal to more people! It's turning out to be Brown against Black, with both major parties exploiting the race card. Where will it end?

I wonder if I did the right thing when I arranged for Thomas to go to the U.S to take the courses in labour management. If he hadn't been in the Embassy arranging his visa, he would not have been harmed. Am I to blame for his situation? He was my last hope for someone to follow in my shoes.

I saw him off today. He has suffered major burns to more than fifty percent of his body. The U.S Embassy has flown him to Washington for medical treatment. He will be in good hands and will receive the best medical care. I'm only thankful that he survived the blast.

Both Reform and Republicans have blamed the other for the bomb blast.

Carl thought about his visit to Thomas in Florida.

His brother had mentioned the explosion at the embassy and the subsequent treatment in the U.S. for his burns. He'd said nothing though, of the real reason why he was going to America. Based on his father's entry, Thomas was going for courses in *labour management.* The Kennedy Administration, through the C.I.A, had used the unions in British Guiana to stir up opposition to the Reform government. Better to have home grown activists fighting the American cause, rather than C.I.A. Was this why Thomas was going to the U.S., to become an agitator for the union movement when he came back? Was this something that Augusto had sanctioned and perhaps even initiated?

In the 1972 journal was an entry about John:

Dropped in to see International Shipping today. John is now in Jamaica. He was previously in Trinidad and Barbados. Heaven knows where he will end up, or what will eventually happen to him. I think that he's wandering because of issues with me, and I know that I could have been, should have been a better father. I hope one day that I can make it up to him. I have tried writing him but letters have been returned unopened. Not sure if he received them or if the letters couldn't catch up with him.

Was this what Augusto was trying to do on John's last visit? He'd done a very poor job of it, if that was the case. John had left, even more hostile than before.

Carl wanted to see the entries in the 1980 Journal, Augusto's last. There might be a clue on Augusto's wishes for the property. Coming down to the end of his life, Augusto's writing had degenerated to a mere scribble; it was like trying to decipher hieroglyphics.

Feeling worse today. Drank the remaining bottle of Madeira last week and no more available to dull the pain that I'm feeling. It's like a volcano raging deep inside. For a few weeks now, I can hardly pass water without a great deal of pain. I have bloody urine sometimes. They want to take me to the hospital but I've been holding off. I'm sure if I go, I will never leave there alive, but it's now reached a point of no return. Perhaps it's even too late.

I have lived a full life and have few regrets. If I had to do it all over again, I would change very little, except perhaps how I would deal with my family. I'm only sorry that I cannot see them to tell them this. Maybe one of them will come before it's too late. If only I can hold on...

Carl looked around, at the shelves lined with books, at the desk, and the cabinets. One of the startling realizations he'd come to, after his Cuban phase, when he'd moved to Canada and joined the bank, was that he'd had a lot more in common with his father than he'd been willing to admit. Going through his father's personal possessions had also confirmed that.

His father had always been something of a dreamer, someone who believed that the old country values of Madeira could be transported to the colony of British Guiana and later to the independent country of Guyana. Carl remembered sitting on his father's lap, a rare event with so many children around, and listening to his father's favourite song that he played often in the study, and the lyrics came back to him:

Beautiful Dreamer. Look onto me. Starlight and moon drops are shining on thee...

He bundled the journals and replaced them in the drawer.

The first drawer with the appointment books was the one he'd initially given a cursory look at, thinking that there wouldn't be much of importance in his father's day-to-day activities. He went back to it –this was his last hope of finding the will, if one existed.

The blue soft-cover appointment books –one for each year, ranging from 1979 all the way back to 1950, were piled up in the drawer, in the same reverse chronological sequence they might have been tossed in year after year. Carl started to rifle through the first one, turning it upside down with the hope of discovering anything that might be lying inside.

A document dropped out of the book, a bank draft for two hundred Canadian dollars, still in mint condition and feeling as crisp as the day Carl had bought and sent it to his father.

He went through all the appointment books prior to 1979, flipping through them one by one, and then reversing the process and starting over. Still no sign of a will.

Shadows had sneaked up on Carl through the windows like thieves in the night. They had cast pools of darkness behind the furniture in the room. The sun sank, swiftly, relentlessly in the tropics and it wouldn't be too long before night fell.

He sat back and bowed his head. It seemed as if his father had given up all interest and in the end, couldn't care less what happened to the property.

CHAPTER 15 -Day Queen Victoria Lost Her Head

The Voice Of Lightning, Official arm of Reform. 17August1964.

POLICE COMMISSIONER CLAIMS ORGANIZED THUG-GERY RESPONSIBLE FOR MURDERS IN THE CITY:

The Commissioner of Police, in a press conference, this morning, said that the CID -Criminal Investigation Division branch of the service is about to wrap up its investigation and will be issuing a report on the more than one hundred murders that have been committed in the country for this year, twenty two of them alone in Georgetown. The Commissioner was outspoken in his condemnation of the murders, and laid the blame squarely on organized thuggery [his words] that was responsible for perpetrating the majority of the crimes. While he was careful to avoid naming names, as charges are yet to be laid in court, the Commissioner left no doubt that he felt most of the crimes had been perpetrated by a group organized by the opposition parties.

This was an item that caught Carl's attention in the newspaper.

He was in the reception room of the Income Tax Department with Wilfred. They'd already gone through the process necessary to obtain their Tax Leaving Certificate. The Certificate, one that verified a traveller had satisfied any outstanding tax liability to the government, had to be presented to officials at Timehri Airport before being allowed to depart.

Cyril was still going through his interview inside the office.

Wilfred had lost interest after glancing at the article.

"You were telling us about this," Carl said. "You knew, didn't you?"

Wilfred nodded.

The newspaper article went on to itemize a long list of incidents that had occurred over the current year, incidents that were meant to corroborate the story about a clandestine group of opposition members formed to commit violent acts against the government and its supporters.

Carl swiftly ran down the list and a few items caught his attention:

February 17th: *UAW strike causes work on all sugar plantations to cease. Blacks were being used on the plantation as scabs to break the strike by East Indians and police vans were being used to transport them in and out.*

March 4th: *Bomb thrown in a bus at Tain, Berbice. It was conveying scabs to Plantation Albion.*

East Indians were resorting to violence to prevent Black replacement workers being used on the sugar estates to run the factories. This was an ironic twist: East Indians had been brought over as indentured workers after the emancipation of slavery and had taken jobs away from Blacks on the sugar estates.

April 10th: *Political advisers from the U.S to coordinate action between the Conservatives and the Republicans. They will a) share costs; b) cooperate in publicity and voter registration; c) refrain from attacking the other party in the coalition; d) discuss cabinet posts in future coalition.*

It was something that Reform and the government had been trying to tell everyone, at home and abroad, for a long time, that the American government was intervening in the internal affairs of the colony. Not too many people had listened.

May 23rd: *Blacks Sealy and wife killed and bodies terribly mutilated.* Then, there was a retaliation by Blacks against Indians at Anna Catherina, Blankenburg and Vergenoegen. At

Bachelor's Adventure and Friendship, houses were set on fire and destroyed. In Georgetown, over 60 people were beaten and robbed.

Carl folded the newspaper and returned it to Wilfred. He was sick of reading about all the atrocities. How could people claim to be nationalists when it was clear that they were allowing themselves to be manipulated under the old divide and conquer rule –the oldest imperialist trick in the history of third world domination by Europeans. When would people eventually start to realize that there was a common foe that had to be fought: the old imperialism of Britain that was still trying to hold on to its empire, and the new expansionism of America determined to establish a world order as the only super power?

Now that he'd obtained his tax clearance, Carl went through his mental checklist of other items that he had to cover before he left. Passport was in order; suitcase packed at home; money order already bought for expenses in Cuba; and the one he'd been procrastinating on since the scholarship was confirmed: breaking the news to Augusto.

Cyril came out waving his certificate in the air. Forever the sceptic, he'd thought that they would face hurdles in obtaining the clearance.

"Got it," Cyril said. "This calls for a celebration –beers on me. Let's go to Rendezvous."

The restaurant was a few blocks away.

"Here's to the future," Cyril said, when they'd settled in at a table.

Carl and Wilfred raised their bottle and echoed Cyril's toast.

"Just think of it," Wilfred said, "in a few days we're going to be in Cuba."

"By the time we come back," Cyril said. "Reform will be firmly in power, British Guiana will be independent, and we're going to have big jobs in the government."

It all sounded very easy, much too easy, Carl thought. In his mind was 1953 when Reform were in power and British Guiana had the highest literacy rate and the most advanced form of self-government in the Caribbean. The British Government had suspended the constitution, throwing the colony back a full decade in its political development. Eleven years later, the other British colonies in the region had moved ahead and gained or were about to gain independence. Deep down, he felt behind-the-scenes manipulation was going to influence the process all over again.

"Let's hope things go according to plan," Carl said.

Wilfred sighed. "If we could only see into the future," he said. "If only we had a time machine, like the one H.G. Wells invented. Remember the movie with Rod Taylor?"

Carl was caught between two extremes at times. Cyril, believed that the future was going to be a rosy one under Reform, and Wilfred, the dreamer who believed in a world according to Hollywood. Still, if he had to choose between his two friends, Wilfred would always come out on top. It was due to Wilfred's intervention that the scholarship had come Carl's way. The three friends had applied the same time to party headquarters and Cyril and Wilfred's applications had been readily approved. The selection committee had expressed reservations about Carl, though. They didn't feel that Carl had what it took to be a dedicated socialist. His father Augusto's connection with the Conservatives did not help matters. Wilfred had pressed Carl's case, even threatening to turn down the scholarship if Carl was not selected.

"Maybe we'll get to meet Fidel," Cyril said.

"Maybe pigs will grow wings and fly," Carl responded.

"Don't be such a sceptic," Cyril said. "We're the first batch of students going to Cuba from this country. He will want to meet us."

"I won't hold your breath, if I was you," Wilfred said. "The man's busy starting a revolution in South America. He and Che Guevara want to reform the whole region."

Cyril seemed to have a sudden inspiration. He said to Carl: "How did Old Man Augusto react to the news about the scholarship in Cuba?"

Carl shook his head. "I haven't told him yet."

The unruly clump of hair on the front of Cyril's head swung back and forth. He slapped his forehead, as if he was trying to still the wavering lock of hair. He laughed, a cynical laugh that conveyed a message of triumph.

Cyril said: "We're leaving in two days and you haven't told your Old Man that you're going to Cuba on a RYM scholarship?"

"Just haven't got around to it."

"You're chicken! You're afraid of your Old Man!"

"Rebel Without A Cause," Wilfred said. "Remember when James Dean was playing the game of chicken and the other guy went over the cliff in the car?"

"There's a time for everything, Cyril. I'm planning on telling him tonight."

"Man, what wouldn't I give to be there when you break the news to him! He's going to flip his lid. I can just imagine him saying," and Cyril stood up and stuck his thumb into an opening in his shirt, imitating Augusto, "No son of mine is going to study in Cuba."

Wilfred said: "A man's gotta do what a man's gotta do."

"There's no turning back now," Carl said. "I'm going all the way, with or without his blessing."

They left the restaurant after a second round of beers. The entrance was cloaked in the long shadow of the afternoon sun and the streets were empty, apart from a few cars passing. Stores in the area were shuttered –the owners afraid of facing the wrath of the strikers. You were either with the strikers or you were against them; there was no middle ground.

A short walk would take them to the hire-car stand outside Stabroek Market where they would catch a taxi to the Walk.

A car passed as they were turning into Regent Street. The driver stopped and waited for them to catch up.

"Where you boys going?" the driver said. "It's not safe to be out on the streets."

"Why? What's happening?" Carl said.

"There's a big union protest march going on and things starting to get out of hand."

Cyril's head jerked right and left, up and down Regent Street, as if he expected to see evidence of what the man had just told them.

"What do you mean?" Carl said.

"Gangs roaming around all over the city, beating up and robbing people who's not opposition supporters."

The term usually meant East Indians.

"How we going to get home now," Cyril said. His voice had grown shrill with anxiety.

There had been no mention in the media of union rallies or opposition marches. Here we go again, Carl thought. There was no end to the unrest.

"I can give you a ride to Brickdam Police Station," the driver said, "and you can try to get a police car to take you wherever you're going."

Cyril wanted no further invitation. He opened the rear door and hopped in. Wilfred followed him. Carl took the front seat next to the driver.

"By the way, my name is Hussein," the driver said.

Carl remembered the driver from pictures and articles in the newspapers. He was the leader of UMP, the United Muslim Party, a splinter group that had formed with the intention of contesting the upcoming elections. Since the British Government's announcement about the introduction of the change in the electoral system to one of Proportional Representation, several groups had announced similar intentions. The most recent was the Justice Party, formed by a disgruntled former Reform cabinet minister. Was this all a part of the plan by the British Government, under pressure from the Americans, to severely restrict the ability of Reform to gain a majority? UMP's intention was to split the East Indian votes by appealing to the Muslim segment of Reform supporters. It was one of the many reasons why Reform was opposed to a PR system –it had the potential to harm Reform most of all.

"I'm the leader of UMP," Hussein said. "We're planning on fighting the next election on a religious platform, so we could do with all the support we can get. Doesn't matter if you're religious or not, whether you're Muslim or not, we'd like your vote."

In his announcement of the formation of his party, Hussein had issued several statements denouncing Reform as Communist, an anti-religious party that would seize church property and ban Islam and other religions. Hussein was painting a picture of the Reform as a party of infidels who had no respect for God in their constitution, something entirely false. Reform, in response, had labeled him as an opportunist.

Hussein's car was a Morris Oxford, of a 1950 vintage. The springs squeaked and groaned and the exhaust system sputtered and backfired as the car started west on Regent Street.

"I have to make a stop at the Law Courts to do some business." Hussein said. "I won't take very long."

Carl looked at his watch: four thirty. He was running out of time and still had a few things to do before he left the country. He knew that in the measurement of time, according to Guianese, *Won't take very long* might mean an hour or more. It was a similar concept to how distance was judged: *Not too far* might end up being at least a mile. Something to do with the tropics? The heat seemed to slow everything down to a crawl at times and the notion of urgency was an alien concept. They were already in the car and on the way and Carl didn't see much of an alternative if they were to avoid the roving bands of opposition members.

Hussein was around fifty, the hair on his head flecked with grey. He wore a white *kurta*, grey surge pants and a fez on his head. He might have been coming from a Masjid where he'd gone for afternoon prayers.

"We all have the same objective," Hussein said. "We want religious freedom. We're not going to get it if Reform remains in power after independence."

More propaganda. Lately, it was being spewed from all quarters. The Catholic and Anglican churches were preaching against the evils of Communism and the Hindu League was demanding that its supporters take a hard look at the constitution of Reform and ask whether it supported freedom of religion, though the leader of the party had repeatedly reaffirmed his support for freedom of expression of all religions in an independent country.

Hussein made a left on High Street onto the southbound artery. The street was divided into two one-way routes, each separated by a trench in the middle. Towering African Flame trees lined a green verge on both sides of the Canal. The car had only travelled half a block when they met with demonstrators heading north. It was a large congregation of a thousand or more people carrying placards and banners: a lumbering, ponderous movement of people that took up both north and south bound arteries.

"Turn around, let's go back," Cyril urged Hussein, panic in his voice.

"Is a one-way. We can't go back, it's against the law."

Hussein slipped the car into first gear and continued going at a snail's pace.

"Don't matter, man, just back up before it's too late," Cyril said.

"Don't worry. I know these people. They're not going do anything to us." Hussein kept going. "They know I'm the leader of UMP and we're all on the same side, against Reform. They won't give us any trouble."

Hussein's voice lacked conviction and Carl couldn't help wondering if the man knew what he was doing.

"Just be cool," Carl said. "They have union leaders in front of the marchers. I don't think they will allow their members to do anything to us."

"Close the windows," Cyril said, as he started to wind up his side.

Within seconds, the demonstrators came upon them and Hussein placed the car in park. The front line marchers gave them querulous looks –*how did you end up here?* Angry expressions, translated, meant: *You're holding us up!* A crush of bodies against the hood. Two people jumped up and took a seat, then dismounted and moved on. It was like being caught in a mudslide moving relentlessly down a hill after torrential rains, momentum taking it along. And, like a mudslide, the crowd slid, slinked and oozed, then, there was a parting of the ways, people pushing their way right and left around the car to continue the march, the car shuddering with every move.

Carl caught fleeting glimpses of pickets and banners:

DOWN WITH REFORM

LABOUR BILL MUST GO

NO INDEPENDENCE UNDER REFORM

DEATH BEFORE COMMUNISM

The pressure increased on all sides of the car. It became hot even though the sun seemed to be blocked out. Some people paused and peered through the windows, banging their fists on the roof and rapping their knuckles on the windows. Carl couldn't hear them, with the windows closed, but words mouthed were clearly obscenities that he'd heard often when people were irate enough to do something rash. He was afraid of this: one or more of the most disgruntled of the lot taking precipitous action and others in the crowd following, leading to a spontaneous eruption against everyone in the car.

They were stuck in the middle of the demonstration for what seemed an eternity before the crowd started to peter out. Just when Carl thought it was all over, men surrounded the car, took hold of the two sides and started to rock it.

"This don't look too good," Wilfred said.

"Grab hold of something," Carl shouted.

"Oh God, we all going to die here today," Cyril moaned.

Carl felt as if he was in a canoe crossing the mouth of the Demerara River at high tide, riding the crest of waves that rose as high as the top of the wharf in the market place. He was careening right and left, bumping into Hussein, into the left door, then back again. How much longer would the driver be able to take it?

"Drive the car, man, drive the car," Cyril urged from the back seat.

Hussein could hardly have acceded to Cyril's demand. The engine had died when the rocking started. It seemed as if the Morris Oxford was almost suspended in mid air. Hussein had a steel grip on the steering wheel that he appeared to be using for support. His glasses hung half off his face and he was flushed, as if he were in the throes of experiencing a massive stroke.

The rocking stopped suddenly and the car was dropped with a resounding crash on its wheels. The springs emitted squeaks of protest, the car bopped right and left and finally settled down. An eerie moment of silence ensued. The demonstrators had passed on.

The tail end of the demonstration was about twenty feet away when Carl, from the corner of his eye, saw someone run back to the rear of the car. The man raised his right hand far back above his head and hurled it forward.

"Duck," Carl said.

A rock came hurtling through the air and landed, creating fissures in all directions on the rear window. Just as sudden, it was over, nothing in the air but the clip-clop of a thousand pair of shoes receding.

"Just drive the kyar, man," Cyril said. "Let we get the hell outta here."

Hussein did not need further prompting. He turned the key in the ignition. The engine whined and sputtered and came to life. He slipped the car into gear and it moved forward with a lurch and a heavy gust of black smoke covering the rear window.

They were halfway down the block, when Hussein said: "See, I tell you that these people won't give us any trouble!"

Carl and Wilfred laughed at the irony of the situation. Cyril ignored the comment –he was too busy looking through the rear window, as if he expected the strikers to reappear at any moment.

In a few minutes they came up to the Victoria Law Courts.

The law courts sat in a sprawling two-story building in a compound that spanned an entire block off High Street. It had been built back in eighteen forty-one, an imposing building with Victorian style architecture, red gables on the roof, and the grounds enclosed by wrought-iron fencing.

Hussein got out of the car. He tucked his shirt back into his pants. "Wait for me, I'll be right back," he said, as he left them in the parking lot and headed up the outer stairs to the second floor.

There it was again, another gross misrepresentation of the measurement of time: *I'll be right back*. Carl shrugged. He looked at his watch: it was 5pm and he didn't expect they would see Hussein for at least half an hour.

Ten minutes had passed when Cyril said: "I don't know about you, but I'm not waiting here. I feel like we're sitting ducks just waiting for them to pick us off." He appeared to have grown paranoid over the number of people who were passing by, looking into the car.

Carl and Wilfred followed Cyril as he climbed the stairs to the top floor. An open veranda ran the length of the building, doors leading to courtrooms, signs outside the rooms indicating where court was in session.

Cyril was antsy. He kept pacing the floor, opening doors, and looking for Hussein. "Is where this man disappear to?" he said. "I want to get out of here before dark."

Carl stood at the rail looking onto the panorama of events unfolding. He'd never seen so many people on the grounds of the Law Courts and outside on the sidewalks. He thought that most of them were strikers or unemployed people. Hucksters were hawking their goods: women had straw baskets with tamarind, mangoes, five fingers and golden apples; men were selling soft drinks; a small boy was peddling boil-channa and potato balls. A cane-juice vendor had his cart parked on the parapet, passing long stalks of cane through the grinder and extracting the sweet nectar for sale to a queue of people.

Directly in front of the building the monumental statue of Queen Victoria sat on a pedestal and cast a long shadow on the lawn. The statue represented a symbol of justice and equality for all. She had sat there on her throne for most of British rule, resplendent in her majestic robes flowing at the back, a mace resting on her lap. Her stern gaze looked down on all passers-by.

"Where is this man?" Cyril repeated.

Carl had resigned himself to playing the waiting game – there was no alternative.

A carnival atmosphere was fast developing.

A group of people was gathered around a teenage boy who was able to belch at will, garrulous sounds originating from deep down in his stomach and rising through his mouth. Loud seismic eruptions exploded above the roar of the crowd.

A second crowd was gathered around a man who was putting on an exhibition.

"Look, is *Law And Order*," Wilfred said.

Law And Order was known all over Georgetown. He'd spent most of his adult life trying to rehabilitate criminals and was now in his sixties. Wherever there was a crowd of people, he was there, preaching his sermon of hell and damnation for all those who followed a path of crime. His cry of *Repent Ye or face the wrath of God* could be heard loud and clear throughout his demonstration.

Law And Oder's small pushcart was rigged with a gallows and trap door. A mannequin, dressed in prison stripes stood with a noose around its neck and a Cat O'Nine tails completed his paraphernalia.

It all looked harmless but Carl was concerned about the fast growing crowd. What if things got out of hand? He doubted that the police would even show up. Since the strike started, police were performing their duties in a limited way. The commissioner claimed that his officers were trying their best to handle a rising crime situation, but Reform was sure the lacklustre performance was due to support for the strikers.

"Repent, before it's too late," Law And Order shouted. He whacked the mannequin several times with the whip and continued his tirade against offenders. "If you don' obey the law, you will be punished." Whack, whack. "Dis is what is in store for you if you go to jail."

The crowd roared: "Give him more, give him more."

Whack, whack. "The law must be obeyed."

Law And Order had a mouthful of crooked teeth with gaps through which spittle cascaded down on the front row of the audience. People were constantly holding up their hands to ward off the deluge or retreating to a safer range.

"If you do the crime, you must do the time," the man said. "What should we do with this criminal?"

"Hang him, hang him," came the cry from the crowd.

Law And Order waved his hand for silence and the crowd was stilled. The man slowly walked up to the cart, took a lever in his hand and pulled it, setting in motion the springing of the trap door. The criminal mannequin fell through the trap door and was left dangling by the neck. The crowd clapped and whistled.

Carl had seen the show many times, but like many members of the audience, he thought there was something rapturous about the way it was choreographed. He looked away from the exhibition. People were huddled around the base of the statue and he thought it strange that they hadn't paid any attention to the demonstration. Suddenly, a man lit something –it looked like a firecracker. Sparks flew in all directions. The man threw the cracker at the statue.

This is no firecracker, Carl thought. It was a stick of dynamite. The dynamite exploded with a sharp crack near Queen Victoria's head, like a bolt of lightning bursting out of a clear, blue sky.

The explosion made a surgical amputation, flicked the head clean off the body and sent it rolling across the lawn like an overripe coconut dropping from a tree. The head hit the fence with a thud and stopped there, where it lay with the eyes staring up to the sky in a silent appeal against the ignominy it was subjected to and the injustice done to it.

The explosion brought Hussein running down the corridor at the head of a group of people.

"What's happening?" he asked.

"Queen Victoria just lost her head," Wilfred said.

Cyril said. "I bet the blame falls on Reform. You just watch and see."

"Let's get going," Hussein said. "We don't want to be around to see what happens next."

The Daily News. August 18th, 1964.

QUEEN VICTORIA LOSES HER HEAD

The flagrant attack on the statue of Queen Victoria yesterday outside the Victoria Law Courts on High Street, remains unsolved at press time. There were hundreds of witnesses but no one has come forward to identify the person or persons responsible. Following the revolting act, the statue was pulled down and carted off by the Public Works Department. This newspaper has managed to trace the whereabouts of the statue and has discovered that it was unceremoniously dumped at the rear of the Botanical Gardens.

Someone in authority, either in City Council or the Government, sanctioned this ignominious end for what has become a symbol of justice and fair play in the colony. It is as if, by doing this, they hope to wipe out a hundred and fifty years of British rule and British jurisprudence. What next? Will they attempt to rewrite history? Will we now see a wholesale obliteration of all things British, from names, institutions, and eventually good government?

CHAPTER 16 - A Different Place And time

THURSDAY 27ᵀᴴ NOVEMBER 1980. AM

Wilfred came through the front door and grabbed Carl in a bear hug, the way someone would greet a long lost friend.

"Senor Carl, como esta mi amigo?" Wilfred said after he'd stepped back and looked at Carl.

"I'm fine, Wilfred, just fine, considering the circumstances," Carl said. "I see you've kept up with your Spanish."

"Just barely. As they say back in Cuba: *pocito*," and he held up the thumb and index finger of his right hand to show an eight of an inch of space between them. "You know what happens if you don't use it –you lose it!" He laughed uproariously at what Carl believed was an attempt at sexual innuendo.

Wilfred continued: "I saw you at the funeral but I had to rush off to a meeting. I thought I'd meet you before you leave, anyhow."

Carl took a closer look at his old friend. The onset of a potbelly, a greying of his sideburns, lines under his eyes, but apart from all of this, Wilfred was just as good looking as he was back in high school. He had the same long, black hair combed back in waves and Carl half expected him to pull out his pocket comb and pass it through his hair, the way he used to.

Carl led Wilfred upstairs to the veranda.

Carl sat in the Berbice Chair on the veranda and Wilfred took a chair opposite.

"I got your message that you wanted to drop in to see me," Carl said.

Wilfred was wearing a white shirtjacket. It had two pockets in the area of his chest and two at the waist and looked as if it had been recently starched and ironed.

"You're looking prosperous," Carl said, pointing to his friend's stomach.

Wilfred rubbed his stomach and sighed. "It's all due to the starch from the rice we eat," he said. "It's not possible to get a balanced meal here, these days, with all the food shortages we have. As it becomes more and more difficult for the government to obtain foreign exchange they keep adding more imported goods to those already banned. They want people to substitute local stuff, but that's not possible when it comes to basic necessities like flour and oil."

"You must have a very big position in the party, after all these years, something that will enable you to afford to put a bit extra on the table?"

Wilfred smiled. "Not really, unless you can call District Secretary a big position. I don't. My job is routine: keep the membership up to date with what's going on in party headquarters, feel the pulse of the local grassroots to hear what they're thinking, raise funds, bring out the voters at election time, that sort of thing." He patted the top of his head, a careful, gentle movement over his hair to check the status of his wavelets. "Not that bringing out our voters at election time really matters –the election is always rigged. The Republicans can't lose."

"I thought you would have made it all the way to the top by now, especially after Cuba."

Wilfred shook his head, slowly. "Sad to say, no."

"Why don't you leave, find something else?"

Wilfred laughed. "Where? All major businesses have been nationalized and you need a party card for employment. It's too late for me to switch sides now, not that I would ever think of doing it."

Wilfred seemed disappointed about the way life had turned out for him, but seemed to have retained his sense of humour.

"What's the party going to do about the election coming up this December?" Carl said.

Wilfred sighed. "There's a big debate about boycotting it. Most think it doesn't make sense to fight when everything is stacked against us and the results are known ahead of time. Why waste the energy?"

"What about the International Elections Commission that will be overseeing the polling? Won't they make a difference?"

Wilfred curled down his lower lip and shook his head. "This government doesn't really care what the international community thinks, at this stage, anyway. As things tighten and the economy worsens, perhaps they will, but it will take economic sanctions to sway them. In the meantime, they're doing everything they can to remain in power, and there's nothing we can do about it, except bide our time and hope they fall on their own swords."

Outside on the driveway, Earl was washing the De Soto. Earl soaked a rag with water from a bucket and with movements that amounted to gentle caresses, carefully stroked the body of the car, left to right and then back again, something that Carl had seen him do every morning since arriving. Earl paused, stepped back and subjected the car to closer scrutiny. What was he looking for? With over one hundred thousand miles, the bright, red body of the car was in great shape. No problem with rust arising from salt on the roads, Carl thought. Earl always seemed to maintain a high degree of eagerness in the way he handled his car; every morning was like an adventure, filled with high expectation. He was like a kid with a new toy on Christmas morning. Carl couldn't help wondering, like the kid who soon grows tired of his new toy, would Earl's feelings for his car pass too, one day?

Wilfred continued: "They're bound to do that, eventually. You remember the Jim Jones story and the Jonestown mass suicide? It was the Republicans that sanctioned the development of this commune in the first place. Some sources say that money was used by Jones to influence the decision. Well, in February this year, two of Jones' aides were murdered before they could testify. In May, another, Layton was found not guilty of murder. The Americans can't be too pleased over this –it was American citizens who died at Jonestown and the truth still has to come out. Also, there's the political assassination of Walter Rodney who founded his own party and was turning out to be a real threat to the Republicans, liable to draw many Black voters away."

"I read about that in the *Caribbean Times* in Toronto."

"It's also well known that the government has a terrorist group that was formed before independence. This group has been involved in all kinds of activities to keep the opposition off guard. They will resort to assassination, even in broad daylight, like how they did with Rodney."

"Hard to believe that something like that can still go on in this day and age."

"You don't know how things operate in this country, now. We're Chicago in the roaring twenties, gangsters running the show, and they gun you down in the streets like a dog if they don't like what you say or do. Our very own Scarface," Wilfred tilted his head in the direction of the Carrington house next door, "is someone who plays a big role in this group, going way back to the disturbances and riots in the sixties."

Wilfred seemed reluctant to say the name, but Carl knew he was referring to Winslow.

Carl remembered Winslow at the airport. "He does seem to have come a far way since we were growing up. I ran in to him at the airport, but he barely glanced at me."

"You can see why: he can't be familiar in any way with someone who's had a connection with Reform."

"Still, there was a time when he would stand up for me. Remember what happened at the cinema with Reds."

Wilfred sniggered. "I wouldn't count on Winslow standing up for anyone who's not Republican. He follows party lines above everything else, and the line right now, is survival of their party."

"Are you still keeping up with the movies, these days?"

"Not really. The cinemas only show very old films. Who wants to see the same old movie over and over again? It's like the elections here."

Footsteps on the stairs announced Sumintra.

"You have a visitor," Sumintra said to Carl. Shirley was behind her.

"Hello Carl, hello Wilfred," Shirley said. She then spoke directly to Carl. "Where have you been keeping yourself for the last day or two? I haven't seen you around."

"I've been busy cleaning up, taking care of the Old Man's business."

"Shirley," Wilfred said. "You're a sight to be held. I've never seen you looking so radiant. Did you dress up specially for me…or is it for Carl?"

Shirley was outfitted in a blue skirt and a white, short sleeve shirt. Both were neatly pressed, the pleats standing out sharp and distinct on the skirt. She looked like someone who was very particular about her appearance. Ringlets dangled around her head as she turned her head here and there to face Carl first, then Wilfred.

"You always so full of sweet talk, Wilfred. I know you don't mean it, but I love you for it."

"Of course I mean every word of it. If I wasn't attached I would have been running after you long before now."

Sumintra said: "Boy, Wilfred, you're a married man with children. How come you be looking at other women?"

"Being married doesn't mean you're dead. I can still appreciate beauty when I see it, and Shirley," Wilfred looked at her and sighed, "in my younger days I would have appreciated you even more."

Carl remembered Wilfred, at school. He was always the best dressed, someone who seemed to be constantly seeking attention and forever with an eye for the girls.

"You a real villain," Sumintra said. "I don't know how you turn out like that. You not at all like Carl."

"Oooh, you don't really know Carl like I do. Ask him about Havana... and Natasha."

Carl smiled but did not jump in to elaborate. Shirley came closer and touched him on his shoulder.

"Havana, huh?" Shirley said. "This Natasha –is she your wife?"

"They had a real strong thing going at the university –he and Natasha," Wilfred said. "She was our lecturer, sent from mother Russia to educate students about the advantages of a socialist economy versus that of capitalism in the decadent west."

Wilfred turned to Carl. "Did the two of you ever continue your relationship after you left Cuba?"

Carl thought about it before he responded. "We did," he said. "We both ended up in Toronto, living together, until early this year when we decided to go separate ways. We're trying to work things out. We have two kids –a boy and a girl."

"So, let me get this straight," Shirley said, her hands akimbo, her dark brown eyes flashing. "You're not really married, but you have two children with this woman?"

Carl looked at her and smiled. Her smooth, dark brown complexion reminded him of the colour of the water in the Canal before the punts passed and stirred up the silt, turning it to black coffee.

"Well, in Canada, living together for a lot less than sixteen years would be considered almost the same as being married." Carl said. "There are even laws recognizing that."

"Why did you break up?"

Carl hesitated. "It's a long story, better left for another day."

Shirley looked at her watch. "Christ," she said. "I'm running late for work. I have to go." She headed for the stairs, Sumintra trailing behind her.

"I will bring something for the two of you to drink," Sumintra said.

Shirley paused at the head of the stairs. "You guys don't forget my party Friday night. I expect to see you both there. No excuses. Everybody else is coming."

Carl followed Wilfred's gaze as he looked through the jalousie slats at Shirley's retreating form. Shirley hurried to the driveway and stepped into the De Soto where Earl was waiting to taxi her to work. Carl thought she was a vision of loveliness: young, vivacious, exuberant and outgoing and he could understand why Wilfred was looking at her with the eyes of a piranha, as if he wanted to devour her body. Minutes after she was gone, her perfume lingered in the air, its appeal and seductiveness remaining to haunt and remind him how close she'd been standing in the short time she was there.

Wilfred sighed, turned to Carl and said, "That girl is going to make someone a wonderful wife, someday."

Carl nodded.

"I'm sorry to hear about you and Natasha," Wilfred said. "You both seemed to know what you wanted back in Havana –each other. What happens when you return to Toronto?"

"We'll see."

"We had a great time in Havana, didn't we, you, me, Cyril?" Wilfred said.

"Another time, different place."

"How about Cyril –did you ever run into him in Toronto?"

Carl sighed. "I hadn't heard from him for years, then, out of the blue, I received an invitation to join this new party, the RDG –the Restoration of Democracy to Guyana party, that he and several Guyanese expats from Canada and the U.S were forming."

"It was all over in the news here, especially the part about them planning to return to Guyana and lead an armed uprising against the Republican government."

"Yes, it also hit the news all over Toronto. Actually, they became the laughing stock of the Guyanese community there and in New York, because they were obviously not very smart about how they went about the whole thing. They were in contact with a couple of U.S Congress men who were sympathetic to the cause, and they took this as support from the American government. Word leaked out about their plan to use armed intervention. Of course, it's against US law to plan or stage an armed overthrow of any government from US soil. This led the FBI to set up a sting operation to sell them the arms they needed. The RCMP in Canada cooperated. Together, they snagged the whole bunch."

Wilfred laughed out loud. "Funny," he said, "it's illegal to stage a coup from US soil but it's okay if the CIA is running the operation in some foreign country. The American public is against the whole idea –but if it happens, just don't tell them about it. The Ugly American –Marlon Brando as the U.S ambassador involved in an attempt to overthrow the Burmese government."

Carl said: "I did something quite stupid. After a lot of persuasion from him, and more for old time's sake, I agreed to attend one of their meetings. To my surprise, I discovered he'd taken out a membership in the party for me, without my knowledge or consent."

"Sounds like our Cyril."

"I only attended one meeting and didn't go back. One session was enough for me to realize that the group sounded really radical, and I'd heard enough of that kind of talk when we were in Cuba. The insane part of it: here I was, minding my own business and the RCMP picks me up for questioning, like all the others, about arms and ammunition being purchased for this uprising to overthrow the Republican government here. I got the shock of my life. I was really angry, though. I told Cyril that I never wanted to see or hear from him again."

"What happened after the RCMP picked you up?"

"Well, my name was on the membership list –it was how they were on to me in the first place. I told them the circumstances under which the membership was taken out in my name and managed to convince them that I had no association with the party executive or the plan. They left me alone after that."

"They didn't dig up your *revolutionary* past life in Cuba?"

"What does it matter, now? All of this happened over fifteen years ago –it's behind me. I don't even know if their records go back that far. I have a job with a reputable bank, a clean record, never been in trouble with the law and have no political affiliations."

"You're lucky you were not living in the US. The Americans would not have let you off so easily."

"I couldn't believe how this happened to me. If it didn't have the potential to turn out so badly, I would have found it comical. Talk about being in the wrong party at the wrong time."

Wilfred laughed. "The RDG was trying to solicit support from Reform at first for this armed intervention. Reform would have no part of it, of course. It's all that the Republicans would need, some connection to the RDG to come down hard on our leadership. We'd all end up in jail, here. What's happened to the case?"

"The Canadians are out on bail; same with those in the US."

"Poor Cyril, he was always trying to make it to the big times. He reminds me of those character actors with small roles. Like Ward Bond and Harry Carey –you find them in every John Wayne movie. They never really make it to the top. If they're lucky, fans might remember their face, only because of the large number of movies they appear in. But, no one really knows the names. Then, one day, one of them dies and you recognize the face in the obituary column of a newspaper, and you say: so, *that's who he was!*"

"I remember how he was in Havana…always trying to impress the lecturers with his knowledge of world history and American involvement in the internal affairs of South American countries."

"More like trying to curry favour with them, I think."

Footsteps sounded on the stairs. Sumintra reappeared with a tray, two glasses of soft drinks on it, ice cubes clinking as she glided across the hallway.

"You must be thirsty," she said.

Wilfred stood up. "Thanks, but I can't stay any longer. I have a meeting to go to. Maybe some other time we can have a drink, you and me, and talk some more," he said to Carl.

Sumintra placed the tray on a coffee table and left.

Carl was suspicious. What more could Wilfred want to say that he hadn't said so far?

"About anything in particular?" Carl said.

"I was hoping we could talk about getting some help from you."

"You mean the party? What kind of help?"

"If we do decide to contest the upcoming election in December, we will need more funding. Would you be willing to help us raise money among the Guyanese community in Toronto? We have supporters there; we just need someone to coordinate the effort."

Carl shook his head. "I've had enough of politics for one lifetime."

"Not even for old time's sake? You were once a big supporter and believed in our quest for a just and equal society."

Carl sniggered. "Sounds like the party line. I didn't think that even you still believed it."

"You have to admit that it's still a catchy phrase and it appeals to the masses."

"Maybe, but for me, it was another life a long time ago."

"Adios mi amigo," Wilfred saluted from the top of the stairs. "In the famous words of Yoda: *May the force be with you.*"

Carl watched Wilfred as he went out the front yard to the Walk.

***

The routine seemed to be quite simple: you were to go to a cage, pay your fee, obtain a number, take a seat and wait.

Carl had already paid his fee, received a number and taken a seat. He was playing the waiting game. Signs plastered all over the walls, written in simple phrases repeated several times, laid out the rules.

He took a look at the big sign hanging over the wicket where he had paid his fee of thirty Canadian dollars for a ten-minute phone call:

YOU MUST FOLLOW THE RULES AND REGULATIONS:

PAY FOR THE CALL

GET A NUMBER FROM THE PERSON IN THE CAGE

WAIT YOUR TURN

ENTER BOOTH PROMPTLY WHEN CALLED

LIMIT TEN MINUTES EVERY CALL

And still more signs:

NO REFUNDS

RATES CHANGE WITHOUT NOTICE

NO MOUTH TALK OR BACK TALK ALLOWED

NO IDLING ALLOWED

ANYONE BREAKING THE RULES WILL BE REJECTED FROM THE OFFICE

IF YOU CAN'T READ THIS NOTICE SEE THE ATTENDANT

The signs were handcrafted. Sure, the spelling was wanting in a few cases, but at least the author had tried to create a process. Was it an attempt to simplify the job? Did the clerks running the office often face disgruntled and belligerent customers, people who were unhappy that the only place in the city they could make a long distance call was at the Telecom Head Office? Or, was it simply an example of the overall approach the dictatorship was employing: people needed to know in clear and uncertain terms what they could expect when they came face to face with the administration –*These are your rights, nothing more!*

Carl counted the number of people in the room –there were twenty ahead of him, waiting for five booths. At ten minutes maximum, plus in-between time for transition to another customer, it might take a minimum of forty minutes before he could place his call. He looked at his watch: it was close to 8:30am. Earl was waiting outside on the street. Afterwards, they were heading up to Uncle Jules in the country, where Carl would spend the night.

One call was completed; the caller left the booth and someone replaced him. Nineteen more to go. Who were all these people waiting? Who were they calling? He'd tried making phone calls from Havana back in 1964 and problems with the system there were no different from the ones now faced in Guyana.

Cuba. Communicating with the outside world was just one of many problems the new regime faced, five years after the revolution when Castro came to power. Carl remembered his stay –the University de La Habana where he spent four years of his life. The Plaza de la Revolucion where he heard Fidel speak to the masses many times. Afternoon walks along the Malecon that reminded him of the seawall and the promenade in Georgetown where he and his friends went girl watching on a Sunday afternoon. *Alerta* –the posters slapped on walls all over the country, alerting Cubans to prepare for another invasion that was sure to come. Nationwide drills on the *Dia de la Defensa*, a day set aside to prepare the country for another invasion by the *Yankee Imperialists who will not give up, even after their humiliating defeat at the Bay Of Pigs.* Soviet trained advisers from the Eastern Bloc countries, the so-called Hispano-Soviets, veterans of the Spanish Civil War who were brought in to consolidate the gains of the Cuban uprising and establish a government worthy of the revolution. And, Natasha, one of the descendants of those Hispano-Soviets …

***

"I see you, how do you say it in English –giving me the over look," Natasha said to him one morning, about two weeks after he started in her Spanish immersion class.

She had asked him to remain after the lecture and they were in her classroom, alone.

"Every student in class is looking at you while you teach, not only me," Carl said.

"Your overlook, it is different, though…" She waved her right hand in the air; she seemed to be searching for the right words.

"Nothing like that."

"That overlook, I see it many times, in Latin men. They, how do you say it, take off my dress with their eyes? They all want to get in to bed, with me."

Carl laughed. She frowned. Undressing her had been far from his thoughts, although he had thought she was attractive from the very first session he'd had in her class. He'd found her fascinating: she was the first Russian he'd been in contact with, someone who came across as fiercely independent, a woman who extolled the importance of the role that women played in the creation of the Soviet Socialist Republic.

"Actually, I am not Latin, although I do come from South America. When you lecture, I can't help wondering where you learnt your Spanish. You're very fluent, as fluent as the Cubans."

"My mother, she is Cuban. I pick up the Spanish from her when she come to Moscow to study. Where from you, in South America?"

"There are only four non-Spanish speaking countries in all of South America. British Guiana is one of them. The other three are Dutch Guiana also called Suriname, French Guiana farther to the east, and of course, Brazil where they speak Portuguese.

"I know only Brazil," she shook her head. "These other countries, still colonies?"

"Yes, the only three colonies still remaining on the mainland."

"They must be liberated!"

For the first two weeks at Havana University, all new students were engaged in an intensive program of what was called *cultural assimilation into a world where the imperialists had shed all their colonial possessions and people all over were free to pursue their own destiny*. In every session they were repeatedly inculcated about the benefits that would inevitably flow down to the lowest layers of society after every country had adopted Marxist-Leninist ideology.

"It's supposed to happen any day now. Some people feel it can't be soon enough."

"What the people in your country like? Muslim? What language speaking?"

"We do have Muslims in British Guiana. It's one of five different nationalities. Everyone speaks English mainly, although some of the older generations still speak a bit of their own language –Hindi, Urdu, Chinese, and Portuguese, like my father."

"Muslim men in the USSR, they like women to dress, how do you say it: conservative? Is that why you look at me, because I don't wear sleeves on my arms, because I wear makeup? Because I don't wear anything under my dress?"

She had come around from the back to the front of her desk and was now leaning against it, facing him where he sat about five feet away. She pushed her short, blonde hair back around her ears –she had a way of doing this, even though her hair seldom seemed out of place.

"I am not Muslim. I'm Catholic, although I haven't practiced the religion in a long time."

"Your English is perfect, so natural. But, your Spanish," and she moved her right wrist back and forth, "is so-so. You have…far to go, many problems that must be fixed. You not like your friend, Wilfred. He have, what you say: the gift?"

"There are many things that come natural to Wilfred, languages is just one of them."

She frowned and it created lines rippling across her entire face. "Why you come to Cuba, if you don't speak Spanish so good?" she said.

Carl scratched his head. "That's a hard thing to explain. Let's just say that I'm hoping it will help me to make a difference when I go back."

"I have a proposal for you," she said.

He was sure she meant a proposition, and was tempted to correct her, but refrained. Instead, he said: "I'm listening."

"My English not so good, your Spanish lousy."

"Ouch," he said. "Lousy is far from what I considered my grasp of Spanish, but I'll take your word for it."

"So, you help me with English and I help you with Spanish. What do you think?"

"Sounds like a good deal to me," Carl said. "When do we start, and where?"

"You be best, speak Spanish like me, by the time you leave Cuba. We start tonight, at my flat. I write for you." She scribbled the address and directions on a sheet from her note pad and gave it to him.

Back then, at that first session, he'd had the impression that she was a woman with a purpose, someone who was determined to get there, no matter what it took. In the following years, he'd been disconcerted many times by her direct approach and lack of consultation.

***

An attendant was calling out for *Number Twenty*, once, twice, three times, a note of annoyance etched in the tone the third time. Carl looked at the number on his card and it was 20. He walked over to an empty booth where an attendant was standing outside. The man glared at him, perhaps wondering why he was breaking one of the rules clearly laid out for everyone to see.

Carl picked up the phone from the cradle. The operator came on, asked him for the number, and made the connection. Carl heard the phone ringing at the other end. He looked at this watch –it was 9:15am. Natasha should be back from dropping the kids off to school; she was probably preparing to leave for an assignment, if she had one.

The phone rang five times and he was just about to hang up when it was picked up. Natasha sounded as if she was breathless when she came on the line.

"Hello," she said, "who's there?"

"Natasha, it's Carl. You sound as if you were somewhere far from the phone and had to run to get it."

"I was just going out the door," she said.

He heard several loud intakes of air and waited for her to catch her breath.

"How are the kids?" he said.

"They're fine. I dropped them off to school. They miss you very much."

"I miss them too. How about you –how are you doing?"

"Good, but I miss you. I have an assignment. Hispanic speaking refugees coming in from Central and South America into Canada and they need translators."

"Sounds as if this one will last a long time."

"I think so. Are you still coming back on Sunday?"

"Yes. Definitely."

He wanted to tell her how much he missed her, that he was hoping they could make another start when he returned, but his attention was diverted by a loud commotion at the cashier's cage. A man was arguing that he hadn't received his full allotment of minutes and was demanding a refund. The cashier was threatening to expel him if he didn't keep his voice down. They were going back and forth, the man holding out for a refund before he lowered his voice, the cashier insisting that he lower his voice before she discussed the matter with him.

"Natasha," he said, "I've been thinking of you, and the kids a lot over the last few days. I know things haven't really been great between us, but I'd like to fix that when I return."

"Are you still there? What's the noise in the background, I can hardly hear you," she said.

"There is no door on the booth so I have to speak very loud. I'm saying that I want us to get married when I return," he shouted into the mouthpiece.

"I still can't hear you. What are you saying?"

The phone went dead; his time was up.

CHAPTER 17 -Refugees

THURSDAY 27ᵀᴴ NOVEMBER 1980. PM

The De Soto slowed to a crawl as it neared Bourda Market in Georgetown. The mid morning traffic in the area was frenzied: hire-cars stopping to let passengers off, lorries and vans offloading merchandise, pedestrians laden with shopping bags as they hopped and skipped around to avoid them all. The air was filled with a chaotic medley of sounds: horns honking, vendors trying to attract shoppers, customers haggling over prices.

After they'd left the Telecom Building, Carl wanted to shop for some foodstuff to take with him on his visit to Uncle Jules. Earl had suggested that the market was the best place, since it was on the way.

"Madness, as usual," Earl said. "It gets worse and worse every day."

They parked a block away and walked back to the market.

The market was spread over a city block, the structure surrounded by a wrought-iron fence with stalls positioned under the cover of a sloping roof of rusted corrugated sheets. Earl led the way to the rear of the building. A secondary market had developed outside and spilled over to the pavement and street. Here, every imaginable locally grown tropical fruit and vegetable was displayed on jute bags: football size papayas and watermelons; scarlet-red cashews and crimson coloured mangoes heaped in high stacks; oranges as large as grapefruits and grapefruits the size of coconuts. Adding to the palette of colours were fresh olive-green okra and plantain; dark brown cassava of different shapes and sizes and red eddoes streaked with a thin film of dark mud.

Carl approached a vendor who was seated on a bench behind her stall of fruits and vegetables, her knees pushed up almost to breasts that hung on both sides of her chest. Her vegetables were neatly laid out in small piles in the middle with fruits stacked up besides them.

A man was ahead of Carl, looking at a pile of mangoes.

The man picked up a mango, squeezed it and replaced it on the pile. He picked up another and did the same thing. A third mango fell to his scrutiny in a similar fashion.

"Eh eh, "the woman said, "why don't you mekh up yur mind? They is all the same, you know!" When she spoke, her mouth opened to reveal a set of jagged teeth with several missing in her lower jaw.

The woman wiped her hands on her apron, reached over and picked up a mango. "Here, try this one," she said, as she held it out.

The woman's wide girth took over the entire bench and the flesh on her huge arms jiggled when she moved them. She wore a white cotton scarf around her head and grey hair protruded from the sides. Her jaws were set and her eyes blazing –she didn't seem to care for the way the man was handling her fruits. He might just as well have been fondling her girl-children in the same manner.

The man ignored her –he picked up another mango and subjected it to his test. Firmness seemed to be a quality that was on the top of his list –an indication of the freshness of the fruit.

"But, is why you playing with them mangoes so for?" the woman said.

"I must check them out before I buy them!" the man said.

"But, you going soften them up and nobody going to buy them after that! If you want to squeeze something like that, go home and squeeze you wife *bubby*. She gat two of them, and they must be just right for you to play with."

The man sucked his teeth. "Big bubby woman," he muttered as he walked away.

"You ever see eye-pass like that?" the woman said. "Just because I don't want he to soften the fruits he don't want to buy from me."

"That man should show you more respect," Earl said.

"I know. I is a poor man child but I still have pride, you know. He got no cause to talk to me like that."

"Can you package a parcel of each vegetable and some mangoes and oranges?" Carl said.

The woman pulled out a plastic bag from a crate. The bag had the imprint of *Honest Ed's –the lowest prices on the planet*, and she filled it with vegetables. Another bag was pulled out and she loaded mangoes and oranges into it.

A plastic bag that had travelled all the way from Toronto, like him, Carl thought. He wondered how it had finally ended up in the hands of the vendor. Had a relative in Toronto sent it; stuffed it into a barrel with other bags, along with cheap canned groceries, as so many expat Guyanese were doing these days to help out relatives caught in the economic bind?

"How much do we owe you?" Earl said as he pulled out his wallet.

The woman did a swift computation on her fingers. "A thousand, son," she said.

Carl did the math. At the going rate of one hundred Guyana dollars to one Canadian dollar, everything they'd just bought was costing no more than ten dollars, a bargain if he'd ever seen one. He couldn't help wondering how people managed to survive at that rate.

"Give her an extra couple of hundred," Carl said to Earl. "She deserves it."

They were on the way.

Carl saw places and buildings that jarred his memory and was amazed how much the city had changed. Once known as the Garden City of the Caribbean, Georgetown was now far from it. Signs of decay were everywhere. Trenches were filled with stagnant water and garbage and tall reeds lined the banks. Buildings were weather-beaten. Streets were perforated with potholes and sidewalks rutted and cracked.

They passed the Bourda Cricket Ground and it took him back to many matches he'd attended –world-class cricket test matches among Commonwealth countries. In another five minutes they were passing the golf course close to the seawall.

Carl turned around and looked, as the De Soto left the city behind.

"I don't see anyone playing golf. Have they given up on the game?" he said.

Earl shook his head. "Not due to choice. They turned it into a National Park after independence. The Republicans considered golfing too bourgeois."

"Used to be the Arawak Hotel." Carl pointed to a rundown building facing the Atlantic. It was the tallest structure in the area: Demerara windows highlighting the top floor. Carl recalled Old Year's Night parties, going home in the early hours of *foreday* morning, as they often called it. The building today was a mere shadow of itself.

"You can still find a room there," Earl said. "Especially if you're looking to hook up with a woman for a one-night stand."

A house of prostitution, Carl thought, with dismay.

The highway started to veer away from the ocean and before long they were in open country.

"I was curious," Carl said, "about your arrangement to take Shirley to work. Is this something you do everyday?"

Earl glanced across at him. "Yes," he said. "I take her and pick her up every working day. Sometimes the family also use me for the odd trip here and there to do shopping in the city."

"Nice girl, that Shirley. How's it that a girl so good looking is still single?"

Earl pulled out a cigarette from his top pocket and stuck it between his lips and left it dangling there. "She's an ambitious one," he said. "I don't think that marriage is in the cards for her in the near future."

"Why is that?" Carl said.

"She wants to leave the country, go abroad to study. She's been planning this for a few years now."

"What's kept her here?"

Earl smiled. "Oh, I suspect lack of opportunity. Back in your days it might have been easy, but since then, things have gotten tighter. With the amount of people trying to get out by any means possible, most countries have clamped down on Guyanese going abroad, even if it's to study. To get a visa to the US or Canada is like a pork-knocker striking it rich in the gold field."

Pork-knocker: Carl hadn't heard the term in many years. He remembered Pussy, the old hermit from the Walk. The man was said to be a Pork-knocker, someone who went into the interior looking for gold, like all those hopeful souls who flocked to the Yukon in Canada.

They came to an intersection where vehicles were backed up and Earl slowed down. A traffic light ahead was not functioning and a policeman was directing traffic.

Earl reached into his pants pocket and pulled out his wallet. From the billfold section, he extracted a two hundred dollar Guyana bill and slipped it into a plastic folder containing his driver's license.

The De Soto edged up closer to the intersection. Earl stopped the car and the police man approached. The man was dressed in a black uniform, white sleeves pulled over his arms to show that he was on traffic duty, his cap pulled over his forehead to block the sunlight. It was growing warmer by the minute and perspiration was streaming down in rivulets from his head.

"You 'ave yur Zone permit?" the cop asked as he leaned over and placed his elbows on the door, all so casually.

Earl handed over his driver's license. The cop opened it up, looked right and left, extracted the note and handed the folder back to Earl.

"Push on," the cop said, as he straightened up and moved down to the next car in line.

Earl slipped the car into gear and pulled away.

"What was that all about?" Carl said.

"Every hire-car is registered to a region."

That would account for the numbers painted on many taxis, Carl figured.

"I'm supposed to get a permit to travel outside GT if I'm taking passengers. I don't have a permit, since I hardly ever get out of the city. I gave him my cash payment."

"I suppose something like that goes on all the time?"

Earl shrugged. "Their way of supplementing their low salary. The government knows they do it, so they justify keeping salaries low. A vicious circle with no end. It's how business is done in Guyana these days, under the table."

"The end justifying the means..."

They were now far from the capital, passing the occasional village on the way: LBI –La Bonne Intention, Success, Beterverwagting, names that had a hint of a long history of Dutch, French and English periods of colonization over the last two and a half centuries. Long stretches of unoccupied land lay in-between villages, on both sides of the highway, and the early afternoon heat was already well on its way to reaching an intensity, the memory of which had slipped far behind in Carl's subconscious. The De Soto had no air conditioning; hot air came in waves through the windows. Carl found beads of perspiration gathering below his shirt and a gnawing emptiness in the pit of his stomach.

"Don't know about you," Carl said, "but I'm hungry. Is there somewhere we can stop for a bite to eat?"

"We'll see what's here," Earl said, and slowed the car as he approached the outskirts of a village.

They passed a lumberyard: planks stacked on high racks under a zinc roof. A man was resting on the top tier, his head propped up on one hand, his right foot crossed at his left knee. The shadow of the afternoon sun had already worked its way to his position and he was just lying there, waiting for time to creep along, watching what little traffic there was as it went by. At the house next to the lumberyard, a man was swaying gently to and fro in a hammock in the bottom-house. A woman and a small girl were on the stairs leading up to the top floor of the house, the girl perched between the woman's legs, her mother passing a fine-tooth comb through her long, black hair. At another house, three men were playing dominoes in the shade of a mango tree in the front yard, bottles of beer laid out on a small table.

Life in the Guyanese countryside: an idyllic scene, if he'd ever seen one, Carl thought. These people seemed not to have a worry in the world. They knew how to take things as they came: slow and easy. What couldn't get done today would be held over for tomorrow, and if they couldn't do it tomorrow, there was always the day after. Wasn't this every man's dream? To escape from a hectic life filled with stress and endless deadlines and priorities?

In the middle of the village they came across a cake shop –The Oasis, and Earl stopped the car and parked outside. The double-door entrance opened to a confined area with several small, round tables and chairs scattered around the premises. A counter ran the entire width of the room. A four-foot steel mesh barricade was strung from the ceiling over the counter. It was something that Carl had noticed in many businesses: steps taken to isolate business owners from customers, for protection.

No one was in attendance when they entered. Earl rapped on the counter and an East Indian woman parted a beaded curtain in a doorway and came in, a small boy dangling on her left hip.

A glass case on the other side of the counter had pastries: pine tarts, Chinese cake, and cheese-rolls.

"Can I have a cheese roll and a soft drink? Doesn't matter which," Carl said.

"Same for me," Earl said.

The woman bounced the boy over to her right hip, reached into a cooler and extracted two bottles, flipped the caps off with an opener attached to the counter, and handed over the bottles. She transferred the boy again to her left hip, opened the glass case with her right hand, manipulated tongs to pull out two rolls that she placed on an enamel plate and turned it over.

Earl paid and they took seats at a table in the corner.

"I can't recall it being this hot," Carl said. "I seem to perspire just by the simple act of breathing."

Earl sipped his drink and bit into his roll. "It's always been this hot," he said. "Your body has just adapted to the Canadian weather."

A dog wandered into the shop, strolled over to the table and stood facing them, less than five feet away. The dog had nipples dangling from her underside as she swayed to the right and left. She passed her tongue along the length and width of her mouth, looked at Carl and Earl, and glanced over to the area behind the counter. Was she looking for the woman? How many times had she been chased away from the premises?

"Ignore her and she'll go away," Earl said.

Carl recalled the bitch that chased him down the Walk after Lincoln had pelted her with a stone. She had been a common breed of dog, just like this one, and like this one, she also had a litter. After that incident, he'd developed a phobia about strange dogs, especially those with pups. This one looked quite innocuous, though; she was whining and wagging her tail.

"Where did you live before you and your mother moved to the Walk?" Carl said.

"We lived in Camp Street after I started teaching, in an apartment."

"And prior to that?"

"Kingston –not too far from the sea wall, in the north end of the city."

"I remember Kingston…well. Whereabouts did you live?"

"We lived on Water Street, in a compound with range houses. Do you remember what they're like?"

Carl nodded. An inflection in the tone of Earl's question suggested resentment, perhaps even anger and hostility. Carl could understand the reason. Range houses were a cluster of flats, four or six of them occupying one building, several buildings grouped together in the compound that was often flooded in the rainy season. There was a solitary standpipe in the centre of the courtyard for washing clothes and occupants shared common washroom facilities. It often led to disputes and bitter arguments over rights and priorities, sometimes even culminating in violence.

"What about your father? I haven't heard you or your mother say anything about him since I arrived," Carl said.

Earl tilted his head and drained the balance of his soft drink. He picked up the uneaten portion of his cheese roll and tossed it to the dog. She caught it in mid-air and scampered out of the shop with it, as if she were afraid that he might change his mind and reclaim it.

"He was not married to my mother. One of those women-on-the side situations that so many Guyanese men indulge in. You know how it is, at times." The intonation in his voice had not changed, only now, it was dripping with bitterness.

The dog was back. She took up the same position in the same spot, licking her chops. The shopkeeper appeared through the opening at the back and the dog retreated out the door.

The woman raised her eyebrows, a silent query whether there was anything else they wanted. Earl stood up and shook his head.

"So, you can say," Earl continued, as he headed out, "in so many ways, that I'm a bastard." He smiled. "Got to give the man credit, though: he did pay for our upkeep and my schooling."

Carl followed him through the door.

The dog was standing outside the shop. She wagged her tail vigorously and followed them all the way to the car. Carl looked back as they pulled away; the dog was still wagging her tail.

They continued east along the highway, passing Bachelor's Adventure. At three in the afternoon, the heat was relentless. Carl could feel the sun penetrating the left side of his body that was receiving the full blast. Soon, they left the highway and travelled inland for another hour. Earl pulled out a scrap of paper and looked at it while he was driving. It was clear that he had lost the way.

They came across a man walking in the opposite direction. Earl slowed down and pulled up parallel to the man.

"Uncle," Earl said to the man, "can you help us with some directions?"

Something else that hadn't changed, Carl thought. Elders were always addressed in a respectful tone and it was still the practice.

The man stopped and turned to face the car. He was bare foot, dressed in khaki short pants and a tattered white shirt. In his left hand he carried a food carrier, the type used by cane-cutters on the sugar estates. In his right hand he carried a cutlass, the sun glinting off its well-honed edge. A battered straw hat provided a modicum of shade from the blistering sun. He was no more than fifty, Carl figured, but time and the ravages of hard work out in the fields had stooped his shoulders and wrinkled his features to the point where he looked more like seventy.

"Is where you going?" the cane-cutter said.

"We looking for Newtown."

The cane-cutter braced his cutlass against his right leg, pulled off his hat and scratched his head. His head had a shock of white hair. A look of puzzlement overcame him. He replaced his hat. "You gat me there boss," he said. "Ah don' really know dat place."

"It's the area where the refugees live."

"Refugees?" The man scratched his white stubble.

"The people who run away. You know, they were chased out of their own village in the disturbances in the sixties."

"Oh, you mean the squatters! Yes, only we don' call it Newtown, boss. Is called Squattown."

Earl looked at the directions again, turned to Carl and said: "Got to be the same place. Your uncle said to ask for the place where the squatters live."

He said to the man, "Yes, the same place."

"You shudda say so a long time ago, boss, and save we all that aggravation." He picked up his cutlass and pointed it to the direction in which the road continued. "You gat to follow this road. You going come to a road leading to Spicetown. Don' turn there. You cross over the old train track through Bonaventure. Turn so," and he moved his cutlass to the right, "you keep going 'till you come to a gravel road. You ky-ant miss it."

"Thank you, uncle," Earl said.

"Can't be too far," Carl said.

"Don't bet on it. It all depends on how far is not too far."

The intersection with the train track through Bonaventure turned out to be three miles away. As they drove over the abandoned track, Carl remembered train rides taken when he was a boy, up to Plantation Madeira, his grandmother's estate. The railway was scrapped shortly after independence, the equipment and rolling stock sold off.

Another two miles and they came to the gravel road that ended at a trench with a wooden bridge over it. The abruptness was startling: a road that ended in the middle of nowhere, as if the local authority had run out of funds for extending it. From that point on, a mud-road continued and it was filled with ridges and gullies, evidence that a tractor had passed through during a recent heavy rainfall.

"This is as far as I can go," Earl said. "The house can't be too far away."

"I'm sure I will find it," Carl said. He got out and retrieved his overnight bag and the plastic bags containing the fruits and vegetables.

"I will come back tomorrow afternoon around four to pick you up," Earl said.

Carl watched the De Soto turn around and head in the opposite direction.

He stood on the concrete bridge and surveyed his surroundings.

Below the bridge, the trench, swollen with overnight rain, gurgled its way through bushes at the edge of the village. About twenty yards down, a fisher man was throwing a cast-net in the trench. The man swung the seine in a circular motion over his head, threw it and slowly reined it in. Carl watched him open the net and extract fishes that he placed in his basket.

The land to the right of the trench was unoccupied –it was all open pasture. To the left was an expanse of houses of varying sizes and construction, a few of them well-built structures on concrete pillars, most of them mere shacks. The people occupying the area would now be in their sixteenth year of displacement and it was easy to see those who had accepted their situation, compared to those who considered themselves transient, hoping to return to their old dwellings. The houses with permanency were well constructed, while the shacks were shaky, like children's blocks stacked haphazardly, just waiting to fall with the first strong breeze that came along.

Carl crossed the bridge and started to negotiate his way around the shallow pools of water lying on the mud-road. As he was passing the first house, an East Indian woman came out on the landing and stood there looking at him.

"Can you tell me where the Dias shop is?" Carl said.

The woman took her time to answer, eyeing him with a frown, as if he had spoken in a foreign language. Finally, she pointed to the right. "Not too far," she said. "Ten houses down the road."

"Thank you," Carl said. It was refreshing to hear the term *Not too far* pinned down to something specific, for a change.

He saw another woman; she was fetching water and he thought she might have come from the trench he'd just passed. The woman was going in the same direction and she was laden with three buckets: one in each hand, a third balanced on her head. He could hear the slosh-slosh of the water as he went past, her body swaying as she adjusted her rhythm to the rise and fall of the dirt road. He thought of offering help, but realized that if he did, he might upset the delicate balance of the load she was carrying.

Along the way, more people came out to look and stare at him. There seemed to be a built-in alarm system that alerted them to a stranger entering their domain. It was bizarre and left him with a sense of discomfort, as if his every action were being scrutinized and evaluated to determine if he were friend or foe. Did they think he was a government agent looking for signs of illegal activity? He thought of recent reports he'd read about a large increase in Guyanese arriving at Pearson Airport, Canadian Immigration subjecting them to a thorough examination –were they there as genuine tourists or simply trying to jump the queue and remain as refugees?

By the time he arrived at the cake shop, he'd gained a thick coat of mud on his shoes and almost fallen twice on slippery patches on the road. Uncle Jules was sitting in a rocking chair on the landing of the top floor. He waved when he saw Carl and came down the stairs to greet him.

***

Carl and Uncle Jules had just finished supper and retreated to the landing.

The sun was sinking fast, bringing a multi hued approach to night, and with it, a painter's palette of reds, crimsons, burgundies and streaks of purple that softened the edges of the horizon and blurred the contours of the landscape. Everything seemed to assume mellow proportions and a peaceful calm descended on the area.

An open savannah lay at the back of the house and about half a mile further was Bonaventure, and beyond that, Spicetown. Bonaventure was where Plantation Madeira had been located. Uncle Jules' rocking chair was facing that direction and his vision never seemed to waver from the view. What was going through his uncle's mind –was he thinking, despite the peace and calm, that the night could hold unseen terrors, like back in 1964, when he and his entire family had fled in the middle of the night and left everything behind them?

Night fell, suddenly, swiftly, as if someone had pulled a large cloak over the area. There were no streetlights, a blackout was in effect and the road was masked in a pall of darkness, except when the full moon came out from behind dark clouds that seemed to be slowly blanketing the entire area, and when it did, streaks of light shimmered off the pools of water on the road.

After closing the shop on the ground floor, Uncle Jules' daughter, Aggie, had lit a candle and left it on the dining room table, before retreating to her room. It was the first time since his arrival that Carl had seen her. Her brother Desmond, was on the night shift at the nearby sugar factory. The oldest, Christopher, had gone to Suriname, where he was working in construction. The second son, Romeo was in Trinidad where he was an illegal immigrant. Carl had not seen or heard from his Aunt Indra so far. All the occupants of the house seemed to be in transit to some other place or were refugees in alien territory.

A cool breeze wafted through the house and blew out the candle, and after that, the only indication that Uncle Jules was in his presence, was when Carl heard his laboured breathing: a rhythmic, wheezing, slow inhalation and exhalation of air.

The mosquitoes came out. Carl had heard them, even before the first one zoomed in on him. It was a high-pitched, angry hum that signalled the intention for the rest of the evening. Carl swatted one that had settled on his right arm. Another zipped straight into his right ear with unerring accuracy, like a laser guided missile that had found its mark. He smacked his ear in desperation and the noise subsided, but it was replaced by a ringing in his ear.

Uncle Jules chuckled. "Boy, them mosquitoes know foreign blood when they taste it," he said. "Don't worry, we have mosquito netting for you in the room."

"Feels like when I was growing up in the Walk. Got so bad at one time that they started spraying the area with DDT to prevent the spread of malaria. They gave us all shots –I still have the impression on my arm from the one I received. Now, we're hearing that DDT is bad for the environment."

"They don't spray anymore –not because of any health reasons. They just don't have the money. They don't have money to do a lot of things these days. Did you notice how the drains and trenches all clog up with silt and weed? When rainy season come and the trenches flood, is when the mosquitoes breed. The government just won't do a damn thing about it."

Uncle Jules didn't seem bothered by the mosquitoes –Carl hadn't heard or seen him take action against them, not once. Other things, like government corruption seemed to annoy and make him livid.

"Where's all the money going?" Carl said.

"In some government top guy pocket and sent abroad. The whole damn country is feeding on corruption. Is like a cancer, spreading from the top all the way to the bottom. To get a simple birth certificate or driver license mean you have to pass money under the table. I don't know when it will all end. Things were never like this in the old days."

Things were never like this in the old days –it seemed to sum up the view of most of the older generation. If Augusto were still alive, he would have said the same thing.

Uncle Jules repeated. "Things were never like this in the old days." Then, he said: "Everybody was much better off under British rule. We didn't have all this nonsense going on."

Which meant that it would also still be a colony. It was a subject that Carl was loath to touch on.

"How are you making out in this new place, Uncle Jules?"

"This is a place to live; nothing more, nothing less." He sighed. "You have to make the most of things."

He said this with an air of resignation, but Carl knew: the house and limited yard space in Squattown were nothing, compared to his estate at Plantation Madeira.

Plantation Madeira, created on land that had been bought by Grandfather Salvador and Grandmother Lilly, had been sitting on a fault line of villages that had the potential for conflict. To the west was the village of Spicetown with majority descendants of Black slaves. To the east, separated by a wide, open pasture, was the village of Endless where majority East Indians traced their ancestry back to indentured workers from India.

"Sixteen years," Uncle Jules said. "Sounds like a long

time, but it feel like yesterday to me."

Carl knew what his uncle was talking about.

Uncle Jules and his family had turned up at Augusto's house in the Walk, back in May 1964, refugees who had fled in the night with nothing but the clothes on their back.

"What really happened that night, the night you had to run and leave the estate?" Carl said. "Do you remember?"

Uncle Jules stopped rocking. He was silent.

"Unless you'd rather not talk about it," Carl said.

Uncle Jules started to rock again. "Everybody around here in Squattown knows what happened. It's no secret."

"How did it all start, anyhow? I thought that the estate employed many Blacks, much more than East Indians."

"I ask myself the same question, over and over again. Were you in the country back in nineteen sixty-eight?"

Carl shook his head.

"Well, we had a minor earthquake back then. Everything seemed to hang in the air before that. Even the livestock and animals on the estate seemed to sense it: hens stopped laying eggs, the cows didn't produce milk, the dogs howling all the time. Well, I was feeling warning signs like that during the disturbances. I was already thinking that with all the problems in GT, trouble was bound to spread to the countryside, sooner or later.

"A rumour started that the Indians living in Spicetown attack a Black area nearby. A whole Black family got wiped out there, the rumour said. That didn't make sense. We had what, four or five Indian families living in Spicetown —everybody else was Black! Why would the Indians do something so stupid to take part in an attack on a Black area? A lot of outside people, opposition party people, been around making speeches, stirring the pot and inciting the villagers.

"I didn't know what to expect. The plantation was the largest employer in the area —logic tell me that the people from Spicetown would not jeopardize their livelihood; very little that was logical those days. All madness, I tell you.

"When night fall, fires start to light up the sky in Spicetown. We could see everything from the veranda. It had to be the East Indian families who live in the village. With that, I realize that the estate itself would be a target.

"I was thinking: if they did come, what could I take? This was the property your grandmother passed down to me and which I planned one day to leave to my children. We build up everything from scratch over the years –your grandmother and me. When first we come here it was no more than a Backdam. We build it up, through all the flooding and the hard times. Was this why we become targets? Was it greed or envy?

"I hear them long before they appear –the sound was drifting in with that cool breeze blowing in from the sea. You can feel the breeze now. You hear the crapoud and crickets? Was just like that. They were coming. They didn't really care who was innocent. They wanted to take revenge on somebody, anybody.

"We run across the pasture, the same pasture you can see out there during the day, through the long razor-grass that slice our bare flesh like a scythe. We stumble over soft pats of cow manure. All the while I can feel my heart going thump-thump, like it going to tear a hole in my chest, and the women crying all the time.

"You ask me if I remember! You bet I remember, every single minute of that night I can remember well. It was a nightmare."

"Who lives on the estate now?" Carl said.

"The same people who killed the Indians in the village and chased us out."

"Did you ever get compensated?"

Uncle Jules shook his head. "With this government in power? You must be joking! We still don't have title to the land here –that's why people call it Squattown."

"You never really recovered from it, did you?"

"There comes a time in a man's life when he realize that it's too late to start again." Uncle Jules shifted his weight in the rocking chair. "If I had the money, the will to do so left me a long time ago."

Uncle Jules once lived in a palatial house with servants catering to his needs and now, here he was, eking out an income from a small cake shop and living a trespasser's existence. Deep down, Carl thought that his father's brother would surely be bitter and resentful over what had happened. With his rocking chair facing in the direction where the estate was once located, and being able to see the coconut trees on the grounds and the lights from the house, they would all be constant reminders of an era long gone.

Uncle Jules shook his head. "Even if I did start all over, what use would it be? There is always something, someone, waiting to pull you down."

CHAPTER 18 - Revelations

RETURN TRIP DAY #4 – THURSDAY 27TH NOVEMBER 1980 PM AND INTO THE MORNING OF DAY #5 FRIDAY 28TH NOVEMBER AM

Carl looked at the luminous dial on his watch: it was four-thirty, Thursday morning, the fifth day of his trip.

He'd remained as late as he could on the landing with Uncle Jules, reluctant to retire to the room assigned to him, knowing that sleep would escape him.

Now, here he was, trying to find the best position on the bed, his thoughts racing from subject to subject, his brain refusing to concede his body's need for rest.

He thought of how things had changed since his departure from British Guiana and how those changes had affected his father and Uncle Jules. Once, the two brothers were wealthy, only to lose it all in the turbulent sixties. Nothing lasts forever, Carl thought. The makeup of the residents in the Walk also had changed radically: a virtual exodus of an entire generation, with a younger generation now trying to leave. Once called the breadbasket of the Caribbean, exporting rice and sugar, the country's main export was now people. No wonder Shirley, vivacious and attractive and youthful Shirley wanted to get out, as fast as she could. Her laughter rang in his ears and he had flashes of her features. It was more than the way she looked at him that had left the indelible impressions that were now haunting him; it was also the way she moved, every gesture and action a study in youthful exuberance.

It had been a very long time since he'd found anyone as fascinating as Shirley. Not since he met Natasha, back in Havana…

***

"You're a bright boy," Natasha said. "Your Spanish is picking up very good. How is my English doing?"

They were in her apartment, a block from the Plaza de la Revolucion, Friday, late afternoon. From where he lay in bed, next to her, through a window overlooking the Plaza, Carl could see the large image of Che, with its slogan in bold, large letters: *Hasta la Victoria Siempre*. Che, one of the architects of the Cuban revolution; he had long since left to transport Fidel's vision to the peasants of Latin America and convert the slogan to reality: *Forever Onwards Towards Victory*.

"Your English is coming along just fine," Carl said, and he meant it. She was a quick learner, someone who seemed to have a natural gift for languages.

He couldn't help smirking, though.

She noticed. She frowned. "Why do you laugh? Are you laughing at me?"

They'd just finished making love, again, after returning from time spent in the countryside in another of the Revolution's mass campaigns –the goal of this one: reverse the ignorance of more than a million illiterate children inherited from the Batista dictatorship. A noble goal, but Carl couldn't help wondering about the means being used to achieve it. Forced labour was becoming an integral part of education, with teachers and students being used in the building of schools and Learning Centres.

"No, I'm not laughing at you. I was just thinking about the first time we made love. How clumsy I was."

"We were both clumsy," she said.

She got out of bed and went to the window overlooking the street. She was naked, her body silhouetted in the glow of the sun that was lying on the horizon, slowly sinking into the ocean like a molten disc of lava.

Carl went over to the window and wrapped his arms around her. She smelled good. They'd showered together when they came back and then rushed into bed. Her skin was still moist from the shower and as he'd climbed on top of her, the thought had occurred to him that there was nothing as rapturous as making love to a woman after she had a bath. He'd consumed her, drinking from her body as if the warm, refreshing, unspoiled waters of an inland creek flowed in every crack and crevice. They'd both been energized, and now, the ecstasy of it lingered in his senses and excited him again.

The city was awakening from its lethargic slumber caused by the afternoon heat. A vegetable vendor, his cart stacked with carrots and okra and beans, was located directly under the window; a group of people, led by a tour guide heading for the Plaza; a man trying to interest the tourists in souvenirs –cups and key chains emblazoned with Che's picture.

Natasha leaned over to have a closer look at what was going on outside and she seemed to be totally oblivious of her exposure to anyone down below. He knew she didn't care. This was one of the things that had attracted him when they first met and became intimate. She had it and was not afraid to flaunt it, a devil-may-care attitude that said: you either accept my way or move on. Her style had been a major obstacle in her marriage back in the Soviet Union: her husband, an older man with his conservative outlook unable to come to terms with the changing times and women's role in the evolving socialist society. He'd moved on.

Carl spun her around to face him. Her breasts were firm, her nipples large and erect. Her torso was milk white, the paleness of the Russian steppes in the grip of winter, in contrast to the tan she'd picked up on her face and legs and feet from the skimpy clothes she wore around and about the city and countryside.

"It's not easy to make love to someone in a foreign language," he said.

He had known no Russian, had difficulty finding the right words in Spanish, and she was of little help with her limited English.

She laughed. "You didn't have no problem, that first time. You know exactly what to do."

He felt his face turning red. The second language lesson in her apartment. He'd come up the stairs. The door was open and she was sitting on the sofa, her legs crossed, a book balanced on her lap. He could see that she wore no underwear when she moved the book around and repositioned her legs. She'd seen him looking. He'd blushed, felt guilty, like a kid caught trying to sneak a peak at an adult magazine.

That first time, she'd practically seduced him. After an hour of unfocussed explanation of nouns and verbs translated between English and Spanish, she came over to him where he was sitting and kissed him passionately. He'd responded eagerly. In the darkness of her bedroom, he'd found himself groping around her body, probing every rise and undulation, like a blind man reading Braille on a page.

Outside, the exhaust of a car sputtered and backfired, someone strummed a guitar, the sound of soldiers' boots resounded on the cobbled street. The Revolution lived on.

She came over to him and rumpled the lock of hair that hung on his forehead. "Sex is a universal language," she said. "Everyone knows how to do it when the time comes."

Making love to her in that first year left him with a rich satisfying feeling, with the sigh of someone who's eaten his favourite meal to his heart's content and still yearns for more.

***

Rain was falling –what started out as a drizzle became a heavy downpour that drummed on the zinc sheets and cascaded off the rooftop, like the sound of a crowd gradually building up in a room, the noise swelling to a crescendo. He'd seen many days like this so far in his short visit back to Guyana.

Carl could hear the gurgling, splashing sounds as the water filled a rain barrel just outside his window. Long after the rain stopped, the drops continued from the gutters into the barrel and he could hear the ping-ping, drip-drip, like a tap that couldn't be shut off completely.

The window curtains fluttered as the bedroom door opened, causing a surge of air into the room. Someone had entered. It was a stealthy movement, the footsteps of a ballerina doing a dance sequence on tiptoes.

Carl sat up. The person came close to the foot of the bed, crossed over to the window and looked out. In the moonlight pouring through the window, he saw a tall and reedy woman, slender almost to the point of emaciation, dressed in a white gown that hung around her body like an old sheet draped over a piece of furniture. She had a matching white hat with a veil halfway down her face, and long strands of unruly white hair spilled down her back to her waist like a waterfall. He saw what looked like a bible that she was clutching in both hands, as if it were her lifeline to salvation. She could just as well be on her way to church, like the women he'd seen in Sunday morning mass at the Brickdam Cathedral when he was a boy.

She turned and looked at Carl. "Who you be?" the woman said. "I don't know you. What you doin' here in this room?"

Carl didn't respond. It was his first meeting with Aunt Indra since leaving British Guiana and his first sighting of her since his arrival. A radical change had come over her. Far from the vibrant, full bodied and attractive woman he once knew, she was now the picture of someone who seemed to be hanging on by a slender thread.

"I'm Carl, one of Augusto's boys."

Her eyes dilated. Was it a sign of recognition? Was it possible that she even remembered him from so many years ago?

The woman started to scratch at white gloves that reached up to her elbows, first the left with her right hand, then the right with the left. Her mouth opened, her tongue flickered in and out and she sucked her lips in and gnawed at both of them at the same time.

"Where be Augusto now? He gone to church?"

No one had told her that Augusto had passed on, it seemed.

"You must go to church and pray to the Lord, you know. You look like a nice boy. Do you go to church?"

Carl was about to respond when she interrupted him.

"Shhh," she placed her right index finger on her lips and tilted her head to the open window. Her eyes opened wide. "Listen. Do you hear?"

Carl listened. He heard the rain dripping in the barrel, a howling dog competing with a medley of crapoud and crickets, a fowl cock crowing, but nothing else.

"They coming," the woman whispered. "They coming for we tonight. They want to get all of we. Run an' hide. Run an' hide before they get you."

She turned and made her way swiftly to the bedroom door. Before she left the room, she paused and turned back to face Carl.

"You be a good boy now. Visit me when we go back home," she said, in a much calmer voice. "And bring Augusto with you next time. We all go to church in the morning." In a few seconds, she had hurried through the door and was gone.

Sixteen years had passed since the relocation, but it seemed as if his aunt was still driven by the idea of returning to her old life. The escape had been a turning point in Uncle Jules' life and Carl thought that the memory of that fateful night had to be burnt into his aunt's subconscious. There are turning points in everyone's existence, he realized, a stage where life, as is known, changes irreversibly, and nothing can ever restore the past. He thought of the milestones in his own life and two of them came to mind readily: the time he left British Guiana for the scholarship in Cuba, and his departure from Cuba for Canada. Today, he was faced with yet another life changing decision: to return to the life he had with Natasha and the kids, or to move on.

The fowl cock crowed again. It was a loud, coarse sound that drowned out everything else around and Carl could picture the proud bird perched on the fence, his breast puffed up, head thrown back as he blasted his morning incantation for the whole village to hear. Long after the cock stopped crowing, the sound reverberated in Carl's ears as he lay there in bed, staring at the zinc sheets in the roof, wondering where his next step would take him regarding Natasha.

He was dressed, lying on the bed, counting the hours until Earl would return for him.

A soft rap on the bedroom door. A woman's voice said: "Breakfast is ready, cousin Carl."

On the way down the corridor, he passed a closed door. He stopped –was it Aunt Indra's? The woman needed professional help and he wondered if it was available in the country these days. In the past, people like her were incarcerated in the Berbice Mad House with little hope of ever seeing the outside again. It was where Aunt Indra's mother had been confined. Such a long time ago. If he saw Aunt Indra in the room, what would he tell her? That he was sorry about things turning out the way they did? Would it make a difference in her life, at this stage? He turned the knob –the door was locked.

When he entered the kitchen, Uncle Jules was sitting at the table, along with his son Desmond and daughter Aggie.

"Did you sleep okay?" Uncle Jules said.

Carl hesitated. How could he tell his uncle that his disturbed wife was running around during the night and had come into his room?

"So much noise in the night," Carl said. "Things I haven't heard for a very long time, and certainly don't hear in a big city like Toronto. But, I did manage to get some shut eye."

"There's chicken curry, fried plantain, pumpkin and roti," Jules said. "And coffee in the pot."

Carl sat down and helped himself.

He scooped up some pumpkin with a piece of *roti* and placed it in his mouth. The taste of the *roti* was different, unlike any of those he'd previously eaten.

Uncle Jules must have been prescient. "You will find that the *roti* is made from cassava flour, not like what you're accustomed to," he said. "The government banned a wide range of imported stuff and they started this *Buy Local campaign* to get people to buy local goods, so there's no flour coming into the country." He shook his head. "They won't tell the people the truth. They just don't have foreign exchange to buy the foodstuff they banned."

"This is just fine for me," Carl said.

"Aggie prepared the breakfast."

Carl turned to his cousin and thanked her.

Desmond spoke for the first time. "What did you bring me from Canada, cousin Carl?"

"Don't be a pest," Uncle Jules told his son.

Aggie leaned over to reach for the coffee pot to pour a cup for Carl. "He stale drunk," she whispered to Carl. "He drinking on de job all de time."

She was a carbon copy of her mother, right down to her features and thin body. Grow her hair long, dye it and give her the white gown and hat, and it would be Aunt Indra standing before him. Aggie was wearing a faded blue cotton dress that looked like a holdover from a school uniform she'd worn back in primary school.

Aggie laughed, covered her mouth with her left hand and said: "One of dese days they going fire him."

She had small, crooked rabbit teeth that were positioned in all directions, and she had a way of covering her mouth with her hand, like someone trying to hide the condition of her teeth, and at the same time drawing attention to it.

"What you saying about me?" Desmond said.

Uncle Jules cleared his throat and coughed. Was it the onset of a cold or was it his demand for peace around the breakfast table?

"I not talking about you," Aggie said.

Desmond sat slumped in his chair, glaring at his sister. He was still dressed in his khaki security-guard uniform, his short sleeve shirt sweat-stained at the collar and hanging loosely around his shoulders. He had large ears –they stuck out from the sides of his head like bat wings and he had the strange ability to move them in different directions, like a cat responding to sounds coming from the kitchen at dinner time.

"What did you bring me from Canada, cousin Carl?" Desmond said, again. It was almost as if the alcohol had wiped out his short-term memory and he couldn't recall that he'd asked the same question just a minute ago.

Carl hadn't seen Desmond eat or drink anything. His cousin just sat there, his hands folded across his chest, a smile frozen on his face, even when he addressed Carl or re-proached his sister.

Aggie sucked her teeth. She covered her mouth and whispered to Carl: "He never got any money. He always drinking it out on payday." She ate with her fingers, breaking a piece of *roti* and pairing it with chicken, but only after she'd moved her food around her plate several times with her fingers, as if she were checking to see whether it was still alive. After she selected a piece of chicken, she would open her mouth wide, stick her tongue out, place the food on it and curl it inwards, like an Iguana reaching for an insect flying in the air.

Desmond seemed to come awake. "Why you eating with your hands like a woman from the country? Why you not using a spoon?"

"Leave me alone," his sister said.

Uncle Jules cleared his throat and coughed, again. He raised his cup to his mouth and drank, his eyes looking over the rim of the cup, like an animal at a water hole wanting to see everything going on around it.

Desmond went off to bed. Aggie went downstairs to open up the shop.

Carl took his coffee mug to the landing with Uncle Jules.

Uncle Jules took his position on the rocking chair.

"I suppose it will be a long time before we see you back in these parts," Uncle Jules said.

Not wanting to hurt the Old Man's feelings, Carl said: "You never know. Things could improve, the bank might open a branch here, they might ask me to come back and lend a hand to set it up."

"That would have pleased your father."

Carl sighed. Pleased his father? There had once been a time, when he was much younger, when he'd wanted to follow in his father's footsteps. He would seek the Old Man's approval and look forward eagerly to a pat on the back. His need for praise had fizzled out in his mid teens. As he looked back, he couldn't figure out which had come first. Had he stopped seeking his father's approval when it dried up, or had his father stopped giving it when he thought Carl no longer deserved it? After a while, he and his father had become two parallel lines, never meant to cross again. There were incidents that still stood out in his mind and had been eating away at him for a long time.

"I'm not so sure, Uncle Jules. I can't say there was very much I did as a young man that pleased my father."

Uncle Jules rose from his rocking chair and walked over to the door. Several columns of black ants were negotiating their way up and down the left doorjamb. He reached over and disrupted the flow and the ants scattered in all directions.

"Them ants come from that tree," he pointed to the orange tree in the front yard. "They working on the ground floor – they have a big nest below it. Soon they going to bring the whole house crashing down 'pon us."

"Is there nothing that you can do about it?"

"That's the way these ants work. Piece by piece, they strip everything and cart it away. This country going the same way: the corrupt politicians only looking out for themselves. They all a selfish and greedy bunch who want more and more."

By the time Jules returned to his rocking chair the ants had resumed their upward and downward trek on the doorjamb, as if nothing had happened.

"Your father might not have said how he was feeling about you. Just the way it is with people like us, from the old school. We don't hand out praise often." Uncle Jules chuckled. "We treat praise like gold sovereigns, and they disappeared a long time ago."

Uncle Jules rubbed his bald dome and focused his thick lens on Carl.

"I know that he was very proud of all of his sons, especially you. He always talked about how you had this way of picking up things quickly, and I remember how much he showed off that you could read before you started primary school."

Carl remembered: he was sitting on his father's lap, reading from a hardcover book with the title *Lives Of The Saints*. Music came from a phonograph in his father's study: *Beautiful Dreamer, come onto me*. He had no idea about the substance or implication of what he was reading back then, and his father hadn't taken the effort to explain it, but the Old Man never failed to boast to visitors about Carl's reading prowess.

Carl stood by the rail overlooking the road, sipping his coffee.

The rain had stopped but there were still nimbus clouds hanging around, threatening, and a light breeze brought scents that Carl could identify. The uninviting odour of decay from the stagnant water of the trench up the road, the marked hint of citrus from the orange tree in the front yard, the unwelcome intrusion of the earthy smell of cow dung from the pasture where cattle grazed.

Carl turned around to face his uncle. "There's something that's been bothering me, something I need to ask you, about my father."

Uncle Jules nodded.

Carl took a deep breath. "It's all very vague, but I seem to remember, as a small boy, my father taking me to visit someone. I can't even remember how old I was, but I must have been old enough for it to make an impression on me. There was a woman and a small baby boy in the house. One of those range houses in Kingston. I remember a priest and a crowd of people, food, soft drinks, ice cream, and there might have been a christening for the baby boy."

Uncle Jules looked away, in the direction of the plantation. "Must have been a long time ago."

"There's more. I remember Grandmother Lilly coming to the house in the Walk. She turned up suddenly one Sunday. She and my father had a big quarrel and it was over a woman that he was seeing outside. My mother was crying. Grandmother was furious with my father; she even threatened to kick him out of the house. Again, I can't remember exactly how old I was, but I know it happened. I remember I was worried: where would my father go if he had to leave the house for good."

Uncle Jules had stopped rocking. "We all have our demons that we have to live with," he said.

"Years later, I remember telling my oldest brother about it and he dismissed it, saying that I must have imagined it."

"I don't think you imagined it."

"So, Uncle Jules, I hope you're not offended if I ask you what you know about it."

Uncle Jules resumed his rocking. "Your father was no saint in his early years, but later, he tried to live a clean life. Sometimes, it's wise to remember the good things and forget about the bad. They can only cause you a lot of sleepless nights and headache for nothing."

"The question that's at the back of my mind is: why did you move Sumintra and Earl into the house in the Walk? I can understand Patsy and her son –they're related, but why Sumintra and Earl?"

"Someone had to take care of the place, and your father needed help."

"Why the two of them? Is Sumintra the woman in my childhood memory, my father's mistress?"

Uncle Jules placed his feet on the landing and stopped rocking. "You sure you want to know?"

"Yes."

Uncle Jules looked in the direction of the plantation. He seemed to be deep in thought. What was he thinking? The plantation –always there, the vision haunting him like the recurring itch from an old scar, coming back to remind him of the wound and the circumstances under which he received it? His father's younger brother had just turned sixty-eight and was now in the twilight of his years. Was he, perhaps, looking back and trying to assess whether it was all worth it?

Finally, Uncle Jules sighed and nodded.

"Then, Earl is my half brother!"

From the road came a shout. "Inside, good mawning neighbour."

"Good morning neighbour Chan," Uncle Jules said, without looking up.

A woman was passing on the road, picking her way around the pools of water, a parasol opened up, even though the rain had stopped. She wore a bright red dress and long boots that were caked with a layer of mud. Far off, in a trench that ran parallel to the last row of houses, was a massive pig, his head moving right and left as he sloughed his way around the bend in the road. A goat was in the neighbour's yard next door; he was trying to poke his way to get out through an opening in the fence, but his progress was hindered by a wooden triangle hanging around his neck.

"Look like we going get some more rain," the woman said.

"Never stops, neighbour Chan, never really stops," Uncle Jules said.

Desperation must have driven Carl's mother to appeal to grandmother Lilly. While lecturing his sons about the need to live a virtuous life, Carl's father had already experienced a phase of dissipation and had his fling with an outside woman. It was so hypocritical: a man, who, having lived his early years engaging in wine, women and song, wanted to impose a strict morality code on his children. Carl shook his head in amusement and thought: there's no bigger fraud than a man who seeks to atone for his period of indiscretions by finding God later.

And the irony of it all: he'd lost his father and gained a brother.

CHAPTER 19 - Visitors

FRIDAY 28th NOVEMBER 1980. AM

Uncle Jules and Aggie were standing on the landing, waving, as Carl left the house.

Carl turned around and took a last look before the road curved and he lost sight of them behind a mango tree. The goodbye had been awkward: a quick hug, a peremptory *Keep in touch*, and then he'd found himself heading down the stairs. Uncle Jules was not planning to see him off on Sunday; he said that he had something important to do. Carl suspected that his uncle knew, like Carl, that it was unlikely they would meet again and he wanted no last goodbye at the airport.

Earl was waiting with the De Soto at the head of the street and he was busy with a rag, working on cleaning the car, when Carl came upon him. The De Soto was splattered with mud and dirty water from the drive into the country.

"Thanks for coming back for me," Carl said, as he settled into the passenger seat in front.

Earl nodded and started the car, heading out to the main roadway.

Carl was soon lost in his thoughts. How much did Earl know? Did Sumintra tell her son that Augusto was his father? Carl recalled the conversation on the way up to visit Uncle Jules. Earl had sounded bitter when questioned about his father. Should Carl tell him? How would Earl react to the news? Would Carl reopen those wounds again if he told Earl that they had the same father?

Earl broke into his thoughts. "We had some visitors yesterday, at the house," he said.

"More of my father's friends come to pay their respects?"

Earl shook his head and reached into his top pocket for a cigarette and stuck it between his lips.

They had now joined the main roadway heading west into the city. Earl was merging into traffic.

Carl raised his eyebrows. "Who were they?"

"One, a tall guy named Ross. The other one, I can't remember his name. Ross said that he was really disappointed in you. He said that you didn't tell them the whole story when you come into the country."

A mini-van pulled out suddenly from the parapet where the driver had been discharging a passenger. Newscasts were filled with reports of traffic fatalities and the East Coast Highway was notorious for motor vehicle accidents that pushed the road-death count to higher levels. Carl braced himself against the dashboard for what he thought would surely be a crash, with him bearing the full force of the impact on the passenger side. The cigarette fell out of Earl's mouth down to the floor as he swerved and avoided the van, with inches to spare.

"Son of a bitch," Earl swore. "You see how crazy these people drive here. Lots of them buy their license and don't know a thing about safe driving, you know."

Earl reached into his shirt pocket and replaced his cigarette. When he settled down in traffic again, he said, "What they talking about?"

Carl shook his head. "No big thing, just a misunderstanding."

Earl glanced over and raised his eyebrows. "Didn't sound like that; Ross was calm and sounded reasonable, but the other one, he was really pissed. He was swearing and talking about you belonging to some group that was plotting to overthrow the government. He even threatened us. I tell you, my mother was really worried."

"Nothing much to worry about. Earlier this year, in Toronto, a very old friend invited me to a meeting that was being held by this group they're talking about. I quickly found out that it was not something I wanted to be involved in. Meanwhile, the guy had taken out a membership in my name, and I had no idea he'd done that."

"What happened after that?"

"I cancelled my membership and never went to any other meeting."

Earl sighed. "The stumpy one say that they throw people in jail for lying to them. Keep in mind that people disappear all the time in this country. You hear rumours. First you hear they gone to the US, then you hear they in Suriname or Trinidad working. Sometimes, you never hear about them, at all. You never know what really happened."

"I'm sure it can be cleared up very easily."

"I don't think it's going to be that easy to convince them."

The machinery of the state bureaucracy grinds very slowly, Carl thought, especially in a centralized one where the top retains the privilege of making all meaningful decisions and passing them down to the lower levels. It was obvious that his brief membership in the RDG Party had been discovered, but it had taken the Guyana Government nearly a week to come to the conclusion that he should be further investigated. If it took that long to arrive at that decision, how much more time would it take to establish that he was not involved?

Earl was negotiating around a hairpin curve and a large building loomed in the middle of the divided highway; the Russian Embassy. After alienating Western governments, especially the British, the American and the Canadian, by nationalizing their businesses, aid from those countries had dried up. The Republican government had turned to the Eastern Bloc and was now receiving large financial support from Russia with hundreds of Cuban advisers in the country.

Along with the aid, had there been lessons on the use of repressive techniques against its citizens?

"They want to ask you some more questions," Earl said. "You must report to them at police headquarters when you go back to GT."

Carl remembered his long session with Ross and Brackett at the airport. Paranoia had ruled. They felt that any arrival from Canada, where the plot originated, might be involved in the attempt to overthrow the government. He did not relish another cross examination with the two men, especially Brackett, who had been boisterous and combative, nor did he want to be turned over to any other agency of the state apparatus. He could see himself languishing in a cell for months while the machinery took its time to clear him. It was typical in a repressive regime: those under suspicion were assumed guilty until proven innocent, and no one would be willing to take the steps needed to clear the accused, for fear of being censored by superiors.

"What did you tell them, about where I was?" Carl said.

"That you'd left and won't be back. Doesn't look too good, I tell you. My mother is really worried."

"I would imagine they'll be watching the house in the Walk for when I return, then?"

Earl nodded. "Most likely. What you going to do?"

"Seems as if I have limited choices. If I return to the Walk, I get picked up. If I try to leave on Sunday, I get picked up at the airport."

"Do you want to check with the Canadian Consulate in High Street? They might be able to help."

Carl shook his head. "Won't do much good. The Consul here offers limited service. They will refer the matter to the embassy in Trinidad. The embassy will contact Ottawa. Foreign Affairs in Ottawa will deliberate over the matter for a while before they contact the Guyana government. Meanwhile, I'll be detained somewhere inaccessible. It could take months before it's all sorted out!"

"You're travelling with a Canadian passport, right?"

Carl shrugged. "Yes. But, the Canadian government makes it very clear: you're subject to the laws of the country you're travelling to. I never saw the need to renounce my Guyanese citizenship, so by default, I have dual citizenship, which means the Guyana government can always claim that I'm under their jurisdiction."

"So, what you going to do, then?"

"I have to see a good lawyer."

Earl snorted. "Wish you luck in that. We still have good lawyers around but not much law for them to practice these days."

"What do you mean by that?"

"The courts have no independence. The President interprets the law in his own way ever since he become President for life in the last referendum, in which only about ten percent of the people voted. You dare not be critical of him or the government today."

"What happened to all those rights that were supposed to be enshrined in the constitution when independence came?"

Earl scoffed. "The constitution is just a piece of paper these days. The government passed an Administration Of Justice Bill and a National Security Act that restricts trial by jury and lands you in jail without bail. It gives more power to magistrates, all political appointees, to carry out the new laws."

"There's more," Earl continued. "An organized group called House Of Israel, led by a man called Rabbi Washington, carries out the government's criminal activities. They break up strikes, attack protesters, and silence anyone bold enough to criticize the President or the government."

"Rabbi Washington, an odd name for someone engaged in criminal activity," Carl said.

"Why they call him the Rabbi, I don't know. He's a Black American, no connection whatsoever with any religious group, Jewish or otherwise. He's involved, though. Everyone thinks so. Whether it's the bombing of Walter Rodney, or strong-arm tactics against opposition supporters, this man is behind it all. Do you remember the Jonestown massacre last year?"

How could Carl forget it? Jonestown was the singular most horrendous event that catapulted a virtually unknown Guyana into the world spotlight and sent people looking up the Atlas to discover the location of the only English speaking country in South America. Overnight, Jonestown and Guyana became catchwords that would be forever associated with cyanide poisoning and mass suicide. For months afterwards, whenever he was spotted around the water cooler at work, Carl would be asked if he was having *one of those drinks*. A vast number of U.S. government investigations, books and movies kept the story public for months and years afterwards.

"It was big news in North America."

Earl said: "A two million US dollar cash contribution to the ruling party in exchange for twenty-seven thousand acres of prime land in the interior, along with no political interference in the activities of the cult, this is what led to Jonestown."

Nineteen seventy-eight, only two short years ago: the Jonestown catastrophe and the year that he was appointed Senior Economist at the Canadian Business Bank. Alexei was four, Irina two, and Carl and Natasha had been living together for five years since her surprise arrival in Toronto.

Earl said: "Well, it was the Rabbi who was the middle man between Jim Jones and the government. I won't be surprised if he got an agent's fee out of the deal."

Carl thought of another priest: Father Martin whom he'd met in the flight coming over. He'd also met the head of the Guyana Human Rights group who was now a member of the International Elections Commission. Both of them were men of influence, but how much influence?

"I don't suppose it will do any good to see anyone else, then?" Carl said.

Earl sighed. "You can take your chances, if you want. Keep in mind, once you're out in the open, they can pick you up very easily. After that happens, who knows what comes next…"

Earlier that month, Ronald Reagan had been elected President of the U.S. and Edward Seaga had been swept into power in Jamaica. Reagan replaced the liberal minded Democrat Carter and Seaga took over from ultra-socialist Michael Manley. The winds of change seemed to be sweeping over the West. Could Carl hope that the autocratic Guyana government would eventually be forced out of power? If this happened it might help his cause, but only in the long run. In the meantime, he was boxed in from all directions.

"I still want to get in touch with a good lawyer," Carl said. "Sure, it's possible there's not much he can do, under the circumstances, but at least he can represent my interests and, most important of all, vouch for my health before I get picked up."

Earl glanced at his watch. "It's after five. Business already close for the weekend. You're not going to get hold of anyone, now."

Carl sighed. "Looks as if I'm running out of options."

Earl was silent. He reached into his shirt pocket and pulled out a lighter. He moved the cigarette around a few times in his mouth. He seemed to be pondering whether to light it or not. What else was he thinking about? Carl still didn't know if his half-brother was aware of the connection between the two of them.

"Do you know what Backtracking is?" Earl said. He'd made a decision on the cigarette –he replaced it in his shirt pocket, along with the lighter.

Carl hadn't heard the term, and shook his head.

"Plenty Guyanese leaving, but not the legal way –they heading through back tracks. Some going overland to Suriname, some through Venezuela, others by boat. They travel through Central America, then crossing over to the States from Mexico. If you went that route, you should be able to get back to Canada."

During the so-called Communist scare back in the fifties in British Guiana, the British Government had rounded up suspects and incarcerated them in a penal settlement on the island of Mazaruni in Essequibo county. They had confined the democratically elected Chairman and his pregnant wife. Was the current government handling political prisoners the same way? The images that his mind conjured up about Mazaruni were something akin to Devil's Island in French Guiana. Essequibo was also where Suddie, the Boys School was located. The Boys School was where Winslow was sent after the fight with Reds. Winslow had disappeared and remained out of touch for a long time. Was that the fate that would befall Carl? Would he even be able to get help from the Canadian Consul if he were sent there?

"I have to get out," Carl said, desperation creeping into his voice. "If they get hold of me, there's no telling how long it will take to resolve the matter. I have my job to go back to... and my family. Do you know of anyone who's done this Backtracking?"

"I know a couple of teachers who had no visa but they ended up in the States. One of them did mention to me about a man named Khan, who operates an import export business."

"Okay, let's go see Mister Khan."

Earl nodded. They were now passing through Vlissengen Road. On the left was the Presidential Mansion, built on land expropriated and carved out from the Botanical Gardens. Carl recalled Sunday afternoon visits to the gardens with his father. A bandstand where the police band played military music, a large pond where manatees surfaced to be hand-fed by visitors, the zoo next door where tigers and leopards paced in their cages, these were all from a distant past.

Carl said, "I don't want to get you and your mother into any trouble. I will need someplace else to stay over the weekend, until I can contact a lawyer on Monday."

Earl turned into Regent Street. "I know a hotel, not too far from here. Is really a beat-up place, but that's just what you need right now. No one will asks questions. We can do that after we see Mister Khan."

***

The sign attached to the door was in bold, black letters:

KHAN'S IMPORT/ EXPORT

WE SHIP ANYTHING ANYWHERE ANYTIME

Khan was on the phone when they entered and he waved Carl and Earl to two chairs in front of his desk.

"You a funny man," Khan said to the person on the phone. "Is a business I run here, not a charity. If you want charity, go see the Salvation Army."

He was a barrel of a man, his stomach hanging over the large desk littered with stacks of paper, his hands negotiating back and forth from a tree-trunk sized torso as he reached for something or replaced it on the desk.

"Gentlemen, what can I do for you?" the fat man said, after he'd hung up the phone.

"We're trying to arrange for a special shipment to Canada," Earl said.

Khan laughed. "You come to the right place. That's what we do. As the sign says: we can ship anything, anywhere, anytime."

Khan had two small burlap bags on the table. He reached into one of the bags, picked up several peanuts, shelled them, placed the shells in the second bag, opened his large, cavernous mouth and threw the peanuts into it.

Khan pulled out a writing pad. "What do you want to ship and where?" he said, in-between crunching the peanuts.

"I want to ship myself," Carl said.

"You?" the fat man sputtered and almost choked on his peanuts. "Gentlemen, you have to go to a travel agency for that. We're not that kind of agency. Go to BeeWee or Guyana Airways, or John Fernandes Shipping if you want to go by boat."

"Didn't you just say that you can ship anything," Earl said.

"Yes, but not people. I was talking about parcels, barrels, goods, merchandise. Anything like that."

Carl wanted to come straight to the point. Either the man could do it, or he couldn't.

"I have to get to Canada," Carl said. "Fast, and by unconventional means."

"I hear that you can arrange for people to go overland," Earl said. "Backtracking."

Khan narrowed his eyes, his brows grew thicker and seemed to merge into a straight line across his forehead.

"Who tell you that?"

"Not important right now. The question is: can you do it?" Carl said.

Khan took another handful of peanuts and started to shell them.

"I'm not saying that I can arrange it. I'm just saying that I know certain people who do that sort of stuff."

"Looks as if we come to the right place," Earl said.

Khan turned to Carl. "It cost much money, up front."

"How much are we talking about?" Carl said.

Khan was perspiring. He moved his right hand around both cheeks and his forehead and wiped his hand on his pants. He pursed his thick lips. "The people who do this sort of thing ask for ten thousand, US dollars."

"That *is* a lot of money," Carl said. "I only have five thousand."

Khan laughed, a laugh that rocked his whole body: his chest moved up and down, his jowls shook, the fat on his hands gyrated. Even after he'd stopped laughing there were still light tremors pulsating in his cheeks, like the aftershock of an earthquake.

"You one funny man," Khan said. "You think I run a charity here?"

Khan grew serious, the first time that Carl had seen humour leave his countenance. He picked up a grappling hook by the handle and reached over the peanuts.

"See this?" Khan pointed to the stack of papers he'd retrieved with his grappling hook, "These all bills I have to pay. You think I run a charity here? Fee is ten thousand. Five down, now, no refunds, and the balance on the day you leave."

Carl had walked with seven thousand dollars, most of it in travellers' cheques. He'd paid for the funeral and had planned on turning over money to Uncle Jules to clear up matters with the property.

"I don't have that kind of money," Carl said. "I only have access to five thousand here, in this country."

Khan roared. "You one funny man. You think I do charity work here?"

The balance was too large. He wasn't going anywhere, Carl thought.

Then, Earl said: "I can raise twenty-five hundred, between my mother and me."

Carl looked at Earl. For his brother and his mother to be able to raise that kind of money would require sacrifices, probably amounting to all their savings, and then some.

"You still short twenty-five hundred," Khan said.

"I'm good for it. I will pay the balance when I arrive in Canada," Carl said.

"You one funny man."

"My word is good."

"Your word is not collateral," the fat man said, and he'd stopped laughing.

Carl was stumped. He had run out of alternatives.

"I have a De Soto, in good condition. On the black market you can get a lot more than that. I will put it up as collateral," Earl said.

The De Soto was more than Earl's pride and joy. It was a major source of income for him and his mother. Without the car to hire out, they might just barely make out on his teaching income.

Khan looked out the window. People were passing outside: a vendor with a large basket perched on top of her head, a man driving a donkey-cart, a small boy steering a bicycle wheel with a stick. The De Soto was parked in front of the entrance.

"You got registration for that car?" Khan said.

Earl nodded. "I will turn it over to you the day Carl leaves."

"I will wire the balance to Earl when I get to Canada and he will hand it over to you in exchange for the car," Carl said.

"Do you have a passport?" Khan said.

"I have a valid Canadian passport."

"I can get five thousand US dollars for it, you know. We split it fifty-fifty."

"Then, how do I get into Canada?" Carl said.

"They sneak you over the border. Is a long border between America and Canada, you know. People crossing over every day."

"No passport in the deal," Carl said.

Khan sighed. He picked up his fly swatter and slapped it on the desk. "I think we have a deal, my friends. I promise I will speak to the people who handle these things and ask them to make the necessary arrangements."

Carl pulled out his money belt and extracted the travellers' cheques. He counted out five thousand dollars, signed the cheques and turned them over to Khan.

"Here's the down payment. Make sure that it's more than a promise," Carl said.

The hotel was in upper Water Street, far from the commercial area, in a neighbourhood that Carl recalled was a Red Light district in his days.

It was late afternoon by the time they arrived.

Before they left the car, Earl said: "Backtracking not going to be easy, you know. If they catch you, is jail for you."

"I know. I have to take the chance."

"All kinds of people you going meet along the way: vagabonds who want to steal your money, cut-throats who don't like the way you look, officials who want a bribe. You might not make it, you know."

"I don't have much of a choice at this stage of the game."

Carl followed Earl through an empty dance floor, to a bar where a man was cleaning glasses with a towel hanging over his shoulder.

"We need a room," Earl told the man.

"A thousand dollars," the man said, as he looked Earl over from head to toe. He shifted his scrutiny to Carl and did the same thing.

"It's going to be for a few days," Earl said.

"Same rate. Pay now for the first night. Pay in advance every other night."

Earl pulled out a wad of Guyanese currency from his pocket, counted and handed over the amount. "A room at the back, with no disturbance," he said.

The man reached behind him and took a key from a drawer. He was a Douglah: Black mixed with East Indian, perhaps in his mid fifties, totally grey, right down to his moustache. He never moved from his position –his feet planted firmly on the floor, as if they'd taken root from many years of working there.

"I know just what you want." The man winked. "Room two-two-two, up the stairs, at the back. Perfect for two, and with privacy."

That was it: a simple non-registration, cash on the barrel, no questions asked.

The man returned to cleaning the glass in his hand but he never took his eyes off Carl and Earl as they went through the door to a hallway in the rear. Was he accustomed to liaisons between two consenting male adults, also? As the door closed behind him, the last thing that Carl saw was a smirk on the man's face, the look of a man who thinks he knows a dark secret about someone else and is storing it away for use when the time is ripe.

Earl led the way, up the stairs, to the end of a corridor and room 222, the numbers fashioned out of wood and screwed onto the door. There had been no pause in Earl's stride, no look of bewilderment, no consternation –he seemed to be fully familiar with the premises. How many times had his half-brother used the room?

The room was sparsely furnished: a double bed made up with a torn white cotton sheet, a hat stand with no hats and a long mirror on the wall. The mirror had a jagged crack in the middle. A solitary chair braced against the wall opposite the bed; an overhead fan that had started when Earl threw the light switch on the wall. What stories the room could tell, Carl thought. The room had the look of being occupied by transients, and had probably witnessed countless clandestine meetings.

"It's not much," Earl said.

Carl threw his overnight bag on the bed. "This will do," he said.

"I'm going to come back tomorrow. Bring some food and other stuff you'll need."

"You've been like a brother to me. I feel that you've done so much already."

Earl shrugged. "It's nothing. I'm only sorry I have to leave you in a place like this." He seemed genuinely perturbed as he opened the door.

"Don't worry about it," Carl said. "I've been around a bit. I'll be alright."

Carl watched his half-brother close the door behind him. After that, he was alone, with his thoughts and memories, and the fan whirring overhead. He went to lie on the bed.

Now, that he was on his own, Carl couldn't help thinking of his decision to go the Backtracking route. Had he been too hasty? The whole trip was fraught with danger. Was he better off turning himself in and taking his chances with the Guyanese government? The frustration of Ross and Brackett at the airport was palpable; it was the exasperation of officials under orders to determine if a suspected uprising might or might not be operational. Carl imagined a situation where the two men were under extreme pressure to produce results. What if they decided to make an example of him, the only person they could lay their hands on? What if they sentenced him to life imprisonment for crimes against the state? Worse, what if they turned him over to the Rabbi?

If he did leave the country through the Backtracking route, he had no illusions about the possible outcomes. What if he were caught in one of the Central American countries, or Mexico, before he even had the chance to cross over to the U.S.? They might imprison him and it would be months before he could get the Canadian Embassy to act. Even if everything went well and he had the good fortune to make it to the U.S. Border, authorities were subjecting the border with Mexico to closer scrutiny recently, to reduce the large quantity of drugs being smuggled into the country.

The uncertainty, the fear of the unknown was driving him, almost to the point of desperation. He felt as if he was going down a dark stairway, missing a step, hurtling into the unknown and having no idea where he would land. He had to admit that he was lost, hopelessly, helplessly, and he didn't know where it would end. He was the man wandering in the desert, looking for an elusive oasis, afraid that his strength would finally give out, while just over the next hill might be salvation.

He had moments like this when he was in Cuba, moments of uncertainty, when he'd questioned his motivation for leaving British Guiana and his decision to take the scholarship. Had he made the right choice? It had gradually dawned on him that, perhaps, he'd done it all to get back at his father. He'd always thought that his father didn't have a very high opinion of his sons, the Old Man never being satisfied with their achievements, constantly driving them to go further and further, always holding himself up as an example of the type of person his offspring could, and should develop into. Try as hard as he could, Carl didn't believe that his father would ever respect or acknowledge his abilities. He thought that his father always looked at him like he did one of his clerks who worked in his store: as someone with no ambition and lacking the ability to get further in life.

Then, Uncle Jules had shattered the myth and told him about his father's boastful pronouncements about his children, especially Carl.

Carl jumped out of bed and headed for the door, but paused just before he opened it. He glanced at his watch: eight thirty, still relatively early in the evening. Where would he go? Music was playing downstairs –the muffled notes crept stealthily through the bottom of the door, the vibration of the speakers penetrating the floorboards and resounding against the walls. He went over to the solitary chair to keep it company but after a few minutes he realized that he was so tired, he was starting to doze and he almost fell off the chair twice before he caught himself. He felt like a bird, its eyes half opened, liable to fall off its perch after a hectic day of being on the lookout for predators.

He was tired, but he didn't want to sleep. He had to keep moving, had to think things out. He began to pace the room.

The doubts had started to surface when he was able to get a firsthand look at what life was going to be like in Cuba, after Fidel and his revolution had succeeded in tightening their hold on the country. His decision to leave Cuba after he graduated was influenced by this unflattering perspective of the revolution that was slowly percolating in his mind, this and other events...

***

Carl and Natasha had just returned from a mass rally: Tens of thousands crammed into the Plaza de la Revolucion to hear Fidel talk about the difficult road ahead in the fight against the Imperialist Yankees. The leader had talked nonstop, going on for more than four hours. It was the way Fidel's speeches were going recently, a marathon runner trying to exceed his previous record. Like most of his recent addresses to the nation, this one had been long on rhetoric and short on substance. Carl was close to collapsing from the build-up of heat due to the relentless sun overhead.

"Thank God, I thought he'd never finish," Carl said, when they arrived back at Natasha's apartment.

Natasha had removed most of her clothes and was down to her underwear –it was the way she handled the heat, she said. She had this way of displaying her nakedness around the flat, like a soldier wearing a sparkling new uniform on parade. During the evening, when the cool breezes of the Atlantic blew across the Malecon, she was known to do this and seemed to display no inhibition, no shame or restraint.

"I have some news," she said, as she paused in front of the fridge that had just started up after a blackout period, an event that was becoming more frequent.

He looked at her.

She continued. "I have a posting as a translator for the Russian delegation to the UN."

She had never hinted to him that she was interested in leaving Cuba.

"Oh, when did this happen?"

"I just hear about it today."

"I'm puzzled. You must have known about it for some time."

"It's been, how do you say, in the works for a while, but nothing was sure, until today."

"What do you mean that nothing was sure? Did you apply or is it a posting with no choice?"

She hesitated, reached into the fridge, looking for something, but the fridge was practically empty –it was a way of life now, almost everything was rationed. She pulled out a bottle half-filled with cane juice, sniffed it, wrinkled her nose, and drank from it.

"I applied, but I wasn't sure it would happen," she said, after she'd replaced the bottle in the fridge.

"When did you plan on telling me?"

"I'm telling you now," she said.

Over four years, he'd grown disenchanted with the way she disclosed information about her background and activities. She was always so secretive, the details coming out in bits and pieces, as if it was all classified information that could be released only on a need-to-know basis. Was it all a symptom of her Communist upbringing that she thought she dared not trust him with all the information, lest he denounce her to the authorities? It was no coincidence that she often told him of how it had been during the Stalinist purges, where many members of her family had been sent off to labour camps in Siberia.

An entire year in their relationship had elapsed before Carl found out that Natasha had been married, and divorced after a year, back in Russia. Vladimir was now employed as an attaché in the Russian embassy in Havana. The man was openly hostile after he found out that his ex-wife was having a relationship with Carl.

"How long are you going to be there?" Carl said.

She came across the room and settled down in the sofa next to him. "Oh, you never know about these things. Could be a month, or a year, two years, I don't know. You go where they send you."

Something occurred to Carl. "By any chance, is Vladimir also going to the U.N.?"

She looked away and stared out the window. The heat had already started to take its toll in June. Reports from the national newspaper Granma continued to extol the virtues of sacrifices necessary for the revolution. Meanwhile, there was no air-conditioning and no relief in sight –the elderly were dying in their flats. People were spending more time outdoors –Carl could hear snippets of conversation floating up and through the open windows.

She turned back to face him and respond. "Yes, he's going."

"By any chance, is he the one who managed to arrange this posting to the U.N.?"

"Yes,"

"I see."

She came closer to him. "My Carlos, my beautiful Carlos," she said, as she ruffled the lock of hair hanging on his forehead. "There's nothing going on. Whatever there was between me and Vlad is dead. We're divorced, remember?"

"I'm to believe that he's doing this only from the goodness of his heart?"

"Yes, for old times' sake."

That, and for favours granted, Carl thought. He'd come to realize that with Natasha, her body was a weapon and sex the ammunition to achieve her objectives.

She stood up and straddled his legs. "I know I can trust you, now." She kissed him. "You have nothing to be afraid of. I made up my mind a long time ago that I was not going back to Russia. There is no future there. Before you know it, the whole system will, how do you say it, implode, and the country will be in ruins. I don't want to be there when that happens."

"What happens after the U.N. posting?"

She ignored the question. "What are your plans, now that you have your degree? Will you return to your country?"

It was 1968. The government in Guyana was two years into its mandate after independence. Already, there was massive state intervention in the economy, shortages of food and other necessities, rumours of nationalization of foreign owned businesses. What was there to return to? Carl had left British Guiana with the best of intentions, hoping he could make a difference when he went back. With Reform now out of office, there was no hope that he would be able to obtain employment since it was Reform that had sponsored his scholarship. What had the last four years in Cuba really done for him? Opened up his eyes: he was seeing a system that was seriously flawed. The patient was almost on its deathbed, badly in need of a transfusion and it was not going to happen anytime soon. The Americans had imposed economic sanctions and Europe was standing back. They were all waiting for the regime to collapse and Castro was just as determined to withstand anything they threw at him.

"I've been thinking of going to Canada," Carl said.'

"Oh?" she raised her eyebrows and kissed him again. "My Carlos is a bad boy. He has secrets that he does not share with me?"

"I went to the Canadian Embassy six months back, when the final courses were coming up, and looked into the possibility of going to a university in Toronto."

"You did all this and didn't share with me?" she pouted and unbuttoned the front of his shirt.

"I can get a scholarship at the University of Toronto."

"Will you remain there, after?"

Carl nodded.

"Where do I fit into this?"

"You're going to the U.N., remember? With Vladimir?"

She was now opening his fly. She reached into his pants, pulled out his engorged organ and guided it into her. "Yes, but Vladimir can't give me what I want, not anymore," she said.

"You seem to be doing okay so far with him."

She started to ride him, slowly, her hands on his shoulder, her head thrown back, eyes closed. "What if I can get away, come to Canada and meet you there? Will you help me to settle?" she whispered in his ear, as if she were afraid that the walls were bugged and her intention revealed.

"How are you going to do that?"

"Remember, I have friends in high places?" she said.

***

Carl barely heard the rap on the door with the constant hum of the overhead fan and the music from the dance hall below. Was it Earl, returning with more news?

He got off the bed and went to the door; he opened it. A woman was standing out in the corridor, leaning against the doorjamb. She was dressed in a low-cut black dress, long sleeves patterned with lace and frills, the overhead light in the corridor reflecting on a trail of sequins hanging below her bosom. She seemed to be overdressed for her surroundings.

"Do you want some company?" the woman said.

Carl shook his head and closed the door. It was two in the morning and what he badly needed was sleep. But, his recollection of his Cuban interlude was something that always broke into his sleep, haunting him, becoming an integral part of his nightmares, similar to the near drowning incident in the Canal so many years ago.

Back in 1968 he'd made his decision and stuck with it. After what he'd seen in post-revolutionary Cuba, there was no way that he would return to Guyana to live, even if his party, Reform, eventually came to power again and imposed a benevolent brand of Communism. He'd already concluded: Communism did not live up to the classless society that it promised. In the Cuba of the sixties that he'd seen, while the Batista dictatorship was no longer in power, the reins of government were now in the hands of a new elite. The successors of the Spaniards were still in the top ranks, while the descendants of the slaves held the lower positions and did the menial jobs. He'd seen enough of that in colonial British Guiana, where the Portuguese dominated commerce and kept it as their own private fiefdom.

CHAPTER 20 -A Party

SATURDAY 29ᵀᴴ NOVEMBER

There was that rap on the door, again –louder this time. Carl stirred in bed. Was it the woman in the frilly black dress returning to try her luck again? Some people never take *No* for an answer.

He looked at his watch: four o'clock. Surely it couldn't be four am; it had to be 4pm. He remembered: it was eight in the morning when he'd finally drifted off to sleep, after the music had stopped and the voices from below ceased to intrude into his air space. He'd slept for close to eight hours!

Another rap on the door.

"I said to go away, damn it!"

"It's me, Earl."

Carl got up quickly and opened the door.

"Are you okay?" Earl said, as he entered the room.

"Yes, fine," Carl said. "I thought it was the woman from last night."

"What woman?"

"Not to worry, nothing happened. I slept away. Just couldn't keep awake any longer."

"What are you doing? You need to clean up. We got to go."

"Go? Where?"

"The party! Remember, Shirley's birthday party?"

Carl sat on the bed and shook his head. "I'm not really in the mood for a party right now."

"You should get away from here."

"I'm really not up to it. You go ahead."

"They going have plenty of food at the party."

He hadn't eaten since the previous day and he was famished, but he said: "I'll go downstairs and get something to eat later."

"Not much good around here to eat. Shirley said to make sure that you come."

He had to admit that the idea of seeing Shirley again was inviting and getting away from the hotel would be good. Another night in his room with the loud music and the woman in black knocking on his door was not something he was looking forward to. Still, with the predicament that he was in, he couldn't see how he would have any fun at the party.

"I can't leave without you," Earl said, "my mother told me to make sure you come to the party. She's going there to help out. Besides, she's bringing your belongings there for you."

A long weekend would pass before Carl saw the lawyer on Monday, and there was no predicting how long Mister Khan would take to come up with arrangements to leave the country. It made no sense for him to remain in his room and mope over the situation.

Carl was standing close to a large group of people, a drink in his hand, watching the goings-on as the night progressed. After the meal, the party had swiftly turned into a loud, raucous affair and it seemed as if the entire village of Repentigny was crowded into the hall. Shirley had to be a very popular person. That, and a combination of free food and liquor would be enough to bring everyone out. The music, most of it Calypso and Soca with the occasional waltz thrown in, was turned up to ear-bursting proportions.

One of the men in the nearby group, a young, tall East Indian, was back on holiday and was telling a story about his visit to New York. The others were listening attentively.

Carl saw Wilfred heading his way. His old friend was dressed in his white shirt-jacket, and he was still carrying the black briefcase that Carl had seen him with the first time at the house in the Walk.

Wilfred said: "Having a good time?"

Carl said: "Didn't expect to find you here."

Wilfred nodded. "They do allow me to go out and have fun, you know. Is not all dogma and discipline. The party slackening the rope these days." He held up a bottle of the local beer to show Carl. "We can even have a drink now and then."

The sarcasm in Wilfred's voice did not escape Carl. He decided to respond in kind. "I suppose your briefcase is where you carry the drinks, then?"

"Look at that Shirley on the dance floor, dancing up a storm," Wilfred said.

Carl managed to pick out Shirley. She was waltzing with a young guy, but was Carl imagining it –was she hailing him? He glanced around: there was no one else looking in her direction. He waved back at her.

Wilfred sighed. "Oh to be young with all that energy. What a girl! Did you think about what we were talking about yesterday?"

"How's that?" Carl said. Yesterday seemed like a very long time ago. With all that was going on, his mind could not come to grips with whatever it was that he and Wilfred had discussed.

Wilfred sipped on his beer. He said: "About giving us a helping hand when you return to Canada, to raise some funds for the coming election."

"No, I haven't really given it any more thought," Carl said.

Wilfred nodded. "How things going, otherwise?"

Carl shrugged. He said: "Could be better, could be worse. I'm not complaining." Something in his old friend's tone suggested there was more to it than just a casual question about Carl's welfare.

Back in Havana, Wilfred had been the point man for the Reform party. All communication to and fro, and what was happening in Guyana as far as it had an impact on the party, came through Wilfred, some of it filtered, as Carl found out later. As the senior party official on site, it was Wilfred's responsibility to ensure that both Carl and Cyril remained loyal and returned to Guyana after their studies were completed; one of the reasons why Carl had held back on disclosing his future plans to his friend.

It had been mere coincidence that Cyril had the same idea as Carl –he'd also applied and been granted a student visa to Canada. When Wilfred found out about his two friends' plans, he was irate. He accused both of them of conspiring behind his back, in his own words: *to make me look bad in the eyes of the party*. Nothing that Carl could say would convince Wilfred otherwise. *You're both a pair of opportunists*, he'd said, *two bloodsuckers only looking out for yourself. You don't really care about what's going on back in Guyana.*

Wilfred said: "You guys really messed up things for me, you know. I got shit when I come back to the country; set me back about five years in the party; had to rebuild my reputation before I was trusted. Not an easy thing to do in this country."

After trying to inflict guilt, if his old friend remained true to form, Carl knew that Wilfred would eventually come around to the subject that was foremost on his mind.

He did. "I hear that you're having some problems with the security people," Wilfred said.

"Word gets around fast."

"We have our ways of finding out what's going on."

"Seems as if there are no secrets in this place."

Wilfred shrugged. "It's a small country. There's always somebody passing information over to the other side."

Carl thought about Havana and the accusations that Wilfred had levelled against him and Cyril. "So much for party loyalty" he said.

Wilfred seemed to ignore the remark. "We can help, you know."

"How?"

"We can arrange to get you out of the country."

The dance was over. Shirley was heading their way.

"What do I have to do in return?"

Wilfred shrugged. "Help to raise funds. Go back to the RDG group planning the overthrow in Toronto, keep an eye on what's going on and keep us up to date."

"In other words, you want me to be your agent in Toronto and spy for you?"

Wilfred said: "You know how it is. It takes two hands to clap."

Shirley was close, now.

"Shirley," Wilfred said, "happy birthday. You look ravishing tonight, as usual, and not a day over sixteen."

Shirley threw her head back and laughed. The curls on her perm dangled right and left and when they finally settled down, she said: "Thanks Wilfred. I know you don't really mean sixteen, but I will settle for eighteen tonight."

"Happy birthday, Shirley," Carl said.

She reached out and held Carl's hands. "How come you didn't ask me for a dance yet?" Shirley said. "Since it's my birthday you have to give me all your attention tonight."

"You've been busy. I didn't think you'd even notice me."

She tugged Carl onto the dance floor. As he was led away, Carl turned to Wilfred and said: "I'll think about it, let you know later."

Shirley elbowed her way through the crowd. "Have you been avoiding me?" she said, when they settled down to dance to a calypso.

Carl shook his head. He'd been looking forward to seeing her from the first moment he arrived at the hall and she lived up to the image he had conjured in his mind about what she would look like on the night of her party. She wore a low-cut red evening gown with slits at the bottom, and as she moved to the fast paced tune, the slit parted wider and revealed well-shaped legs. Something about a woman in black stockings managed to mesmerize him every time.

"What do you have to think about to let Wilfred know?" She had to lean closer to his left ear to speak to him, her voice almost drowned out by the music.

Carl looked at her. Was it possible that she also knew he was on the run?

He shook his head. It was futile trying to form a conversation with the music so loud.

She must have read his thoughts. "Let's go outside on the veranda," she said. "I find it really hot in here."

Shirley led the way through the crowd. Carl almost lost her when two young guys tried to grab her and return her to the dance floor, but she fended them off as if she were holding on to a prized possession and had no intention of losing it.

Carl was glad to get some distance between him and the dance floor. There were two other couples out on the veranda and Shirley staked out a place some distance from them.

Shirley said: "Where you been all yesterday? I looked out for you in the Walk and didn't see you."

"I was in the countryside, visiting Uncle Jules."

"I have to ask you something very important."

Carl raised his eyebrows. A direct approach again, very little or no preamble. "Oh?" he said.

"You're going back to Canada soon, right?"

Carl nodded.

"I remember you saying a couple of days back that you're not living with your woman anymore. This is so, isn't it?"

"Can't say it's not, but..."

"Well, I have something to ask you."

Carl leaned against the wall of the veranda. He felt bloated and uncomfortable from all the food he'd eaten. He'd overcompensated for his hunger by eating much more than he was accustomed. On top of that, he'd had two bottles of beer.

Shirley said: "I tried for a student visa to America, but I didn't get through. You know how it is these days, too many Guyanese going there and disappearing when is time to come back. They make things bad for everyone else."

"I've heard about that."

"So, I decided to go to Canada, instead."

Carl waited.

"If you marry me I can get a permanent visa for Canada," Shirley said.

"You want me to marry you?" Carl sputtered. "Just so you can get a visa?"

Shirley nodded. "It will only be for a short time. As your wife I will be able to get residence in Canada."

She seemed to have it all figured out.

Another couple drifted out to the veranda, looked over the situation and returned to the hall. Down below, on the street, a dray cart was passing, wheels squeaking, a lamp hanging on a pole.

"I'm willing to pay you; five thousand dollars; Canadian."

"I'm sorry, I can't do it."

"Why not? People do it all the time. There will be no obligation on your part and you have nothing to lose. You're not married and you said yourself that you don't live with the woman anymore."

"I just couldn't do it."

"Is it the money? Isn't it enough?"

"It's got nothing to do with money. I just couldn't do it."

She said: "I'm willing to go to ten thousand dollars."

Carl sighed. He suspected that she'd built up a great deal of expectation in her plan. Desperation was now creeping into her tone and her voice was starting to crack. Before long, he suspected that she would start to cry. If she did, what should he do: try to comfort her or walk away?

She turned away from him and looked out to the dark night outside.

"You don't understand," she said, when she turned back to face him. "I have to get out. There's no future here anymore."

A gap of three feet separated them and she narrowed the space and came over, within inches of him. She looked up. She had tears in her eyes.

"I have to get out," she said. "I will do anything to get out."

The implication was very clear to him. Anxiety had a way of driving people to do strange things. His situation was similar in many respects. Was he desperate enough to accept Wilfred's offer?

She came closer. She was at least three inches shorter and she looked up at him. He could see a sparkling gold necklace on firm breasts, a pendant with a fish resting between her cleavage. She was whispering now. Was she afraid that someone would hear, or was this all part of the appeal?

She started to cry. "You have no idea what it's like to live here," she said, between sobs. "Life is terrible. I'm either going to end up being stuck in my dead-end job with no prospects of going anywhere, or getting married with a dozen children. Either way, there's no future for me."

Carl shook his head. "I can't do it," he whispered.

She placed her arms around his neck. Carl felt her grip tighten as she tried to pull his head down towards her. He could smell her odour –it was an intoxicating, exhilarating mixture of perspiration and perfume.

"You like me, I can tell," she said. "I can make it worth your while, I promise."

Carl shook his head. "I wish I could help you, but the truth is, I'm hoping to patch up things with Natasha when I return to Canada. I'm even going to ask her to marry me."

"You can still help me out. We can get married before you do that and then after a year we can get divorced."

Someone behind him said: "Oh, this is where you disappeared to." It was Earl. "Are you ready to go back?"

Carl was relieved. Shirley broke away and turned to look out over the veranda.

"I'm really sorry," Carl whispered, as he turned to go with Earl. "I hope things work out for you. I really do."

Earl led the way to the rear of the hall, to the kitchen where Sumintra was working on cleaning up dishes. She dried her hands on her apron and offered to make a cup of tea and Carl readily accepted.

The three of them, Carl, Earl, and his mother sat around a table.

"Earl tells me that you might go Backtracking," Sumintra said. "Is this the best thing to do?"

"I don't think there is much of a choice, at this stage," Carl said. "Wilfred offered to help, but I don't know how much I can trust him. Our past relationship didn't end up too good back in Cuba. On top of that, he has some conditions that I can't accept."

"Is a pity that things worked out like this," she said. "I wish there was something we could do to help."

"You've both done enough," Carl said. "I couldn't ask for anything more." Time was running out and there were things that he had to discuss before he left. "I've decided to turn over the house and property to you and Earl, the property to be shared with Patsy and Mike junior."

Sumintra raised her eyebrows. The spots on her face seemed to expand. She looked at Earl, who shrugged, as if to say that it was the first time he was hearing it.

"What will your brothers say about this?"

"I don't think the other members of the family will care much, one way or the other –no one wants to come back here."

"I don't know what to say," Sumintra said. "We didn't expect anything."

"I know, but I think that if anyone deserves to live in the house, it's you and Earl, especially after the treatment you received. I'm going to see a lawyer Monday. I'll ask him to draw up the papers before I leave. After I get back to Canada, I'll get affidavits from all the others, relinquishing their claims and transferring title. Earl can handle things from this end."

"How about you, though, won't you want to come back and live here? This is where you born and grow up."

Carl shook his head. "Guyana is no longer my home. It doesn't matter where you live, home is where your family is, and mine is in Canada."

Muffled sounds came through the door: people talking, music from the loudspeakers, feet stomping to a calypso tune.

"I know everything," Carl said.

"Everything?" she said.

"Yes, I spoke to Uncle Jules last night and he confirmed what I suspected for a while now."

Sumintra got up and went to the sink, her back to Carl. She was sobbing. In her reflection in the window, he saw her wiping the tears with a kitchen towel.

"It couldn't have been easy for you over the years," Carl said. He looked at Earl, who was leaning back on the rear legs of his chair. "Or, for Earl for that matter. I'm only sorry that you had to wait so long to get what you deserve."

When Sumintra turned around to face Carl again, she had a sunken look below her eyes. He could see that she was distraught. The area below her eyes had ridges as deep as the Canal in rainy season and tears had lodged in them, despite her effort to wipe them away.

"I really liked your father," she said. "I never intended to break up your family home. Sometimes, things just happen."

Carl nodded.

"He was a good man. He made sure that we never lacked anything while he was alive."

Carl glanced at Earl. His half-brother had a vacant appearance about him. He looked like a man who'd awakened from a coma and discovered that the world had moved on, leaving him far behind.

"The Old Man should have done a lot more," Carl said. "The least he could have done was to come out in the open with Earl."

"Don't judge him too harshly," Sumintra said.

That was exactly what he'd been doing over the years, Carl realized.

Carl recalled his last conversation with Augusto, the night before he left for Cuba. The discussion had swiftly degenerated into a shouting match, the Old Man refusing to sanction his trip, bitter that Carl would even think of going to Cuba or be affiliated in any way with Reform and its Communist connections. Carl had gone to his room., but his father's words rang in his head for many hours into the night. Eventually, everything had settled down, like the way dust settled on the furniture overnight. But, he'd known that while dust could be easily wiped away, the ill feelings generated between him and his father would linger for a long time to come.

"Believe me, I'm trying not to," Carl said. "It's really hard, considering what I knew about him, and what I've found out since coming back."

"He tried his best, for all of us."

"The man's dead and gone. Let him be," Earl spoke for the first time since the conversation began.

Carl was taken aback. He'd thought that Earl's vacant look was one of consternation and recrimination.

"Why do you look so surprised?" Earl said. "Is it because you think I should be bitter?"

"You have every right to be," Carl said.

"I remember the number of times that I came into the store to buy something and saw the Old Man," Earl said. "I even saw you in the store a few times. I'm sure you can't remember that. Why should you? I was really nobody that you could connect to. The Old Man always gave us anything we wanted. I can't complain about that. I was bitter for a while, but, the more I thought about it, the more I realized: did I really get a different kind of treatment than you or our other brothers? Not from what I know. What did I really miss?"

"Is true –he always did see that we were never short of anything," Sumintra said.

Earl said: "I know he was the father I never had. He was still my father. He rarely showed his affection or handed out praise. True, isn't it? At least, he lived up to his responsibilities."

Carl thought about it. He had to admit that Earl was right.

Sumintra had stopped crying. She was smiling, now, like someone who'd just been to a fortune-teller and received good prophecies.

"I remember you as a small boy," she said. "Your daddy bring you around for Earl's christening."

"You can remember that?"

"Yes, you were such a beautiful boy. It made me realize how lucky I was to have a son of my own...with your father."

Carl was amazed at what he was hearing. He'd expected nothing but bitterness from Sumintra and his half-brother, and here he was, being taught a lesson in humility and forgiveness. Listening to the two of them, it made him realize that his father, despite all his flaws, was someone who lived a life defined by principles that guided him, and even though he'd made mistakes, he did the honourable thing and tried to rectify them.

CHAPTER 21 - Paradise Hotel

SUNDAY 30TH NOVEMBER 1980/ MONDAY 1 DECEMBER 1980.

Carl awoke with a start and sat up in bed. Someone was shouting at the top of his voice. Heavy footsteps followed in the corridor.

It took a few seconds for him to realize that he was back in room 222 at Paradise Hotel, where Earl had dropped him off shortly after three in the morning.

He half expected to hear a knock on his door. He waited; the footfall came closer, louder, was directly opposite, passed, finally receding in the opposite direction.

Carl looked at his watch: it was 10am. There were two broken wood slats in the jalousie window and sunlight was streaming through, one of the beams focused directly on his face. He'd been dreaming, again, about the Canal. Another hot day, all his brothers at school; a convoy of punts having just passed, and Carl had it all to himself. This time though, he'd jumped into the water, of his own free will. He was swimming, taking long, graceful strokes, pleased that he'd conquered his fear of water.

"Look, dad," he shouted to his father who was standing close to the partoff, "I can swim on my own."

The Old Man looked young and full of life. He'd smiled and waved. He was wearing his three-piece suit, the same one that he'd worn in the family picture, taken when Carl was around a year old. In that picture, Carl was on his father's lap while the Old Man sat in a rocking chair, Carl's mother, Mary, next to him, the older siblings Joseph, James and Thomas surrounding them. Augusto had been buried in the same suit.

Carl had swum to the far side of the Canal, turned around and made his way back. By the time he reached the bank where his father had been standing, the water had changed, from dark cocoa-brown, to a thick murky sludge, and he had to struggle to make his way over. Augusto had fallen into the Canal. Three feet away, his head was showing above the water and he was slowly sinking into the thick muck. Carl got two feet closer and his father was covered up to his eyes, and when Carl reached out for him, the Old Man vanished.

Then, Carl had heard a door slam across the hall of the hotel and he'd awakened. There were several more voices – the denizens of the hotel were coming alive and the activities of another day were starting.

Even before Carl left the country in 1964, the water in the Canal had turned murky and black. Just like the Canal, his life had now turned into a deep miasmic mess from which he was constantly trying to negotiate his way out and around.

The picture in his dream: what had happened to it? He'd last seen it hanging on a wall back in the old house on the Walk but it was never rehung when the house was renovated, just replaced by another picture taken when his younger brother John was born in 1952, the same way Carl's had replaced the one with Thomas, three years earlier.

There were so many things that he wished he'd done while his father was alive, so many things he should have done when he and Natasha were still together. It seemed as if he'd always focused on the negative aspects of his relationship with the people close to him, when he could have built on the positive qualities…

***

It was October 6, 1973, a Saturday, and he was at home in the evening, eating dinner in front of the TV. He'd come home after a full day at the office and had been pleased at what he'd been able to accomplish with the usual distractions and interruptions of the workweek behind him.

He was looking at the news on CBC. The lead item was the breakout of war between Israel and a coalition of Arab states, led by Egypt with a push into Sinai and Syria recapturing some of the Golan Heights. The U.S and the U.S.S.R were rushing arms and armament to their respective allies. Here we go again, Carl thought. His immediate response was that it would create chaos on financial markets and the world economy. He would go to work on Monday and find that clients were moving funds around in massive amounts, shedding investments in the equity markets and moving to gold. The financial section of the news confirmed it: the price of natural resources was starting to climb through the roof. Oil and bauxite futures had already risen dramatically, all of which would be a boon for resource-rich countries, like Canada, and Guyana, of course with its abundant bauxite reserves. More money would flow into the Guyanese treasury, to prop up the dictatorship of the Republican government and increase the level of corruption.

The phone rang. He picked it up. A long-distance operator had a collect call from Natasha Petrenko, and will he accept the charges?

It came as a complete surprise to Carl and rendered him speechless. He had been in touch with her on and off since he left Havana over five years ago; the occasional phone call from the U.N in New York or from a phone booth somewhere in the city; a written note scribbled and mailed from a post office to tell him that she was thinking of him and hoped they could get back together one day.

"Sir, will you accept the charges?" the operator repeated.

"Yes, I will," Carl said.

He heard a click on the phone as the connection was made.

"Hello, Carlos, are you there?" the voice on the other end of the line said.

"Natasha! What a surprise. Where are you calling from?"

"I'm here at Ni-agarah Falls," she said. "Can you come and get me?"

"Sure, but why didn't you let me know you were coming?"

"Oh, a long story. I will tell you when I see you."

He picked her up and brought her back to his apartment in Toronto. On the drive back, she told him that she'd finally managed to break away from the Russian Embassy, make her way to Niagara Falls and cross over to the Canadian side where she'd claimed refugee status. She had given his name and address as a reference and they'd released her on the condition that she turn up for a hearing at a date to be set.

"Why didn't you tell me you were coming?" Carl had asked.

She'd already navigated around the apartment once and inspected it, opening cupboards, checking out the washroom, bouncing up and down on the sofa. She'd gone into his bedroom and poked at the mattress, and now she was doing the rounds again. It reminded him of their time in Havana. She'd always been infused with a surplus of curiosity. She was like someone coming from a country behind the Iron Curtain and marvelling at the wonders that the western world had to offer.

"You know what it's like at the embassy: you're under constant surveillance –is that how you say it? Every minute of the day. You can't even go to the washroom without somebody watching you. I had no way of letting you know ahead of time."

"What about Vladimir? Is he still there at the embassy?"

She stopped moving around and came over to where he sat on the sofa.

"Oh my sweet Carlos," she said, as she sat on his lap and stroked his hair. "I know what you really want to ask me. The answer is still that it's over between us, since a long time ago, even before Havana. You don't have to feel insecure."

"Where is he now?"

"He was called back to Russia early this year."

So, had she come to Canada because she'd lost her benefactor, or was it easier to flee, now that Vladimir was no longer there? Where Natasha was concerned, nothing was ever spontaneous. She planned everything down to a detail and executed it with flawless timing.

"What do you plan on doing, now?" he said.

She kissed him. "So many questions," she said. "You act as if you're not pleased to see me again, after so many years! We have time for questions later."

He was sure that she would eventually share her plans with him, in bits and pieces. They made love, all night, on the floor, in bed, in the washroom. Afterwards, she traipsed around the apartment, naked, and he had fond recollections of Cuba.

Things had worked out well. Natasha was eventually granted residence and he'd completed his Masters and started with the Canadian Business Bank. By 1978 he'd been appointed Senior Economist, responsible for new business ventures. This was after Alexei and Irina were born. She had never raised the question of marriage and he'd been satisfied to let the situation continue without it.

***

He got out of bed and went to the window. The hotel was located in the commercial district and there were few pedestrians or vehicular traffic moving around for a Sunday.

A kiskadee landed on the lantern-post opposite his window, looked around and flew off in the direction of the seawall. A man was asleep on the sidewalk, a lean dog was rummaging in the garbage, and a mangy cat was waiting its turn. All down the street, trash lay in heaps, uncovered, waiting to be collected, if there was such a service provided by the city. The place was a dump. Carl felt that it was not somewhere he'd want to die. He had visions of his body being thrown out with the refuse and lying there unclaimed.

Shadows had already lengthened on the pavement and the sun had started its climb across the skies. In a few hours it would be crossing the horizon, making its way to Canada, and Natasha and Alexei and Irina. He was so far away from it all.

Tomorrow, he would see a lawyer. Later in the week, he would be travelling overland or by sea or both, back to Canada. He had no assurance that it would work out. He'd never been so lonely or felt so solitary. He thought of evergreen trees in his yard covered with burlap sacks, standing like lone sentinels, braced against the bitter cold winter wind, swaying and quivering, moaning, the wind sneaking through holes in the bags, widening the gaps.

Why did he even have to get out of bed? He'd been comfortable there, even though the sheet was stained and the blanket looked as if it hadn't been washed in weeks. Safely ensconced under the cover, all things seemed possible and it filled him with optimism. Only, when he got out of bed, reality had a way of sneaking in and dispelling the confidence he'd built up. He could feel desperation setting in, again.

He went back to bed.

***

When he woke again, it was seven. He heard more activity in the corridor: footsteps, doors opening and closing, muted conversations. It seemed as if the fact that it was Sunday did nothing to curb the trade in the establishment.

Carl dressed and headed for the stairs. He passed a man leaving a room, pushing his shirt tails into his pants; a woman opened the door of another room, saw Carl coming and closed the door; a couple stood outside the door of a third room, the man embracing the woman from behind as she tried to open the door with her key.

The woman laughed. "Can't you wait till we get inside?" she said.

The dance hall was packed. How was it that so many people were having fun on a Sunday night when the next day was a workday? Maybe they were trying to put off the closure of the weekend, he concluded. The woman in the black dress was standing by the bar and as Carl passed her she winked at him.

He went to the bar. Despite the number of people lining up for drinks, the bartender smiled at him and asked him what he wanted. The man's temperament seemed to have changed, like *pepperpot* left to foment overnight for a noticeable improvement in the taste. Carl ordered a local beer and took a table in a corner of the restaurant area, facing the front entrance.

A waitress came over with a menu.

Carl ordered a chicken fried rice and another beer and the waitress left.

More people were entering through the front door.

The noise level had increased. The din was overwhelming. He imagined that it was like this in the Berbice Mad House, everyone trying to talk at the same time, no one listening.

Carl's food arrived, a heaping portion, twice what he typically ate, but he was hungry and did it justice. He was almost through when he noticed Earl coming through the rear door. Earl surveyed the room and spotted Carl. He came over.

"I went upstairs to your room but didn't' find you, so I thought I'd check out the restaurant," Earl said.

Carl said: "Are you going to have something to drink and eat?"

Earl shook his head and took a seat.

"No good staying in one place. I think we need to move you, tonight, so you should get your things after you finish and let us go."

"What's happened?" Carl said.

"You remember Winslow?"

Carl nodded.

"Winslow was over at the house, asking about you this morning. Said he wanted to get hold of you."

"Did he say what he wanted?"

Earl shook his head. "He works for Special Branch. There could only be one thing he wants."

"What did you tell him?"

"We told him that we had no idea where you were. Looks as if they searching for you all over. I think we need to move you around to a few different places until the time for you to leave."

"Sounds like a good idea."

"I don't know how much you know about Winslow, but he can't be trusted. There's stories floating around about him."

"What kind of stories?"

Earl had to raise his voice to make himself heard above the loud music and this seemed to be making him uncomfortable, as if he thought he might be overhead and what he was saying might be held and used against him. Carl had met many people like him when he was gathering information about prospective clients looking for a loan. People were always leery about providing information that might come back to haunt them later.

"Winslow worked his way up in the Republican party. The story is that he was involved in some shady things going on during the disturbances."

Winslow had certainly made his way up in the world, for someone who had barely completed primary school. Carl remembered a time when the man couldn't even read the Nelson West Indian Primer that was used in classes. He'd relied on Carl many times to help him with his homework.

Carl shrugged and took another sip of his beer. "Doesn't seem to be anything wrong with that."

Earl looked around again. "How do you think Winslow worked his way up?"

"I have no idea."

"Have you ever heard of the X-13 group?"

Carl remembered: back in 1964 Wilfred had talked about Winslow being part of an Opposition group, but he'd never supplied the name.

Carl shook his head. "Who are they?"

"Back in 1963, the Republican party, which was in the opposition then, created a security force, supposedly with the purpose of protecting high ranking party members."

"Every party had the same thing going."

Earl snorted. "Security force protecting party members, my ass! They were a terrorist group."

"What does this have to do with Winslow?"

"Winslow had just finished serving his time in Suddie Boys School, when he became a member of the group."

Carl shrugged. "Reform had an organization like that, too. I suspect the Conservatives also had one."

Earl sighed. "The police force had its own Special Branch, responsible for investigating political crimes, but they were infiltrated by this security group, and before long, Special Branch started operating as an arm of the Republican party. You don't know the half of it. The X-13 group was trained in explosives and weaponry. You weren't here, but you must have an idea about the terror campaign carried out against Reform members. Government buildings were bombed, people were killed. I give you one guess about the source of it all."

Carl had heard stories about this campaign from Wilfred, even as far away in Havana. Back then, he'd thought it incredible and improbable. After all, the country was still under British rule. How would they allow something like that to go on?

Earl continued. "Orders for this campaign came from the highest level of the Republican party."

"Do you mean the current President?"

"Maybe. They had a number of cells that carried out the operations. They bombed the Ministry of Labour, Health, Housing, the Rice Marketing Board, the houses of several Reform supporters, and the Paramount cinema."

This was their way of spreading discontent with the government and demoralizing its supporters. The Rice Marketing Board catered to rice farmers, and the majority of these farmers were East Indians who were government supporters.

Earl seemed to choose his next words carefully. He didn't look directly at Carl when he said: "There was even talk that the Conservatives and its leader knew about this X-13 group and supplied them with funds."

"You're trying to say that our father might have been involved in this?"

"It's possible it was only known at the highest level of the Conservatives. I don't discount the possibility that the he knew about it. He was planning to run for the Legislature, wasn't he?"

"How do you know all this? Where did you get your information from?" Carl said, a bit irritated that nothing seemed verified.

"A teacher friend of mine, a Republican, was one of the original thirteen in the group. He didn't like the change in direction, from protection to terrorism. He had to run. He went to the US."

"Seems a bit farfetched that somebody like Winslow, who didn't even go to high school, would end up in a top position in the party."

"I believe that Winslow did go to high school. But, you'd be surprised at who runs the government, now. All you need is a party card and the right connections and any position is open to you. You have post men who can't even read the address on the envelope, trying to deliver mails; teachers who can't even spell properly; civil servants who can't add. All I can tell you, is, don't trust Winslow if you come across him, or anyone else connected with the Special Branch."

"Too late," Carl said. He motioned towards the entrance.

Earl turned around to follow Carl's gaze. Winslow had just entered the restaurant and was scanning the dance floor and diners.

"He must have followed me," Earl said.

"It doesn't really matter."

"I can stall him while you head out the back," Earl said.

Carl shook his head. "I don't want you to get into any more trouble than you already have. I want you to leave, now. Make sure you get hold of that lawyer tomorrow and tell him that Winslow is the person who can provide information on where they're taking me. Can you do that?"

Earl nodded. He looked like a man who had been caught in the middle of an earthquake and had the wall of a building collapse on him. He rose from his chair and left, swiftly making his way out through the dance floor to the rear entrance of the hotel.

Winslow made his way across the floor. He came through like a bulldozer, brushing aside the dancers with his immense bulk.

CHAPTER 22 - Thank You, Father

SUNDAY 30TH NOVEMBER 1980/ MONDAY 1 DECEMBER 1980.

At the airport, when he came into the country, absorbed with the interview with Ross and Brackett, Carl hadn't paid much attention to Winslow. Now, he could grasp the enormity of the next-door neighbour in the Walk: powerful, broad shoulders and massive arms.

The scar had remained as a permanent reminder of a violent life. Was he still the same?

The man Carl had known so long ago was someone who cared little for his appearance. However, he was now decked out in a black suit, white long sleeve shirt and black tie. Everything about his appearance indicated a man of means. Someone who could afford the best. Perks that came with Winslow's job?

"You coming with me," Winslow said, with no preamble.

"Where are we going?" Carl said.

"Don't ask questions. I already doing you a big favour by letting Earl go. Don't push your luck."

"I want to know where you're taking me."

"We going collect your belongings, then we going for a ride."

They went to Carl's room; Carl collected his suitcase and carryon bag and then, Winslow led the way to the back of the building where a black van stood alone in the parking lot.

"Get in," Winslow said, after he opened the rear door.

"Where are you taking me?" Carl repeated. "I have a right to know."

"Just get in."

Carl stepped up and entered the van. When he was in British Guiana, a van like this was used for transporting prisoners to and from jail. Called the *Black Maria* –it was notorious as a dreaded symbol of someone about to be caught up in the justice system.

The vehicle was completely sealed off: no windows, no access to the driver in front, a row of benched seating on two sides. Carl was alone, and as the door closed behind him he understood that he was now a captive, completely shut off from the rest of the world.

He felt the driver's side sag with Winslow's weight as the man entered behind the steering wheel. Carl walked up to the front. A glass pane separated them and it was painted black.

"Where are you taking me?" Carl shouted.

Only silence up front.

Carl banged on the glass. "I have a right to know," Carl shouted. "Where are you taking me?"

Earl had told Carl not to trust Winslow. Was Winslow now taking Carl to some way-off destination from which there would be no return?

Carl sat down on the bench. It was pitch black: he couldn't even see the fingers on his hands. He was trapped in a cell, a moving cell but a cell non-the-less. From the luminous dial on his watch, he could tell that it was fifteen minutes after ten, Sunday night.

He gave up trying to communicate. Either he was not getting through or Winslow was ignoring him.

The van rolled along, sometimes at a fast clip, at other times it slowed when they went around a bend –he could tell, he and his baggage were sent careening against the other side when this happened. A few times he was tossed towards the door and he had to pick himself up and return to the bench. After a while he gave up and sat with his back to the door. When they had started out, they had paused several times, for traffic-lights, he thought, as the van started off with a lurch and picked up speed soon after. He heard a few vehicles outside: the honking of a horn, a car door slamming, and an engine revving. After that, they picked up speed and continued without pause. They had to be heading into the country somewhere, he figured, but where? He had no idea.

They came to a stop two hours from the time Carl last looked at his watch; midnight. He heard voices: someone asking for papers, Winslow identifying himself. He felt the van start off and continue for another two minutes; the door opening; Winslow appearing.

"Follow me," Winslow told him.

Carl got out. Silhouetted against the night sky and spotlights mounted on tall poles, he could see a high mesh fence with barbwire strung on top, a gate with a guard tower on each side. From what he could see of the building itself, it was a long concrete structure stretching off into the night, no windows, a flat roof topped with corrugated sheets. It looked like a concentration camp.

"This way," Winslow said.

Carl followed to a doorway where a guard was stationed. Winslow produced his ID and the guard opened the door –a solid door that closed behind them and led to a lobby where there was another guard behind a desk. Again, Winslow produced his ID and was given permission to enter through another door.

Only one thing missing, Carl thought: a sign over the door saying *Give Up Hope All Ye Who Pass Beyond These Doors*, and he was concerned that it was the last time he would see the outside.

They traversed down a long corridor with cells on both sides and the incipient sounds of occupants filtering through closed doors. A cough, a scratching sound, and a banging. How long had the occupants been behind those closed doors?

"This is not right," Carl said. "You have to allow me to contact my consulate and speak to a lawyer."

Winslow opened the last door on the right and stood aside for Carl to enter the room.

"Take a seat," Winslow said.

Winslow closed the door behind him and left Carl alone in the room.

What would come next? Browbeating, followed by strong-arm tactics to force a confession for something he hadn't done? If they used force, Carl had no doubt that he would be unable to hold out. Pain was not something that he could withstand for long periods. Where would that leave him? Would it seal his fate or would he be able to broker a deal? What could he offer them?

The downside was that he might never be able to get back to Canada, and with that Carl's thoughts drifted to Shirley. It was ironic that she wanted him to be her passport into Canada, and yet, here he was in a position where he might never be able to get there himself. He wondered what Shirley would do next. Would she seek out someone else who would be willing to provide the service? Carl was sure that in the end, Shirley would survive. Much more than that, she would get out of Guyana, one way or the other. There would be no stopping her.

Carl couldn't help reflecting. Both of the women he'd been interested in had been after him with the same objective: obtaining a free pass to Canada. There were other similarities in the two. They were outspoken, attractive, knew what they wanted, and were not afraid to use their sexuality to achieve their goal.

Back in Cuba, it hadn't been much different with Natasha. He'd known that from the start, but when she came to Canada, he had developed a closeness to her that was unlike anything he'd ever felt for someone. Apart from a few minor issues, everything was going smoothly, until that day it went off the rails...

***

He'd had a particularly rough day at the bank.

Bad news piled up during the day with all the financial indicators pointing to a recession in North America, and perhaps even worldwide. Unemployment in Canada stood at seven percent and was on the rise. Government debt stood at over forty-five billion dollars and this had driven inflation up to over eleven percent. Before he left the office at the end of the day, there was worse to come: the Dow had dropped over fourteen percent and the Toronto Stock Exchange was down eleven percent. Optimists were saying that the worst had passed, but Carl was sceptical: he thought the downward spiral would continue on Monday when the markets reopened.

When he got home the news hadn't been good either.

He was examining his bank statement that came in the mail. He discovered withdrawals made from his and Natasha's joint checking account, driving it over the edge to a negative balance, something he always took pains to avoid, being a bank employee. Sums had been withdrawn that he was unaware of, not the type of news that he wanted to receive, with all that was happening with the economy.

"I'm sure I told you about it," Natasha told him, when he asked her about it.

He'd been very busy at work. Was it possible that he'd forgotten? On the other hand, she had a history of telling him that she'd mentioned something when he had no clear recollection of hearing about it.

Like how she'd claimed that she'd told him about the difference in their age.

Back in Cuba, Carl had suspected that there wasn't much of an age gap between them. She always managed to maintain a girlish appearance that belied her maturity and worldliness and she'd told him that she was two years younger than him. When the time came to endorse her application for refugee status in Canada, however, he discovered that the age gap was wider and she was eight years older. He'd asked how she could have let something like that slip through without telling him and her response was that she thought she had mentioned it.

"I can't recall any conversation where you mentioned about the money," Carl said. "It doesn't matter, now. Just tell me what the money was for."

"I told you before. My mother is sick. I sent some money to her in Moscow to help her out."

Carl had never met the members of her family. He didn't even know that she was still in touch with them back in Russia.

"I'm really tired of all these matters you were supposed to have told me and I have no recollection of hearing about them!"

"Are you saying I make things up?"

"All I'm saying is that you seem to have a convenient way of neglecting to tell me certain things and when I find out, you claim that you told me."

"I'm sure I told you about this. You just have too much on your mind to remember."

"I would have remembered this. Is she the only one you're sending money to?"

She was washing the supper dishes. She had stopped and turned around to face him.

"Just what are you saying? Why don't you come right out and ask me?"

"I am asking you: is she the only one you're sending money to?"

Her eyes narrowed. "You mean Vlad, don't you?"

"Yes, I mean Vladimir."

"Why would I be sending money to Vlad?"

"That's what I'm trying to find out."

"I can't take this. You have a very suspicious mind, Carlos. It makes me feel like I'm back in Russia or Cuba again."

"I can't take all your lies anymore," he'd said.

"What are you? KGB? Do I have to answer all these questions!"

He headed for the door and picked up his car keys from the rack.

The last thing he heard her say was: "In case you're interested, they believe my mother has got cancer."

He'd left without even saying goodbye to the two kids.

***

Ross and Brackett entered the room, followed by Winslow. It was now one am.

"We've been looking for you," Ross said.

"What for?" Carl responded.

Brackett shouted: "Dias, you know damn well what for. You deliberately lied to us and you been hiding out, knowing we wanted you for questioning."

Ross and Brackett sat in the two chairs across from Carl. Winslow remained standing, braced against the wall where the only exit was located. He had a file folder in his hands.

Carl said: "I had no reason to hide. I haven't done anything wrong. I'm just a Canadian citizen back here for his father's funeral."

"Come now, Mister Dias," Ross said. He was still the polite one. "Only a man on the run would hang out in a dump such as the Paradise Hotel."

"You deliberately lied to us, about your connection to the RDG in Toronto." Brackett said. "We're on to you. We know everything, now."

"When I came in there was no restriction placed on where I could stay. Aren't people free to go and stay where they want to in this country?"

Brackett said: "We know you're a member of the RDG. We know about your mission: you and your party wants to overthrow the government. We know you come here to recruit more people to work from inside the country."

Carl placed as much sarcasm in his voice as he could collect. "I suppose too, you think that I arranged my father's death just to have an excuse to enter the country and carry out this so-called mission?" Carl pointed to Winslow. "Ask him about the funeral –he lives right next door."

Winslow did not react.

Brackett continued: "You people stupid or what? What make you think you can come into this country and get away with something like that?"

He sounded like a man sent to suppress a prison riot with a machine gun, someone who didn't care how many innocent people were killed in the process, as long as the riot was quelled.

Ross said: "Doesn't look good for you Mister Dias. Why don't you come clean and tell us everything."

"How can I tell you what I don't know?"

"We got all the evidence we need," Brackett said.

"You've got no evidence, but it looks as if I've been tried and convicted already. It's just left for you to incarcerate me here and throw away the key."

"Incarcerate," Brackett snorted, "that's a big word. Do you t'ink you any smarter than us because you know a few big words?"

"The Canadian Consulate knows I'm in the country. I'm registered with them," Carl lied.

"We don't give a damn about the Canadian government," Brackett said. "You're in Guyana now. We can hold you for as long as we want. They won't even know where you going be."

"This is ridiculous!" Carl said. "I haven't done anything wrong. Ask Winslow –he lives right next door to my father's house. I'm sure he knows about the funeral and what happened."

Winslow hadn't moved from his position; he continued to play an emotionless role in the proceedings.

"Do you mean you're not a member of this RDG party?" Ross said.

"No, I'm not."

"But, your name's on the membership list!"

"You're lying," Brackett said. "I don't believe a word of what you're saying. Give me your passport."

"My passport is the property of the Canadian government," Carl said. "You have no right to it." But, he knew that they eventually would be able to take it from him. He decided to appeal directly to Ross. "Look, you're a reasonable man. I'm telling you: I never intended to be a member. It was all a mistake."

"You're saying you never went to meetings and you don't know people in the party?" Ross said.

"I did go to one meeting, I admit that. Only one, but it was all a mistake. I never planned on joining the party, but before I knew it, the person who invited me to the meeting had taken out a membership in my name; not something that I can control!"

"Who is this person?"

Carl was about to respond when he realized that he would be implicating other people. He had no way of knowing how far the Guyana Government had woven its web. Were they capable of reaching out as far as Toronto, to the people who were members of the RDG?

"I can't remember and it doesn't matter. The main thing is that I never intended to become a member. I told them to take my name off the membership list soon as I found out. If this is all you have against me, you don't have much."

"You're lying," Brackett said. "Why did you go to the meeting if you didn't plan on becoming a member. How come you can't remember who signed you up?"

Carl said: "The RCMP already investigated me. They cleared me. Check with them, if you want."

"We don't give a damn what the RCMP did," Brackett said. "You're under Guyanese jurisdiction now."

Ross said: "We want to know about the connection between the RDG and Reform. Tell us about Reform involvement. Did Reform know and sanction the plot?"

So that's what it's all about. They were looking to connect dots between Reform and the RDG and going after Reform, perhaps even having an excuse for putting away the top echelon of the party.

They were firing questions at him rapidly, one after the other, without giving him the time to respond. Carl thought: so this is what it feels like to be interrogated by the secret service of a third world country! The elements missing, so far: the intense glare of a bright light, truncheons, pliers and water hoses.

"I have no idea what you're talking about," Carl said.

"So, someone invited you to the meeting? Who? You told them to take your name off the membership list? Who?" Ross said.

"I told you, I can't remember. That was a long time ago."

"Come on, give us something, anything, Mister Dias," Ross said. It sounded almost as if he was pleading with Carl.

"You have a very convenient loss of memory," Brackett said. "We can make you remember."

Ross shook his head. "You're not making it easy for us to believe you, Mister Dias. I want to accept what you're saying but you're being very uncooperative."

"I told you all that I know."

"You're lying," Brackett said.

"Look," Ross said. "We have three options. We can kick you out the country as an undesirable. We can charge and try you with belonging to a treasonous group intent on overthrowing the legal government of Guyana. Or, we can detain you indefinitely until we're satisfied, one way or the other."

"I say we continue to hold him until he tells us the truth," Brackett said.

"I have no connection with any group whatsoever," Carl said. "So, how can you detain me?"

"We're going to give you some time to think this over," Ross said, as he paused by the door.

Brackett glared at Carl as he left the room. "You better tell us the whole story when we come back."

Winslow remained. He came over and dropped the file folder on the table.

"You in big, big trouble," Winslow said. He took a seat.

"What's this?" Carl said.

Winslow pulled out two documents and pushed them over to Carl. "You might t'ink these people making jokes but this is serious business," he said.

Carl scanned the two documents. One page had his full name, address in Toronto, and the address of the house in the Walk; his affiliation with Reform; his scholarship to the University of Havana and his membership in the RDG party. The RDG was described as being extreme right wing, formed with the sole purpose of overthrowing the government of Guyana by any means possible. The second page contained an ACTION ITEM: subject to be detained for questioning to determine if he's part of an advance guard entering the country with the intention of looking for recruits. If so, how many has he recruited so far, and who are they?

Carl pushed the two documents across the table. "I already said, many times, this is all ridiculous. I came back for my father's funeral, nothing else."

Winslow replaced the documents in the file. "They don't believe you, especially Brackett, and especially after you buried yourself in the Paradise Hotel, knowing they wanted to talk to you."

"Looking back at it, going into hiding was probably not the smartest thing for me to do, but I had no idea what I was faced with. The only reason I came into the country was for my father's funeral –that's the truth, and you should know that."

"How about this membership in the RDG party? Your name on the list?"

"I've already said that was all a mistake."

Winslow got up, limped over to the far wall and braced against it.

"Seem to me you make your share of mistakes, including joining Reform and going to Cuba on scholarship."

"Maybe so. As far as the scholarship, that was over sixteen years ago. I gave up any connection with Reform after I left Cuba. This can't be of any importance now, so many years after the fact."

"You still going to Cuba, though. Reform still got Cuban connections they could use."

"I didn't hide my recent visits to Cuba –anyone could see that from my passport. The trips were all on business for my bank."

"How 'bout recruiting people to join this plot, you all want to overthrow the government?"

"Look, I've been in contact with no one, apart from the many mourners who came to express sympathy. I've discussed politics with no one, been nowhere outside the Walk except for a visit to Uncle Jules and a party for Shirley, the girl next door. You remember Uncle Jules, my father's brother, don't you? You must have seen him sometime when he came to visit us in the Walk?"

"I remember him. Is not true that you had no other contact, though. We know you been talking to Wilfred. The third person in Cuba, Cyril, his name on the list for the RDG. All three of you went to Cuba. You still going to Cuba to get training?"

"Oh Christ!" Carl almost exploded. "You're trying to put a bad slant on everything I say and do."

"And it seem you got all the answers ready –that's what we thinking."

"I'm telling the truth."

"I remember your father well. I know he was a Conservative party man. How come you join Reform and went to Cuba to study?"

"That's a long story."

"I don' t'ink your father liked that."

"There are a number of things that me and my father didn't see eye to eye with and we both made mistakes in our relationship. I made a lot more than he did, I admit it, but that's something I have to live with."

Winslow came over and sat in his chair. He looked intently at Carl. The scar on his cheek that looked like an imbedded centipede, started to flare. Winslow rubbed the scar, tracing it from the top to the bottom.

What was going through the man's mind? Was he thinking at what point he should resort to use force to get the information needed?

Winslow shrugged. "I think I actually believe some of what you tell us," he said.

Carl sighed. "I'm glad someone does."

"Your story don't end there. You have four problems: Ross, Brackett, this file, and not cooperating with the investigation."

"If you're convinced I'm innocent, why can't you persuade them?"

"Ross is not a problem –he's a smart man, smart enough to add up the pieces. It's Brackett you must worry about. He's power hungry and ambitious. He want to get somebody so badly that he don't care if the person is innocent or not. Then, there is the file." Winslow picked up the file and traced his right index finger around the perimeter. As large as the eight by eleven file was, it looked small in his hands. "Files got a way of disappearing. You should see the filing system we got down at headquarters. Steel shelves crammed with folders and they fill up with all kind of useless shit."

"Whenever all is said and done, there is no reason for them to hold me. They have to let me go. Can you talk to them?"

"Why should I put my neck on a rope for you?"

Carl waved his hands. "Because you know me, because it's the truth, and you know it's the right thing to do."

Winslow rubbed the scar. "You thinking that this is like fighting Reds all over again back at the cinema? Them days long gone."

Carl shook his head. "I don't know what to think anymore. All I know is that I need to get out of here and back to Canada, to my family."

"Tell me the truth, now. What really happened in Canada with you and RDG."

"I already said it, several times. Nothing happened."

"You have to give me something to show you want to cooperate. Who was the man who get you the membership in the RDG? Who else in the party? Where they getting the money from? Where they plan on starting this revolution from?"

Carl shook his head. "I've been through this. That was too long ago. I can't remember."

"You don' trust me, but you expect me to help you?"

Winslow picked up the folder, opened the door and left the room.

The door was slammed and the sound reverberated in Carl's ears long after Winslow left the room. There was no doubt in Carl's mind that Winslow was his last hope. Could he really trust the man to intercede?

Earl had told Carl that he shouldn't trust Winslow. His half-brother had also talked about the Rabbi Washington group that was implicated in political assassinations. Was he suggesting that Winslow might now be involved in that group?

Carl had never felt as exposed and helpless. At the bank he made decisions every day that affected the lives of people. Here he was, now, his future about to be determined by three people and he had no say in how it would turn out. Three people who had the power to deprive him of his freedom, possibly for the rest of his life. It was only with the threat of the loss of that freedom that he appreciated how valuable it was. He would give anything for the right to return to Canada, to his family, Alexei and Irina, and Natasha. For his wellbeing, he knew he had to focus on the positive aspects of his life, like the tender moments he'd once shared with Natasha...

***

They were in the apartment in Toronto. The city was sweltering in one of those midsummer heat waves for which it was famous and Hydro had called for voluntary reductions in electricity consumption.

They'd just finished making love and were lying in bed, naked. Carl could feel perspiration beading on his back from the humidity. His digital clock radio was showing 7:00. Ten floors below, sounds of children playing in the park floated upwards on a solitary breeze and came through the window.

"Do you ever wonder," Carl whispered, "what life would have been like if we hadn't gotten back together?"

Natasha whispered: "I always did know I would come to meet you here. I said it when we were back in Havana."

Old habits died hard. Neither of them had told the other to speak in undertones, the way they had communicated back in Cuba. It was how all of Havana, perhaps the entire island discussed things. The country was a nation of whisperers and citizens engaged in clandestine activities. Neighbours spied on one another; children reported their parents to the authorities for anti-revolutionary activity; people found they could no longer count on friends to suppress remarks critical of the revolution.

He said: "Why are we whispering?"

She laughed. "I know; we're no longer in Havana. We're in Canada –freedom and a bright future."

They'd just marked the second anniversary of their post-Cuban relationship and he was feeling optimistic about life and living. He was working long hours at the bank and he was up for promotion.

"I was supposed to return to Guyana, to serve the party, and the people," Carl said. "It's something that weighs on my mind, sometimes. I wanted to make a difference. How about you? Do you have regrets about leaving Russia and Cuba?"

She sighed. "I don't know what your party in Guyana plans for the future. They all start out with the best intention. Like how it was in Russia; how is now in Cuba. Eventually, they all keep the people down because they think they know best for everybody. There is no freedom to speak about."

"Surely the Russian revolution changed things for the better?"

"That's like saying anything is better than the rule of the Tsar. At first the revolution did make many good changes. Everybody was excited –they got rid of the Tsar and his kind. The party talked about rule by the common man. Who do you think replaced the Tsar and his aristocrats? Just a bunch of common dictators, that's who. It's like, how you say it in English? The inmates run the jail?"

"What if I had decided to return to Guyana after leaving Cuba. Would you have come with me?"

She rolled over on her side, away from him and said: "I would have followed you anywhere you went. I still would…"

***

Carl looked at his watch: it was seven-thirty. Winslow had been gone for over an hour. What was happening? He could understand how a prisoner on death row would feel, coming down to the last day of his life. His last-minute appeal had been made, now he was waiting to hear the decision.

He heard the creak in the hinges of the door as it started to open and he wondered who was coming this time. Was it a repeat performance of Ross and Brackett? Was it Winslow coming to bring him bad news?

Winslow poked his head in the opening and said: "Let's go."

"Where are we going this time?"

"To the airport, to catch your flight."

Relief flooded through his entire body; he felt giddy and weak in his legs. Was it really true or a trick to soften him up further? He'd heard of persecutors who dangled freedom in front of political prisoners, playing psychological games to lull them into a sense of security, and when they'd built up their hopes, everything came crashing down to the point where they would do anything, say anything, write anything to obtain their freedom.

"What happened?"

"It's all settled –you being kicked out of the country."

"What do you mean? They still think I'm guilty of something but they're letting me go?"

"The best deal I could get for you. Consider yourself lucky."

Carl followed Winslow through the building, a reversal of the process in which he'd arrived, and they ended up in the parking lot, boarding the same van, only this time Carl was allowed to sit in front, next to Winslow.

Winslow started off, heading out the parking lot.

They came to a highway and drove in silence for a while. The morning sky had come alive: the sun had created pink, purple and crimson layers on the horizon and wisps of dazzling white clouds floated in the foreground.

"I want to tell you something, about your father, and what he did," Winslow said.

Carl shook his head. Was Winslow going to confirm what Earl had already hinted: that Augusto was aware of the X-13 group and might even have been involved in its terrorist activities?

"There's nothing you can tell me about my father that I don't already know," Carl said.

"I might surprise you."

"I know that my father was not the greatest, but I believe he always had the best in mind for us and the country. So, don't tell me anything disparaging about him –I won't hear it."

It was Winslow's turn to shake his head.

"What I want to tell you is that your father help me a lot. If not for your father, I would have ended up in jail, or worse."

"I don't understand. My father was not a Republican. Why would he have helped you?"

"Your father pay my school fees for high school."

Carl was shocked. "Why would he do that?"

"Do you remember when I went to Boys School at Suddie, after the fight between Reds and me? Well, I been going down the wrong road long before that. Before I went off to Suddie Boys School, your father come over to our house one day and talk to me. He tell me that he want to make a deal with me. If I finish primary school when I was in Suddie, he pay my school fees to go to high school later. I did get to finish primary school. And, he did keep his end of the bargain."

This would have happened back in the early sixties, most likely after the riots and after the store was burnt down, at a time when Carl's father could least afford it. Yet, the Old Man had kept his word.

"You remember how I used to come over to your house and you and your brothers would help me with my homework sometimes? I know: I was really dumb, back then, but your father say to me one time: Don't you want to be as smart as Carl? Something that really help to push me in the right direction."

"My father said that?" Carl said.

"Your father was the only one who really take an interest in me. We used to be in the demonstrations outside the Legislature, only I was Republican and your father was Conservative, but that didn't matter to him. All he was interested in was to get Reform out of office, same thing we did want. I get hit in the head by a police rifle butt one time. Your father take me to the hospital and had it fix up. He also bring me home in his car."

This was a side of his father that Carl never knew or identified. It was amazing how long one could live with someone and yet not know the person.

Winslow took his time before he continued. "He was even willing to pay my fees to go to University, but I had enough of education. I wanted to work for some money. In the years before independence, I didn't see your father much even though I still live next door. The few times I did see him, I say hello, but he didn't look at me. He never look me in the face again."

"Why is that?"

"I think he was ashamed of me."

"Why would my father have been ashamed of you?"

"I believe he know."

"What?"

Winslow spoke softly; Carl had to lean forward to hear him.

"About X-Thirteen."

Winslow continued: "I seen some terrible things done back then by the group. There isn't a day that pass that I don't think of some of them. At first the group obstruct the government, make it hard for them to govern, make their supporters turn against them. When that didn't work out, the group get orders to take a hard line."

How active had Winslow been? Had he taken part in crimes? Was he still involved in the Rabbi Washington group?

"I seen some terrible things," Winslow repeated. "If there is a God, when the time come, he will make me pay for the things done."

Carl shook his head. In everything he'd said so far, Winslow had referred to the X-13 members as the *Group* and hadn't expanded on his own role. For over a decade and a half, Winslow had carried around this secret with him. Was he now looking to unload his burden and perhaps get absolution?

They were now in the airport parking lot. Winslow got out of the van and pulled out Carl's suitcase and overnight bag from the back.

Something occurred to Carl. "How did you manage to convince Ross and Brackett?" he said.

Winslow sighed. "It wasn't easy. I had to give up something in exchange."

"Like what?" Carl said.

"Special Branch gets sweeteners from all kinds of people – to speed things up in the system. We got our fingers in lots of things going on in the government. We fix things up for people. Is how the system work –I didn't make it, I just work there. I had to give a bigger share of mine to Brackett to keep him happy."

It was clear what Winslow meant when he talked about sweeteners. The system was rife with corruption.

"And Ross?"

"Ross is an okay man; he didn't want anything. He already think you innocent. So it was two for you and one against."

"I want to thank you…for everything," Carl said, as he followed Winslow into the airport.

Winslow shook his head. "You can thank your father."

The final parting words that he heard from Winslow: "Remember, we don't want to see you in these parts anymore."

***

The plane was taxiing down the runway as the sun rose higher in the sky. The captain made his announcement: "Our flight time is five hours twenty-two minutes. The weather is a balmy fifteen Celsius in Toronto. I'm sure you'll be happy to get back to some cooler temperatures after the heat in Georgetown."

Carl looked out the window. The plane was picking up speed and the landscape was changing as the aircraft took to the sky. Would he ever see the family home in the Walk again? He doubted it. And, he realized that, apart from his memories, he had nothing to remind him of his father. There had been no time to collect anything from the house in the Walk –no pictures, journals, or memorabilia in the study.

A man should have something to remind him that his father once existed; something that he can pass on to his own children. Then, he remembered; he pushed his hand into his jacket pocket and felt the watch that Uncle Jules had given him.

"Thank you, father," Carl whispered as the plane climbed into the clouds.

ACKNOWLEDGEMENTS

WRITTEN WORKS
Thanks to the following works:
Scenes from the History of the Portuguese in Guyana, by Mary Noel Menezes, RSM, from which I drew some historical data on the arrival, life and times of the Portuguese immigrants in British Guiana.
Report of the Wismar, Christianburg and Mackenzie Commission, Editor Dr. Odeen Ishmael from which I drew some historical information.
Sundry works on British Guiana U.K., U.S. relations during the pre and post British Guiana/ Guyana independence eras, including declassified files and documents from the British Archives, from which I drew some historical data.

SONGS AND LYRICS
Title of the song *Hit The Road Jack* aired over radio stations during the strike; lyrics by Percy Mayfield.
The opening line from the song *Beautiful Dreamer*; lyrics by Stephen Foster (1826-1864].
The line *Sweets for my sweets, sugar for my honey*; lyrics by C.J. Lewis.

ABOUT THE AUTHOR
Ken Puddicombe's writing and stories have appeared in various publications over the years.
Born in British Guiana, he came to Canada in 1971 and currently lives there with his family.
Contact him at kenpudwriter@gmail.com
www.kenpuddicombe.ca/Writer/Welcome.html

Made in the USA
Charleston, SC
06 October 2013